THE LIFE AND TIMES OF HUGH MILLER.

BY THOMAS N. BROWN.

"A star hath left the kindling sky,
A lovely northern light:
Many a planet is on high,
But that hath left the night."

NEW YORK:
RUDD & CARLETON, 130 GRAND STREET.
(BROOKS BUILDING, COR. OF BROADWAY.)
MDCCCLIX.

AUTHOR'S EDITION.

R. CRAIGHEAD,
PRINTER, STEREOTYPER, AND ELECTROTYPER,
Caxton Building,
81, 83, *and* 85 *Centre Street.*

Contents.

—o—

INTRODUCTORY.

It is somewhere said by Goldsmith, that the life of a literary man seldom abounds with adventure. His fame is acquired in solitude; and the historian, who only views him from a distance, must be content with a dry detail of actions by which he is hardly distinguished from the rest of mankind. Though embodying a general truth, the observation we have quoted does not exactly sum up the life we have chosen to illustrate. Its even tenor was, indeed, not much disturbed by adventure, but it can scarcely be said of Hugh Miller his fame was acquired in solitude, or that his actions were not in a very marked degree distinguished from the actions of the mass of mankind. On the contrary, the more closely his life and writings are scanned, the more clearly will Scotchmen begin to discover that, amongst the men of genius these latter times have produced, Hugh Miller is Scotland's representative man.

This statement is made with a full appreciation of its

import, and with a perfect knowledge that names will instantly rise in many minds, disputing the pedestal on which we seek to place the Cromarty stone-mason. It may, therefore, be well the reader should distinctly understand that, in claiming for Hugh Miller this representative character, no comparison is instituted, and no superiority is asserted for him over such men as Burns and Scott, either of whom may be supposed, by a large class of admirers, to possess superior claims to the position we seek to assign the late editor of the *Witness*. It may even be acknowledged that, in native intellectual force, Scott and Burns equalled—nay, in certain special mental attributes, excelled—Hugh Miller; while yet it is asserted, that neither so fully gathered up into himself the ideas, sentiments, and passions, that mark the representative man.

Notwithstanding his geniality and breadth of character, Sir Walter Scott was rather a relic of feudalism than a representative of modern times. Without the conscious and pronounced loathing of the present, everywhere to be met with in the writings of another great countryman, Scott turned instinctively to the golden glories of the past—his spirit revelled in the jousts and tournaments of the age of chivalry; but for all that had been done in Scotland subsequent to the Reformation era he had little sympathy, and certainly no enthusiasm. It was this chasm of centuries—lying a great gulf between Sir

Walter and the ideas and sentiments of his countrymen—which, though coloured with the exaggeration of controversy, gave a tone of truth to the elder M'Crie's assertion, that his characters were for the most part moss-troopers and Border reivers, rather than genuinely Scottish. The laureate of chivalry fallen upon an age from which chivalry was gone—whelmed in the wide-weltering chaos French democracy had created—Scott's mission was to gather up that minstrelsy of the Scottish Border, and in those metrical and prose romances with which his name is now so indissolubly and so gloriously associated—the image of the vanished age—bequeathing to democracy a mirror in which it might evermore behold a faithful portrait of the glories laid in the dust in its march to universal dominion. That mission accomplished—the literature of chivalry carried to the ends of the earth—Scott's work was done. "No sky-born messenger, heaven looking through his eyes," was the Lord of Abbotsford; and no voice from the celestial land did the literary Vandyke of a demi-savage age bring near to the children of men. A couple of trivial and seemingly unimportant facts brought together, will better illustrate the antithesis, on the spiritual side, between the characters of Scott and Miller than a whole chapter of dissertation. If we recollect aright, it is the Ettrick Shepherd who relates how charmed Scott had been with the conversation of an intelligent mechanic, whose acquaintance he had made on the lands of Abbotsford; but on discovering that this intelligent operative, from whose converse he had enjoyed so much delight throughout the week, was a Baptist preacher on Sabbath, Scott never spoke with him more. Hugh Miller, in his "Scenes and Legends of the North of Scotland" (his first prose work), has not scrupled to present his readers with one of the finest illustrations of unostentatious Christian philanthropy, in the person of an humble Baptist shoemaker.

Burns did embody at once in his intuitions and ideas—very distinctly embody—the spirit of the age, in certain of its aspects; he had, indeed, an affection for the antique, but the dead past did not, as in the case of Scott, swallow up his sympathies for the living present. What, then, was necessary to complete his representative character? assuredly neither native force nor established and diffusive fame. The foremost man of all his time, after gauging his intellectual capacity, pronounced him fitted to excel in whatever walk of ambition he had chosen to exert his faculties. And in our day we are witnesses of what could scarcely have been predicted in his own, the voice that first rose in lowly cadence in that "auld clay biggin' by the banks o' bonny Doon," is now "heard on every wave, and sounds on every sea." Yet, despite his superior endowments and pre-eminent fame, there is a fatal flaw in the character of Burns which prevents us assigning him the position we claim for Hugh Miller. We allude, as our readers will easily comprehend, to the discord between the poet and the man, which has always constituted the chief difficulty with the critics of our national bard. There is a point of view from which Burns appears altogether lovely; and there is a point from which he appears quite the opposite of attractive. As either of these phases of his character is dwelt upon too exclusively, we obtain a false, or at best, imperfect view of Burns as a whole. Few, indeed, of his biographers, have been able to hold the balance with that scrupulous exactness even-handed justice demands—extenuating nothing, nor yet setting down aught in malice. Certainly it is with no feeling of regret we have observed, the more attractive features of his character are the features on which writers in general have loved to linger. It is perhaps well that such should have been the case. Gloating over the errors of humanity or the aberrations of genius, displays no amiable feeling; and his must ever be a thankless task who seeks to break the spell by nature bound around the voiceless dead. Yet without gloating over, while in point of fact mourning, the errors of the bard, we cannot forget the jarring and the dissonance between his higher and his lower, his nobler and baser self. The powers of light and darkness seem to have been mated within him, and to have waged a terrible, and but too equal strife, during his entire earthly pilgrimage; now beckoning him to heaven, now bending him to earth: and alternately, as either principle waxed or waned, Burns is seen soaring into the region of the holiest sentiment, or sunk in the mire of an odious sensuality. Nor let it be supposed there is anything incongruous in all this. Man is neither an angel nor a demon; the wheat and the tares grow together in the soil of the human heart; and unless we shut our eyes to facts, there is no denying that black and polluting passions were often the tenants of the breast which poured forth the address to the mountain daisy, and that the bosom which heaved with emotions of the most touching tenderness and exquisite sensibility, was often set on fire of hell.

We say not these things because we have any pleasure in calling attention to the failings and shortcomings of one of whom Scotland has so much reason to be proud. Nor do we homologate, in any measure, the untenable opinion held by certain narrow souls, that Burns was wanting in what modern moralists have called the religious sentiment. The very opposite we believe to have been the case. Again and again throughout his letters we meet the genuine outbreathing of this sentiment. It is related by his brother Gilbert how very profoundly Burns was impressed with the solemn beauty and power of the words, "Let us worship God." That this simple utterance, heard from childhood beneath the paternal rooftree, known by him as the call which summoned thousands of Scottish households, to offer up to heaven the morning and the evening sacrifice—should have so completely penetrated his soul, and bowed it beneath a sense of the awe and mystery of the infinite and the unseen, tells in language neither to be mistaken nor misinterpreted, the depth of religious feeling which, like a fountain sealed, lay struggling for utterance within his soul. Pity it was that this religious sentiment, naturally so deep and ardent, was not permitted to work itself clear of the dross which had gathered round it, "staining the white radiance of eternity." The men and the times on which he had fallen, in great part prevented this. That latent scepticism which good old Wodrow, in his Analecta, mourns as having entered the Church of Scotland, had, in Burns' day, borne some of its most noxious fruits. A false philosophy had eaten out the heart of the historic religion of Scotland amongst Scottish literati and Scottish theologians. The church of Knox, Melville, and Henderson, was now represented by Dr. William Robertson and Dr. Hugh Blair. Unhappily, the New-Light priesthood found in the rustic bard at once a powerful and popular ally; for, without doubt, the controversies into which he plunged with its approbation, exerted a most sinister influence, at a most critical hour, on his religious nature. Cut off, not by any innate want of sympathy, but by a fatal misdirection of his faculties, from the creed of his country—nay, publicly pitted against it, as the fighting man of the illuminati of his age—Burns missed becoming Scotland's representative man.

Thus has it come to pass that neither in Abbotsford nor in Ayrshire—not by the banks of the Doon, but by the Bay of Cromarty, must we seek the embodiment of the genius and tendencies of our country. We again repeat, that however great, however potential in their respective individualities Scott and Burns undoubtedly were, the defects we have pointed out are fatal to their claims as representative men. A nation with such glorious souvenirs of freedom, could not crown the laureate of feudalism; and though he who sang "A man's a man for a' that," and "Scots wha hae wi' Wallace bled," has infinitely higher claims, yet a nation whose religious struggles surpassed even the splendour of her conflicts for civil freedom, cannot call the author of the "Holy Fair" a type of the children of the covenant.

In his "Sartor Resartus," Carlyle, with that felicitous pictorial power for which he stands unrivalled among modern writers, has gathered up into a single sentence that photographs on the mind for ever, a magnificent image of the influence and the unity of mankind. "On the hardest adamant some footprint of us is stamped in—on the last rear of the host shall be read traces of the earliest van." Subordinated to this general unity, and infolded in its ample circumference, lie the various national unities; and he who would adequately represent a nation must be himself the heir of all the epochs through which that nation has passed. The puerile rant indulged about Scottish nationality by certain writers and speakers during recent years, has so burlesqued the subject, that it is all but impossible to obtain the public ear for the soberest and most philosophic statement of its claims. Fortunately, the object we contemplate in adverting to the topic now, will be sufficiently served by the recapitulation of a few facts which even the most sceptical will not attempt to challenge. It may be asserted with something like axiomatic accuracy, that the peculiar character of a nation is determined by the spirit with which it rises equal to those great crises in its history which sooner or later overtake all peoples in the development of the drama of the world. Three such epochs have occurred in Scottish story, and it has been the fortune of Scotland, on each occasion, to encounter the fiery trial through which she was called to pass, in the most heroic and dauntless spirit.

The first crisis was the patriotic struggle for Scottish nationality in the actual, not in the heraldic sense Blind Harry's heroes were men of a very different stamp from the windbags who, a short while ago, set England a laughing at Scotland and Scotchmen. And, however easily *Punch* snuffed out the babblers about nationality in our own day, we believe southern chivalry found it no laughing matter to deal with the thirteenth-century defenders of Scottish rights.

The conflict of which Wallace was the representative, fused the various races which had come together on the soil of Scotland, but had hitherto dwelt apart without community of interest or unity of feeling. The battle with England, fought out so gloriously, so victoriously, animated the victors with a passion for nationality, such as never before possessed them. The unity of the nation, thus perfected through suffering, was destined to exert a most salutary influence upon the fortunes of another great struggle which was soon to call, not Scotland only, but Europe to the conflict. What Wallace was in the thirteenth century, such was Knox in the sixteenth. The foe is now no longer England, but the Pope; not a powerful sovereign, but a powerful superstition it is the people are called to combat. We need not say how more completely here than in any other corner of Christendom, if perhaps we except Geneva, the work was done. Yet once more was Scotland summoned to the battle-field. Again the conflict is mainly ecclesiastical. She has been equal to the occasion hitherto, whether the foe was England's sovereign or the Roman pontiff: will she be equal to the conflict when the enemy is her own king? Deep-seated in every Scottish heart was the attachment of the people for the descendants of the hero of Bannockburn. Through long centuries that royal race had gone out and in before them, and, whether in the halls of debate or in the field of battle, had not been wanting to the nation. Much, very much, did Scotland suffer from the Stuarts before, stung into rebellion, her sons took the field against them. Yet generous and ardent as had been their devotion to their kings, in the camp of Leslie the highest earthly royalty was esteemed but as the dust in the balance, when weighed against the claims of Christ's crown and covenant.

From the elements which mingled in this last struggle it was necessarily very protracted. During thirty years did the best and bravest of our people wander the wilderness, pouring out their blood like water in defence of the good—the holy cause. The battle descended from sire to son, and even in what seemed its triumph, though a period was put to the fierce persecution which had devoured the nation, the principle for which Scotland had taken arms against Charles Stuart was not conceded by William of Orange. We deem it of some importance to note this fact; for, in the definite perception, that so far as Scotland's ecclesiastical position was concerned, the revolution of 1688 was rather a drawn battle than a victory, lies the key to the comprehension of some of the most important events that have transpired in our times. These being the phases through which the nation has passed, we should expect to find its representative man imbued with the passion for civil freedom which fired the soul of Wallace, inspired with the zeal for religious liberty which animated Knox, and panting to decide in the light of the principles of the great Reformer, the drawn battle the revolution bequeathed—a bone of contention to the men of our times. If, in addition to rehearsing the storied past, we found this man had fully caught the scientific spirit of the present, incredulity itself were vanquished. It is our belief that more completely than any other Scotchman, Hugh Miller sustains this complex representative position, and in the development of the leading incidents in the life, and in the salient features of the character of our great countryman, we hope to inspire our readers with a kindred conviction.

KINNING PARK, GLASGOW, 10*th March*, 1858.

HUGH MILLER.

CHAPTER I.

ANCESTRY AND EARLY LIFE.

THOMAS CARLYLE, some time ago, lamented with a very sincere regret the lack of material for the study of English history, in the want of good and reliable portraits of historic characters. We can easily understand that regret: a genuine likeness would sometimes go far to solve a historical problem. By the aid of such insight as portraits would supply, the annalist might gather up something like a conception of the blended influences different families had exerted upon each other, whose blood had mingled together. How interesting such a collection might be made, we know from the interest that attaches to even the portraits of a single eminent individual, taken in the successive stages of life. Seen as passing through life's seven ages, we catch a glimpse, through the canvas of the painter, of the vicissitudes which time and circumstance exert upon man. We have not the fortune to possess such a gallery of the ancestors, by either the male or the female line, of the subject of this biography; but we are fortunate enough to possess in Hugh Miller's "Schools and Schoolmasters," what, in the want of such a gallery, may supply the gap its absence creates—the traditionary reminiscences of that ancestry for several generations. Judiciously enough, these traditions are not rendered unnecessarily prolix, while yet sufficient of incident and of character are reproduced, to enable us to form a very definite idea of the tributary human streams from which the Cromarty stone-mason sprang.

In fashionable and aristocratic biographies, one often meets some statement like the following; meant, no doubt, to overawe the plebeian mind, and gratify the pride of birth:—the family is one of very ancient date, having, it is believed, come into England with the Conqueror. Hugh Miller honestly tells us that his progenitors were a long line of seafaring men, skilful, adventurous sailors, who had coasted along the Scottish shores as early as the times of Sir Andrew Wood and the bold Bartons, and mayhap helped to man "that very monstrous shippe, the *Great Michael*, that cumbered all Scotland to get her to sea." These sea-kings appear to have been a worthy race; superior, we opine, to the shaggy northmen who accompanied Duke William to the conquest of England. But the buccaneers of the earlier period, who, "by the splendour of God," took seizin of the soil of the Saxon, were ennobled; while old John Feddes and his comrades, whether disappointed in love or otherwise, who did business on their own account in the Spanish Main, though quite as honest, were not quite so fortunate. We obtain a very penetrative glance into the basis of kindness on which the energetic characters of Hugh Miller's progenitors reposed, from the following story of his father's early life. His mother had consigned him to the care of an aunt married to a neighbouring farmer, that in the acquisition of agricultural tastes, he might be saved from the hereditary fate of the family, who, in its male members at least, had, during many generations, all of them made ocean their tomb. But destiny was not thus to be foiled; the family fate was not to be so avoided. Sent from the farm-house to drown a litter of puppies, the boy, after some intermittent fits of irresolution, took his way to his mother's house, arriving there in the dusk of the gloamin, with the doomed doggies tucked up in his kilt. The good woman in consternation at his appearance in such circumstances, exclaimed "O my unlucky boy!" "Mother," said the youth, "the little doggies, mother; I couldna drown the little doggies, and I brought them to you." The unlucky boy having no ambition to become a model farmer, was ultimately sent to sea, and exhibited throughout a checkered, yet not unsuccessful career, the best qualities of a British sailor. The tender-hearted youth, "who couldna drown the doggies," afterwards did very effective execution upon the Dutch off the

Dogger-bank, on that day, memorable in the annals of British naval warfare, doing the work of two men.

Pressed into the service of his country without his consent, Miller is one evening found absent without leave, and the next glimpse we have of him, he is master of a craft that sails from his native Cromarty. Fortune smiles upon the shipmaster; he builds a new house beside the ancient cottage of his buccaneering grandsire, of more imposing proportions than satisfied the modest ambition of old John Feddes. The dangers of the sea are proverbial, both in song and story; and nowhere does adversity follow faster on the heels of fortune in individual instances, than on that element which has built up the greatness of Britain. Early in November, 1797, Miller's square-rigged sloop, which had lain for some days wind-bound in the port of Peterhead, left its moorings on the gloomy night of a gloomy day, and bore out to sea. The breeze, which had lured the craft from her haven, speedily freshened into a gale, the gale into a hurricane; and despite the most herculean efforts, and the most skilful seamanship, his bark, the *Friendship*, next morning is in spales on the bar of Findhorn. His fortunes thus wrecked, Miller was on the eve of selling his house at a disadvantage, to provide himself with a new vessel, when a friend interposed and advanced the money required. The new sloop, though not quite equal to the lost one in point of size, was wholly built of oak, every plank and beam of which he had superintended in the laying down; and so, though he had to satisfy himself with the old house, with its little rooms and its small windows, and let the other house to a tenant, he began to thrive as before. Shortly after this the master of the sloop, who had been now for some years a widower, married a second time, and in 1802, not 1805, as some popular biographies assert, Hugh Miller was born in the low long house built by his great-grandfather, the buccaneer. The memory of the child awoke early; his recollections dating from some months before the completion of his third year. Most of these reminiscences are of a pleasing character. "The young spirit has awakened out of eternity, and knows not what we mean by time; as yet time is no fast hurrying stream, but a sportful sun-lit ocean; the fair garden, life, rustles infinite around, and everywhere is dewy fragrance and budding hope."

But sterner memories are at hand. The cloud that is to cast so dark a shadow over his fortunes, already hangs on the skirts of the horizon. As agent for the Leith Glass-works, his father had been for some months sailing round the Hebrides, collecting kelp; and towards the end of October, 1807, deeply laden, he had threaded his way round Cape Wrath, and through the Pentland, and across the Moray Frith, when a severe gale compelled him to seek shelter in the harbour of Peterhead.

From this, to him ill-fated port, on the 9th November, 1807, he wrote his last letter. On the following day he set sail from Peterhead; soon a storm arose, more terrible than the tempest in which the *Friendship* went to pieces. Miller's vessel was last seen by a townsman and shipmaster, who, safely moored in an English harbour, marked the square-rigged sloop in the offing from morn to night, exhausting every expedient of nautical science to keep aloof from the shore. Skill and perseverance seemed successful; for, clearing a formidable headland, mottled with broken ships and drowned men, the sloop was seen stretching out by a long tack into the sea. "Miller's seamanship has saved him once more," said the Cromarty skipper, as quitting his place on the outlook, he returned to the cabin. But the night fell wild and tempestuous, and no vestige of the hapless sloop was ever more seen. Thus perished a man, whom his comrades called the best sailor that ever sailed the Moray Frith.

No foreboding of the catastrophe had reached the bay of Cromarty. The Peterhead letter had shed light and hope into the master's humble dwelling. The night after the reception of this missive, the sailor's household are gathered around the family hearth; the mother plies the cheerful needle by the cottage fire; her son, a boy of five years of age, is sitting by her side—when the house door, which had been left unfastened, fell open, and the youth is despatched to shut it. Of what followed, the man shall tell the recollections of the child. "Day had not wholly disappeared," says Hugh Miller, "but it was fast posting into night, and a grey haze spread a neutral tint of dimness over every more distant object, but left the nearer ones comparatively distinct, when I saw the door open. Within less than a yard of my breast, as plainly as I ever saw anything, was a dissevered hand and arm stretched towards me. Hand and arm were apparently those of a female; they bore a livid and sodden appearance; and, directly fronting me, where the body ought to have been, there was only blank transparent space, through which I could see the dim forms of the objects beyond. I was fearfully startled, and ran shrieking to my mother telling her what I had seen. I communicate the story as it lies fixed in my memory, without attempting to explain it. The supposed apparition may have been merely a momentary affection of the eye, of the nature described by Sir Walter Scott in his Demonology, and Sir David Brewster in his Natural Magic. But if so, it was an affection of which I experienced no after-return, and its coincidence with my father's death seems at least curious." We shall best respect the memory of the dead, and best consult the tastes of the living, by leaving the story of this singular apparition as its author has left it, unexplained. Right or wrong, we like as little as Hugh

Miller possibly could, to draw aside the veil of enchantment in which he obviously loved to shroud this vision from the too curious scrutiny of science. We know the fishers of Cromarty are, or at least were, a superstitious people, devout believers in all sorts of demonology and witchcraft; and it may be possible that, living on the confines of the fisher-town, the vivid imagination of the boy had become tinged with the superstition of the place. Friends, we are aware, have offered this explanation of the vision, and probably it is the true one. But we pass from all attempts to furnish the rationale of the apparition, simply remarking that seldom indeed have we found much either of goodness or greatness in any man whose young heart was not profoundly imbued with a love of the marvellous. Before departing from this topic, we may mention that, though just turned five years of age, this was not the first vision seen by the boy. Old John Feddes, his buccaneering ancestor, dead fully half a century before, had already appeared to the youth in the identical light-blue coat he wore when in the flesh. There are more things in heaven and earth than are dreamt of in our philosophy. And those dreams and visions of which we sometimes hear the wondrous story, may they not have their origin in mental phenomena which the plummet of philosophy will never be able to sound?

But whatever opinion may be entertained about the

reality of the apparition, there can be none about the loss the boy had sustained; and he tells how, day after day, he used to climb the grassy protuberance of the old coast-line immediately behind his mother's house, that commands a wide reach of the Moray Frith, and to look wistfully out, long after every one else had ceased to hope, for the sloop with the two stripes of white and the two square-topsails. But months and years passed by, and the white stripes and the square-topsails he never saw. Those who have seen life in its gloomiest aspects, and sorrow in its saddest forms, have often wondered what preternatural power it was that gave such marvellous fascination to the grief of a child. The secret of the spell we apprehend to be this:—Light-hearted as children generally are, and for the most part their sorrow only an April shower, there is yet a pensive melancholy of which childhood is susceptible, lost in youth and early manhood, that comes back upon man when his powers are matured by reflection and mellowed by experience, uniting by a mysterious bond, subtler far than any electric affinity, the gloamin of his years with "the love of life's young day." Perhaps in all men a measure of this feeling is to be found; but in the man of genius it receives its special and most marked development. And far truer herald of genius do we deem it than any dux medal of even the best-appointed public school—that this boy of five years of age should, day after day and month after month, long after hope had died in every breast save his own, be seen climbing that grassy knoll from which was beheld the most glorious of prospects stretching away into infinitude, yet utterly oblivious of every marvel of nature with which he is surrounded; his eye sweeping the farthest verge of the horizon, intent only on discovering amid that yeast of waves the bark which has borne his father from him never to return. Hugh Miller mourning his sire reminds us of the first great sorrows of Cowper, of Kitto, and of De Quincey, all of whom were early taught in the deaths of dearest friends how soon "shades of the prison-house begin to close around the growing boy." It was the death of Kitto's good grandmother that constituted his first great sorrow. A sister's death was De Quincey's earliest grief. Kitto's impressions upon receiving the tidings that his grandame was no more, recorded in his workhouse journal, remind us, in their dirge-like plaint, of De Quincey's wail by his sister's bier, with only this difference, that while the expression of anguish is in both cases nearly equal, the sorrow of Kitto has in it less of the fantastic and imaginative. There is a pomp of woe—an affluence of grief about the wail of the child of fortune—wanting in the plaint of the workhouse-boy. Cowper, fifty years after the event, dedicated one of the noblest of his minor poems to the memory of a mother lost in childhood.

Hugh Miller, in opening manhood, embalmed in verse the record of the catastrophe which so early made him acquainted with grief; but poetry was not Hugh's province, and though not destitute of a certain rugged force, and vigour, and sensibility, the stanzas on his father's death have about them little of the true minstrel fire. That sorrow was too deep to find adequate utterance in any verse which "a journeyman stone-mason" could write; and probably it had been better he had never attempted the theme. The painter who could not express the excess of grief, covered with a veil the face of Agamemnon.

CHAPTER II.

THE DAME'S AND GRAMMAR SCHOOLS.

YOUNG Miller's loss of his father, so keenly mourned, was supplied, as far as the best earthly friends could make up a bereavement so sad, by his two maternal uncles; types of a class of men that, from age to age, have been the ornament of the peasantry of Scotland, but who, generation after generation, are permitted to pass away without any adequate memorial of their many virtues. We, therefore, gladly pause to read the inscription on the stone of remembrance, which, in his "Schools and Schoolmasters," Hugh Miller has erected to that pair of noble brothers. "My elder uncle, James, added to a clear head and much native sagacity, a singularly retentive memory, and great thirst of information. He was a harness-maker, and wrought for the farmers of an extensive district of country; and as he never engaged either a journeyman or apprentice, but executed all his work with his own hands, his hours of labour, save that he indulged in a brief pause as the twilight came on, and took a mile's walk or so, were usually protracted from six o'clock in the morning till ten at night. Such incessant occupation, of course, left him little time for reading; but he often found some one to read beside him during the day; and in the winter evenings, his portable bench used to be brought from his shop at the other end of the dwelling, into the family sitting-room, and placed beside the circle round the hearth, where his brother Alexander, my younger uncle, whose occupation left his evenings free, would read aloud from some interesting volume for the general benefit—placing himself always at the opposite end of the bench, so as to share in the light of the worker. Occasionally the family circle would be widened by the accession of from two to three intelligent neighbours, who would drop in to listen; and then the book, after a space, would be laid aside, in order that its contents might be discussed in conversation. In the summer months, uncle James always spent some time in the country, in looking after and keeping in repair the harness of the farmers for whom he wrought; and during his journeys and twilight walks on these occasions, there was not an old castle, or hillfoot, or ancient encampment, or antique ecclesiastical edifice within twenty miles of the town, which he had not visited and examined over and over again. He was a keen local antiquary; knew a good deal about architectural styles of the various ages, at a time when the subjects were very little studied or known ; possessed more traditionary lore, picked up chiefly in his country journeys, than any man I ever knew. What he once heard he never forgot ; and the knowledge which he had acquired, he could communicate pleasingly and succinctly, in a style which, had he been a writer of books, instead of merely a reader of them, would have had the merit of being clear and terse, and more laden with meaning than words. From his reputation for sagacity, his advice used to be much sought after by the neighbours in every little difficulty that came in their way ; and the counsel given was always shrewd and honest. I never knew a man more entirely just in his dealings than uncle James, or who regarded every species of meanness with a more thorough contempt."

Uncle Alexander was of a different caste from his brother both in intellect and temperament, but he was characterized by the same strict integrity ; and his religious feelings, though quiet and unobtrusive, were perhaps more deep. James was somewhat of a humorist, and fond of a joke ; Alexander, grave and serious. An old sailor, he had served under Nelson at Camperdown, taken part in the campaign under Abercrombie in Egypt ; and though wanting his brother's fluency, yet by his descriptions of foreign plants and animals, he succeeded in inoculating his nephew with his own special tastes. In his lengthened rambles on the wold or by the sea-shore with the old naval hero, young Miller was initiated into the study of natural history: Uncle Sandy was in point of fact his earliest, his only professor.

Before his father's death, Hugh Miller had been sent to a dame's school, where, under the tuition of an old lady, its superintendent, who, most likely, had she been living in our days, would not have received a government certificate, or been favoured with any pupil teachers, he groped his way through the Shorter Catechism, the Proverbs, the New Testament, and at length entered her highest, *the* Bible class. Even thus early was that peculiarity, which we shall afterwards meet as nearly marring his prospects, fully developed. In deference to his superiors he had, after a manner, made a kind of acquaintance with the rudiments of knowledge; but having no adequate sense of the tendency of his lessons, all was dark and chaotic. There are certain minds that probably might not have felt in any perceptible degree uncomfortable in such circumstances; but Hugh Miller was not one of these minds. He could not go on day after day getting crammed by some superior, without questioning whereunto that cramming should grow; he liked to see the reason of things—sought above all else to know the central principle around which the details, either of business or of study, grouped themselves. In this strongly-marked mental peculiarity is embodied every pregnant hint for educationists. So soon as Hugh Miller made the discovery, that the art of reading was the art of finding stories in books, all the darkness and all the drudgery fled. Have the friends of education kept sight of this important fact? we are afraid that, in too many instances, the powerful lever it would place in the hands of the teacher has been left to rust unused.

Having seen that reading was the key that unlocked a boundless store of mental pleasure, young Miller's progress, which had hitherto been nothing extraordinary, accelerated in something like a geometric ratio. The story of Joseph, the stories of Samson, of David and Goliath, of Elijah and Elisha, all were speedily mastered. And from these Hebrew tales—the joy of many generations of the youth of Scotland—Hugh Miller turned to those classical romances of childhood, Jack the Giant-Killer, Jack and the Bean Stalk, The Yellow Dwarf, Blue Beard, Sinbad the Sailor, Beauty and the Beast, Aladdin or the Wonderful Lamp; and passed from these without break or conscious line of division to the Odyssey: for even so early had he seen that no other writer could cast a javelin with half the force of Homer. At this time, too, it was he found in that marvellous production of the tinker of Elstow—"The Pilgrim's Progress"—a sacred Iliad; and subsequently he made the acquaintance of that class of works which we may designate, not inappropriately, our Scottish Martyrology —"Howie's Scots' Worthies," "Naphthali, or the Hind let loose," "The Cloud of Witnesses," &c.; blending, in his mind, by a perfectly natural transition, the patriotic and religious struggles of the nation whose story these works record. It was the tone and colouring that the heroism of those humble men, "men who lived unknown till persecution dragged them into fame," had given to the mind of Hugh Miller, that, when in 1831 he came a stone-mason to the metropolis, so instinctively led him to Dr. M'Crie's humble chapel. None of the great men he saw in Edinburgh on this his first visit, produced the same powerful impression upon the wanderer from Cromarty, as the biographer of Knox and Melville.

The best part of his father's library had perished with his parent. Still there were a few books, curious and rare, that had been left behind. Among these were the "Miracles of Nature and Art," to which we find Dr. Johnson referring, in one of the dialogues chronicled by Boswell, as scarce even in his day. It contained, also, what to one who subsequently became so great an admirer of Goldsmith must have been a volume of no little interest, the only copy he ever saw of the "Memoirs of a Protestant" condemned to the galleys of France for his religion; a work which had been translated from the French by the author of the "Vicar of

Wakefield" in his day of obscure literary drudgery, and which exhibited the peculiar excellencies of his style. Books of theology and books of travel made up the rest of the collection. Flavel's works, Henry's Commentary, and Hutcheson on the Lesser Prophets mingled with the voyages of Anson, Drake, Dampier, and Raleigh. It might not, indeed, be such a collection as the Useful Knowledge Society would have altogether approved of placing in the hands of a youth; nevertheless, we believe it to have been just about the kind of collection to suit the versatile tastes of young Miller. The aim of the Useful Knowledge Society was no doubt excellent, and, like most things done with good intentions, it was productive of some beneficial results. It failed, however, because it attempted to make of the rugged steep man must climb in quest of knowledge, never to be scaled without earnest toil and endeavour, a kind of macadamized road which all might travel with nearly equal ease and equal progress. The error was indeed an error into which the author of the "Novum Organon" fell, but the delusion was not less pernicious because shared by Lord Bacon. We do not, therefore, wonder that Hugh Miller should have designated the works with which that society sought to flood the nation "intolerable nuisances, tenebrious stars, shedding their blighting influence on youthhood." About this time Hugh Miller's uncle, James, put into his hands Blind Harry's "Wallace."

When he had read how Wallace killed young Selbie, the constable's son; how Wallace had fished the Irvine Water; and how Wallace killed the churl with his own staff in Ayr,—his uncle, with that dry humour that makes a joke tell, said to him the book seemed rather a rough sort of production, which he need read no more of unless he liked; but young Hugh rather did like—what boy ever did not?—to read of Wallace. He was intoxicated with the fiery narratives of the blind bard—all he had previously read of the marvels of foreign parts, of the glories of modern battles, seemed tame and commonplace; in a word, he was now a Scot. From the story of Scotland's hero-guardian, he passed to the story of her hero-king, and in Barbour's "Bruce" read the glorious consummation of the work Wallace had so gloriously begun.

After some twelve months' instruction from the old lady who taught the alphabet in the antique style, young Miller was duly transferred from the dame's school to the grammar-school of Cromarty. The master of that seminary was, what not seldom happens, a good scholar, but by no means an energetic instructor; at college he had distinguished himself in mathematics and the languages, and if a boy wished to learn he could certainly teach him; but if a boy wished to do nothing, he was not required to do more than he wished. He was in the habit of advising the parents or relations of those whom he deemed his clever lads, to give them a classical education; and, meeting one day with uncle James, he urged the worthy harness-maker to put his nephew into Latin. Uncle James, on data of his own, having arrived at a similar conclusion to that of the schoolmaster, his protégé was transferred from the English to the Latin form. In the Latin class, however, it would appear Hugh Miller had either forgotten his axiom about the art of reading, or thought the story of old Rome not worth the trouble of mastering a language to know. The account he has given of his progress in acquiring the Roman tongue is quite explicit enough to show that, even with greater perseverance, he was not likely to have become a rival to Cardinal Mezzofante. "I laboured," says he, "with tolerable diligence for a day or two, but there was no one to tell me what the rules meant, or whether they really meant anything; and when I got as far as *penna*, a pen, and saw how the changes were rung on one poor word that did not seem to me of more importance in the old language than the modern, I began miserably to flag and to long for my English reading, with its amusing stories and picture-like descriptions. The Rudiments was by far the dullest book I had ever seen—it embodied no thought that I could perceive, and certainly it contained no narrative. None of my class-fellows were by any means bright; and yet, when the class, which the master very soon learned to distinguish as the heavy class, was called up, I was generally found at its nether end." Thus was thrown away Miller's only chance of acquiring the tongue of Cicero and Cæsar. In "Memorials of His Time," Lord Cockburn tells us that, when at school, the beauty of no Roman word, or thought, or action, ever occurred to him; nor did he fancy Latin was of any use except to torture boys. In youth-hood the future geologist and the future judge seem to have thought very much alike on this matter. Nor were their fates very different. If Miller was generally at the nether end of his class, Cockburn never got a prize, and (a more humiliating reminiscence than any the stone-mason has recorded) once sat booby at the annual public examination. Some critics have lamented Miller's inaptitude for Latin, as having left his style destitute of the majesty and rhythmic cadence of Milton, Gibbon, and Macaulay. In reply to such regrets, we have to say that we should not desire to have seen his style other than it is. We admire—who does not admire? —that illustrious triad of English classics; but we certainly should not have more, but less admired Hugh Miller had we discovered in his pages either the cadences of Cromwell's Latin secretary, the balanced antithesis of the "Decline and Fall of the Roman Empire," or the sonorous rhetoric of the historian of England. Style, it should not be forgotten, consists quite as much in knowing exactly what to say, as in the excellence with which it is said. That delicate taste, which spontaneously rejects a false word with the same unerring instinct that the musician rejects a false note, is something native, not something acquired. How else could we account for the multitude of eminent linguists who yet remain through life the most indifferent English writers, and whose styles, so far from being musical, are in a very special degree destitute of that mingled strength and beauty, that rhythmic cadence, which the admirers of the classics suppose the masterpieces of antiquity pre-eminently bestow?

Some of the wealthier inhabitants of Cromarty, dissatisfied with the small progress their boys were making under the parish teacher, got up a subscription-school, to which their children were transferred; and uncle James, sharing the general impatience, sent his protégé thither also. Unfortunately, though rather a clever young man, this teacher proved quite as unsteady as he was clever. Getting rid of him, a licentiate of the church was procured, who promised well; but getting immersed in the Baptist controversy, he resigned his charge. A third teacher was got; but he too soon lost health and heart, and in a labyrinth of perplexity also gave up. Young Miller's opportunities for rambling the coasts, and exploring the caves of Cromarty, were, in consequence of these mishaps, quite as great as before.

The many wanderings in which he indulged at this time, besides permanently forming his taste for the study of natural science, and laying the foundation of that very extensive and accurate knowledge of the marvels of nature, which remain for ever unknown to unanointed eyes, have enabled us to catch a glimpse of what was the condition of the Highlands before the Highland lairds had made the very notable discovery of how much a sheep was better than a man, or had hushed the hum of humanity in the glens of the north by the cry of the curlew and the wail of the plover. Hugh Miller's recollections of excursions into the interior made by him at this early period, lift the veil which, during fifty years now, has been falling over northern society, and discover to us somewhat of the condition of the Gael ere the march of modern improvement had transformed "the land where Fingal fought and Ossian sang" into sheep walks and deer forests. In these reminiscences, shadowy and imperfect as they may seem, are not wanting traces of the germs of a transition-era; the bloom of a new civilization loomed on the future of that interesting people; but all has been suddenly and, we fear, for ever arrested by a ruthless political economy, which, during the last forty years, has realized itself in the clearance system.

Schoolmaster, number four, has now been appointed to the subscription-school of Cromarty—a combination, it would appear, of the coxcomb and the pedant, and being such, naturally enough soon became obnoxious to his pupils. Throughout life as little as possible of either pedant or coxcomb, it is not surprising that Hugh Miller did not keep long on the most amicable terms with the new teacher. The antique pronunciation of the alphabet, which he had learned at the dame's school, still clung to him, and in spelling he had to translate the old Scotch into English sounds; thus rendering the operation not only somewhat painful, but tedious. Neither had he been originally taught to break the words into syllables. The result of this neglect was a serio-comic termination of his school career. "When required one evening," says Hugh Miller, "to spell the word *awful*, I spelt it word for word without break or pause, as a-w-f-u-l. 'No,' said the master, 'a-w-*aw*, f-u-l *awful;* spell again.' This seemed preposterous spelling; it was sticking in an *a*, as I thought, into the middle of a word where I was sure no *a* had a right to be; and so I spelt it as at first. The master recompensed my supposed contumacy with a sharp cut thwart the ears with his tawse, and again demanded the spelling of the word. I yet again spelt it as at first; but, on receiving a second cut, I refused to spell it any more." A fight followed, which no sooner finished, than young Miller takes down his cap from the pin and marches out of school, never more returning to do homage to the

Cromarty pedagogue—having got as little good from teachers as probably ever did any man of equal eminence. Though, perhaps, there is nothing wonderful in this, quite as often as otherwise it has happened that those distinguished in after have been little distinguished in early life; while, in not a few instances, early eminence has only been the presage of after obscurity. Academical distinctions are by no means badges of permanent celebrity. "In the world's broad field of battle," the booby of the schools has not seldom snatched the laurel from the dux. The distinguished have thus no cause for presumption; the dullards not much reason to despair.

Surrounded by images of the fleeting and evanescent, whence comes that passionate desire to baffle mutation, which so early takes possession of man, and leads him on to all those devices to conquer time's tyrannic power, and perpetuate, amidst every change, the memory of his noblest and most cherished associations? Are we wrong in assuming that it comes up from out those deeper feelings of our nature that mysteriously ally the present with all its changefulness to the eternally unchangeable? In this instinct, if we may dare to call a thing so sacred by such a name, lies the source of the sorrow with which we interchange the farewell word with the friend from whom we are about to part for ever, or take the last fond look of the scenes to which we have bid a final adieu. A crisis had now arrived when Hugh Miller and his comrades were about to partake of this sacrament of sorrow. The band of which he had been the leader, hitherto more famous for rambling than for study, was about to break up; some going to sea, others going south to complete their education. Before, however, they are scattered abroad, they shall erect a memorial of their fraternity. The common school-book story of the Persian shepherd, who, when raised by his sovereign to high place in the empire, derived his chief pleasure from contemplating in a secret apartment the pipe, crook, and rude habiliments of his happier days, suggested to their chief that the band should also have its secret apartment, in which to store up for future contemplation, their bayonet, pistol, pot, and pitcher. The proposal was favourably received; and selecting a solitary spot among the trees as a proper site, and procuring a spade and mattock, they began to dig. At length the mysterious chamber was completed, a huge pit, six feet, lined with spars. Unfortunately, while exultant over their success, Johnstone, the forester of the district, discovers the pit, and being altogether a one-idead man, not able to fancy it was meant for any nobler purpose than the maiming of cattle, began to talk about a proclamation and a reward for the apprehension of the excavators of the cattle-trap. Miller's known acquaintance with all kinds of books on natural history, led the forester to some very definite conclusions about his share in the work. He was certain the rascal had acquainted himself by books with the mode of entrapping wild beasts in the forests abroad, of which this trap for his master's cattle was a copy. Thus speedily confounded and brought to nought was this humble memento of the joys and companionships of youth, and the band left to console themselves with the philosophic reflection that "the best laid schemes o' mice and men gang aft agley."

CHAPTER III.

THE QUARRY.

The hour has come when Hugh Miller must gird himself in earnest for the real business of life. Nearly all his early companions are gone from the scenes of their boyish and youthful rambles; his mother, after a long widowhood of eleven years, has entered anew into the married state; and now, after tasting so much of uncontrolled liberty and enjoyment, he finds himself standing face to face with a life of labour and restraint. The necessity of ever toiling from morn to night seemed a dire one, and fain would he have avoided it. But there was no escape. Unwilling, however, that labour should wield over him a rod entirely black, and remembering the long winter holidays of his cousin George, he selected the profession of his cousin as his own, trusting to find, like him, in the amusement of one-half the year, compensation for the toils of the other half. And yet, it was not altogether amusement which he sought. Even at this time, notwithstanding what he calls the antecedents of a sadly mis-spent boyhood, he looked to higher than mere amusement, and dared to believe that literature, and mayhap natural science, were, after all, his proper vocation—a belief which, we doubt not, that sadly mis-spent boyhood went a long way to kindle. For the future geologist, we could scarcely conceive a better training than it was the fortune of Hugh Miller to receive. What lectures on natural science, by professor however eminent, were to be compared to those rambles with uncle Sandy, in which he became acquainted with nearly every organism about Cromarty? It was the deep love of nature which this early familiarity with its every feature inspired, that threw around Hugh Miller's scientific treatises, so many of the charms of poesy. When resolving to be a mason, with literature and science as his ultimate aim, he also resolved that much of his leisure should be consecrated to the study of our best English authors. Such resolution fairly carried out, will place the stone-mason on a vantage-ground which multitudes who are wasting their guineas at the university will never attain. The grandest human intellects—are they not enshrined in books? have they not shed their souls into those types and that printer's ink? What is the art of printing, but the art of making us familiar with the best thinking of the wisest and the best in every age of the world's history? Is there aught that men have done, devised, or discovered, that is not to be found in books? How truly did Milton say, " a good book is the ethereal and fifth essence, the life's blood of man embalmed and treasured up for a life beyond life." In the existence of books, and in the access which all men have to their pages, we discover the hollowness and the pedantry of the distinction made so much of in some quarters between educated and uneducated men.

The resolution to become a stone-mason sorely vexed both Hugh Miller's uncles, especially James; they had expected to see their nephew entering and attaining eminence in some one or other of the learned professions, and here he was about to become a mere operative mechanic like themselves. Though the labour of their hands was their only wealth, they offered to assist him in getting through college; nay, he might, if he chose, come and live with them, the only condition exacted being, that he should give himself as sedulously to his lessons as, in the event of becoming a mason, he would have to give himself to his trade. To the suggestions and to the entreaties of both his uncles, with characteristic pertinacity, Hugh Miller demurred. He had no wish, no peculiar fitness, to be either lawyer or doctor; and as for the church, that was too serious a direction in which to look for one's bread, unless he could regard himself as called to the church's proper work, which he honestly could not. This deeply conscientious feeling now interposing itself between him and a life of learned leisure, we shall have occasion frequently to notice. Nor were his uncles, though anxious to see their nephew rise to eminence, at all desirous he should do violence to any honourable and sacredly conscientious feeling. Better, said they, be anything honest, however humble, than an uncalled minister. Whatever may have been the difference between the spiritual conditions of the uncles and the nephew, here they shared in common a hereditary conviction. The echo of the protest of old Donald Roy against the intrusion of an unworthy, an uncalled minister—which so startled the reverend intrusionists that they retreated precipitately from the scene of their unhallowed work, much in the manner in which we might suppose some guilty king of Israel to have cowered and fled from the terrible warnings of the prophet of the Lord—seemed yet to ring in their ears. The Reformation let in upon the Scottish mind a clearer light upon this topic, than was let in upon the mind of all Christendom besides. The wholesale manufacture of priests without any pretensions to peculiar fitness for the sacred office, had disgusted the nation with the old religion. The satiric muse of Sir David Lindsay of the Mount preceded the sermons of Knox, in denouncing the traffic in the holy office. This feeling, which Hugh Miller has well said was the strength of the recent conflict in the Scottish church, lay at the very basis of the Scottish Reformation. In the instincts of the spiritual children of that great revolution did the reformers seek their consecration to the sacred office, not in priestly manipulation. Any other system produces parrots, not teachers; conduits, not fountains; men who speak not that which they do know, but only that which they have learned.

Slowly and reluctantly did Hugh Miller's uncles resign their nephew to a life of manual labour: at length, however, consent was wrung from them, and their protégé, whom they would gladly have sent to the university, becomes a mason's apprentice, has agreed to serve for a term of three years, and may now be seen arrayed, not in the gown of the scholar, but in a suit of moleskin and pair of heavy, hobnailed shoes.

With Miller's dreams of ambition there had also mingled strange dreams of the luxury of a life of solitude. Something of the same reluctance to mingle with the world had taken possession of his mind, and seemed to hold his spirit entranced, as compels the religious devotee to shun the society of man, and to seek in the solitude and seclusion of the cloister that deep and unfading repose that seems for ever denied to ordinary mortals. In Miller's case, however, it was not religious feeling that awakened this predilection, but simply "the timidity of the yet undeveloped mind that shrinks from grappling with the stern realities of life, overshadowed by the formidable competition of men already practised in the struggle." With such feelings mantling his spirit did Hugh Miller, just turned of seventeen, commence his labours in the quarry of Cromarty, the masons of his native place combining both occupations. The necessity that made him a quarrier taught him geology, and now he is to reap the first fruits of his excursions with uncle Sandy. Confined to this quarry, which formed part of an upper member of the Lower Old Red Sandstone, he was not long in discovering among its ancient strata the same phenomena he had witnessed on the sea beach when laid bare by the ebb tides. In his new occupation, and working surrounded with the loftiest images of grandeur, of beauty, and of liberty on every side, the young spirit of the future geologist speedily shook off the shrinking and timidity with which it had been seized, and the remembrance of how unworthy were his fears and how gloriously they had all been falsified, inspired the apostrophe to labour with which he has adorned his "Schools and Schoolmasters." "Noble, upright, self-relying toil! Who that knows thy solid worth and value would be ashamed of thy hard hands, and thy soiled vestments, and thy obscure tasks,—thy humble cottage, and hard couch, and homely fare! Save for thee and thy lessons, man in society would everywhere sink into a sad compound of the fiend and the wild beast; and this fallen world would be as certainly a moral as a natural wilderness."

The ills he so much dreaded on entering the school of labour had proved only imaginary, but some real evils fol lowed his toil which he had not calculated upon. Even so early as this, his seventeenth year, do we discover premonitions of the malady which, in the maturity of his powers, so suddenly called him hence. The seeds of that mysterious combination of physical and mental disease, which at length did its work in so very terrible a manner in his solitary chamber in Portobello, were sown in the quarry of Cromarty. In page 149 of his "Schools and Schoolmasters," Hugh Miller thus describes his appearance at the age of seventeen. "Short, seven inches, of my ultimate stature; and my frame—cast more at the time in the mould of my mother than in that of the robust sailor, whose 'back,' according to the description of one of his comrades, 'no one had ever put to the ground' —as slim and loosely knit; and I used to suffer much from wandering pains in the joints, and an oppressive feeling about the chest, as if crushed by some great weight. I became subject, too, to frequent fits of extreme depression of spirits, which took almost the form of a walking sleep,—results, I believe, of excessive fatigue, —and during which my absence of mind was so extreme, that I lacked the ability of protecting mysel: against accident, in cases the most simple and ordinary. Besides other injuries, I lost at different times during the first few months of my apprenticeship, when in these fits of partial somnambulism, no fewer than seven of my finger nails." In some of the symptoms here enumerated there was nothing peculiar, nothing alarming, being incidental for the most part to youthhood. But that absence of mind, so extreme and so painful, was a symptom calling for the exercise of peculiar care; and though he experienced no after-return of it until long subsequently to the period of his apprenticeship, it is manifest the disease had never been got rid of, but had continued lurking in his system, and, like a traitor who has stolen into a beleaguered fortress, only waited the favourable moment to accomplish its purposes of destruction.

Uncle David, by whom Hugh Miller was initiated into the mysteries of mason-craft, was a person of plodding, persevering industry, a most conscientious workman, and something of a character. At first he was of opinion that his friend would do but little credit to him as a workman; but in the course of a few months, he acquired the mastery over the mallet, and one morning astonished the old man by setting himself to compete with him, hewing nearly two feet of pavement for his one. In the midst of the oppressive toils of the operative, young Miller was assailed by the temptations which the drinking usages of our country are constantly casting in the path of virtue, and taking his own statement as not exaggerated, stood on the brink of a very perilous precipice, from which the love he bore to learning only saved him. Here is his narrative of the crisis:—"When overwrought, and in my depressed moods, I learned to regard the ardent spirits of the dram-shop as high luxuries; they gave lightness and energy to both body and mind, and substituted for a state of dulness and gloom, one of exhilaration and enjoyment. Usquebaugh was simply happiness doled out by the glass, and sold by the gill." On going home one evening, after having assisted at drinking a "royal founding pint," Miller found on opening the pages of a favourite author, the letters dancing before his eyes, and that he was no longer able to master the sense. Disgusted with himself for this indulgence, in that hour he resolved never again to sacrifice his capacity for intellectual enjoyment to a drinking usage, and, through God's help, he was enabled to hold by the determination. We have sometimes wondered that one who had himself confessedly so narrow an escape from the ruin that awaits the confirmed tippler, saw nothing more in the temperance movement, than "a useful fanaticism." The question was, however, one which he had never studied for himself, and probably looking at it only in the light of the characters of its chief apostles in the metropolis, the self-glorification, egotism, and enormous vanity of these leading lights disgusted him, as they might very easily have disgusted a man with even a less nice sense of propriety than Hugh

Miller possessed. Those who are ever mistaking the blowing of their own penny trumps for a music which the world should hush itself to hear, are more likely to find men of the intellectual calibre of the author of the "Old Red Sandstone," laughing at than listening to them.

In nothing, perhaps, is the modern mind more favourably distinguished from the mind of antiquity, than in its love of nature. Amongst the ancients, the passion for art swallowed up all admiration of natural scenery. Even Homer does not impress us with any vivid love for nature as existing in his soul; and we have the authority of Humboldt, in "Cosmos," for saying that no description has been transmitted to us from antiquity of the eternal snow of the Alps, reddened by the evening glow or the morning dawn, of the beauty of the blue ice of the glaciers, or of the sublimity of Swiss natural scenery, although statesmen and generals, with men of letters in their retinue, continually passed through Helvetia on their road to Gaul; and even Julius Cæsar, the foremost man of all his time, when returning to his legions in Gaul, employed himself, while passing over the Alps, in preparing a grammatical work, without once troubling himself with the marvels of nature with which he was everywhere surrounded. It is not a little peculiar, and would almost seem to indicate that sympathy with the beautiful and sublime in the world around us is an emanation of Christian sentiment. So soon as Christianity had shed a gleam of its glory over the darkness of Paganism, we find this love kindled in the breasts of its disciples, and a taste for solitude and contemplation taking possession of some of its finest minds, and colouring the style and language of the times. The tendency of the Christian mind to prove from the order of the universe and the beauty of nature the greatness and goodness of the Creator, gave rise to a taste for natural description, of which it may not be amiss to cull a few examples from the work already alluded to. Basil, in his Homilies on the Hexahemeron, describes the mildness of the constantly clear nights of Asia Minor, where, according to his expression, the stars, "those everlasting blossoms of heaven," elevate the soul from the visible to the invisible. When, in the myth of the creation, he would praise the beauty of the sea, he describes the aspect of the boundless ocean-plain in all its varied and everchanging conditions, "gently moved by the breath of heaven altering its hue as it reflects the beams of light in their white, blue, or roseate hues, and caressing the shores in peaceful sport." We meet with the same sentimental and plaintive expressions regarding nature in the writings of Gregory of Nyssa, the brother of Basil the Great. "When," he exclaims, "I see every ledge of rock, every valley and plain, covered with new-born verdure, the varied beauty of the trees, and the lilies at my feet decked by nature with the double charms of perfume and of colour; when in the distance I see the ocean, towards which the clouds are onward borne, my spirit is overpowered by a sadness not wholly devoid of enjoyment. When in autumn the fruits have passed away, the leaves have fallen, and the branches of the trees, dried and shrivelled, are robbed of their leafy adornments, we are instinctively led, amid the everlasting and regular change in nature, to feel the harmony of the wondrous powers pervading all things. He who contemplates them with the eye of the soul, feels the littleness of man amid the greatness of the universe." Whilst the Greek Christians were led, by their adoration of the Deity through the contemplation of his works, to a poetic delineation of nature, they were, at the same time, during the earlier ages of their new belief, and owing to the peculiar bent of their minds, full of contempt for all works of human art. Thus Chrysostom abounds in passages like the following:—" If the aspect of the colonnades of sumptuous buildings would lead thy spirit astray, look upwards to the vault of heaven, and around thee on the open fields, in which herds graze by the water's side. Who does not despise all the creations of art, when, in the stillness of his spirit, he watches with admiration the rising of the sun as it pours its golden light over the face of the earth; when resting on the thick grass beside the murmuring spring, or beneath the sombre shade of a thick and leafy tree, the eye rests on the far--receeding and hazy distance!"

These passages serve to corroborate the opinion we have ventured to state respecting the connection of Christianity with the revival of a genuine love of nature. We may not trace here the varying fortunes of this feeling, or mark with any degree of precision the epochs in Europe's history when it waxed or waned. It is, however, impossible to overlook the important influence modern poets have exerted in rekindling this admiration. Pre-eminent amongst these for the influence they have exerted, is William Wordsworth. At an epoch when Europe was steeped in a materialistic philosophy, and when a sneering and critical spirit mocked at all that was deep or sincere, his was the voice of one crying in the wilderness, calling men to return from their false worships and literary idolatry, and, renouncing the gods of their poetical pantheon, listen anew to the melody of the voice of nature, which even now in the old age of the world sounds fresh and solemn as on creation's dawn. Wordsworth more than any other poet, if, perhaps, we may except Dante, has seized the evanescent points of nature's beauty. The daisy with its eye of gold looking up into the sky o'erhead, the solitary star shedding its reflex on the November ice, the mists that mantled his native mountains or slumbered over the stillness of the lakes, all that ever-shifting yet beautiful scenery midst which he dwelt was familiar to him, not merely in outline, but in each minutest detail.

Quite independently of Wordsworth's influence, though after a similar manner, had Hugh Miller become a worshipper in the same temple; amidst the serenity of the external world his mind became attuned to nature's harmonies; the scenes amidst which he laboured were, even more than books, the ministrants to his genius—the hidden manna on which his spiritual nature fed. He communed with rock, flower, and stream, until each inanimate object was clothed in attributes and surrounded with associations that awoke within him feelings of almost human affection. Quitting the long-wrought quarries of his native town, and crossing the Moray Frith, Hugh Miller began to work in one recently opened in an inferior member of the Old Red Sandstone. He had not been long employed on this northern shore, ere he discovered by the hill of Eathie, a liasic deposit, amazingly rich in organisms. The description he has given of this early discovery, will, we think, amply sustain all we have just said of his sympathy with nature, while illustrating the range and delicacy of his descriptive powers. "I can scarce hope to communicate to the reader, after the lapse of so many years, an adequate idea of the feeling of wonder which the marvels of this deposit excited in my mind, wholly new as they were to me at the time. Even the fairy lore of my first formed library—that of the birchen box—had impressed me less. The general tone of the colouring of these written leaves, though dimmed by the action of untold centuries, is still very striking. The ground is invariably of a deep neutral gray, verging on black, while the flattened organisms, which present about the same degree of relief as one sees in the figures of an embossed card, contrast with it in tints that vary from opaque to silvery white, and from pale yellow to an umbry or chestnut-brown. Groups of ammonites appear as if drawn in white chalk; clusters of a minute undescribed bivalve are still plated with thin films of the silvery nacre; the mytilaceæ usually bear a warm tint of yellowish brown, and must have been brilliant shells in their day; gryphites and oysters are always of a dark gray, and plagiostomæ ordinarily of a blueish or neutral tint. On some of the leaves curious pieces of incident seem recorded. We see fleets of minute terebratulæ that appear to have been covered up by some sudden deposit from above, when riding at their anchors; and whole argosies of ammonites that seem to have been wrecked at once by some untoward accident, and sent crushed and dead to the bottom. Assemblages of bright black plates, that shine like pieces of japan work, with numerous parallelogrammical scales, bristling with nail-like points, indicate where some armed fish of the old ganoid order lay down and died, and groups of belemnites, that lie like heaps of boarding-pikes thrown carelessly on a vessel's deck on the surrender of the crew, tell where *sculls* of cuttle-fishes of the ancient type had ceased to trouble the waters. I need scarce add that these spear-like belemnites formed the supposed thunderbolts of the deposit. Lying athwart some of the pages thus strangely inscribed, we occasionally find, like the dark hawthorn leaf in Bewick's well-known vignette, slim-shaped leaves coloured in deep umber; and branches of extinct pines, and fragments of strangely-fashioned ferns, form their more ordinary garnishing. Page after page, for tens and hundreds of feet together, repeat the same wonderful story. The great Alexandrian library, with its tomes of ancient literature, the accumulation of long ages, was but a meagre collection—not less puny in bulk than recent in date—compared with this marvellous library of Scotch Lias." This description were of itself enough to indicate that here was a mind not meant to vegetate among the flats and shallows of science, but possessing sufficient strength to scale her loftiest heights, or penetrate her most abysmal depths and subterranean recesses, clothing the while every nook and cranny, and mantling even her sternest cliffs with the enamel of its own gorgeous and picturesque vocabulary.

The profession of a mason had been chosen by Hugh

Miller because of its winter leisure; and now his first winter is come, his year of labour is over, and the next three months are all his own. His cousin George is about to visit his father-in-law, an aged shepherd residing in the upper recesses of Strathcarron. Hugh is invited to accompany him, and gladly he accepts the invitation. The road from Cromarty to Strathcarron was a dreary moor unopened by any public way. The journey enabled him to see something more of the devastating influence of the clearance system. The noonday refreshment of the cousins was eaten in an uninhabited valley, among the ruins of fallen cottages, where once had dwelt some of the best swordsmen in Ross, lost to Scotland by a compulsory emigration. Cousin George came out strongly against the lairds. On arriving at the cottage of their friend, the shepherd, a highlander of large proportions, but hard and thin, and worn by the cares and toils of at least sixty winters, sat moodily beside the fire. Disease had smitten his flocks, and his mind was filled with strange forebodings. He had gone out after nightfall on a previous evening to a dark hollow in which many of his sheep had died. The rain had ceased a few hours before, and a smart frost had set in that filled the whole valley with a wreath of silvery vapour, dimly lighted by the thin fragment of a moon that appeared as if resting on the hill top; when suddenly, the figure of a man, formed as of heated metal, sprung out of the darkness, and after stalking over the surface of the fog for a few brief seconds, as suddenly disappeared, leaving an evanescent trail of flame. The old shepherd had merely seen one of those shooting lights that in mountain districts so frequently startle the night traveller; but the apparition now filled his whole mind, as one, vouchsafed from the spiritual world, of strange and frightful portent—

> "A meteor of the night of distant years
> That flashed unnoticed, save by wrinkled eld
> Musing at midnight upon prophecies."

This visit enabled Hugh to view in the forest of Corrychalgan the last remains of that arboreous condition of our country, to which the youngest of our geological formations, the peat mosses, bear such significant witness, which still largely existing as the condition of the northern countries of Europe, remains to attest, more than even the records of history, the youthfulness of our civilization.

Returned from his highland tour, he made, or perhaps, to speak more correctly, he renewed acquaintance with William Ross. Five years before, Ross had come from the neighbouring parish of Nigg, an apprentice to a house-painter; but though known to each other, there was then too great a disparity between them for friendship. William was a lad of genius, drew truthfully, had a nice sense of the beautiful, and possessed the true poetic faculty; but of melancholy temperament and extremely diffident; thin and pale, fair hair, flat chest, and stooping figure, already a drooping and withered flower; in seven years afterwards, he is in his grave. He had been unfortunate in his parents; his mother, though of a devout family of the old Scottish type, was an aberrant specimen—she had fallen in early youth, and had subsequently married an ignorant, half-imbecile labourer, with whom she passed a life of poverty and unhappiness; of this unpromising marriage William was the eldest child. From neither of his parents did he derive his genius. His maternal grandmother and aunt were, however, excellent Christian women. With them William had lived from an early age. His boyhood had been that of a poet; he had loved to indulge in day-dreams in the solitude of a deep wood beside his grandmother's cottage, had learned to write verses, and draw landscapes, as no one in that locality had written or drawn before; and, as the nearest approach to an artist in those primitive regions was a house-painter, William was despatched to Cromarty, to cultivate his taste for the fine arts, papering rooms and lobbies, and painting railings and wheel-barrows. The house-painter and the stone-mason having once fairly re-established old recognizances, the new friend went a long way to supply the gap which the breaking up of the band to which we have alluded, left in Hugh Miller's acquaintanceship. In their converse together, they beat over all the literature with which they were in common acquainted, and though the literary tastes of William were more circumscribed than the tastes of Hugh, in the field of nature both perfectly harmonized. Many a moonlight walk had the friends together, visiting after nightfall the glades of the surrounding woods, listening to the night breeze as it swept sullenly along the pine tops. It is deeply interesting to note the marked difference in the kind of enjoyment which the youths drew from those lofty images of the sublime and the beautiful with which they were equally enamoured. Hugh Miller, full of hope, joy, and life, yearning for the large excitement the coming years would yield, already looks out upon nature as a companion with whom he is destined to enjoy at once a lengthened and most familiar intercourse. William Ross already carried about with him the consciousness that, in a very special manner, here there was for him no continuing city. The shadow of the cypress shed its sadness into his soul. The joy with which the contemplation of nature filled him, was overcast by the melancholy foreboding that soon her raptures would be for other eyes than his. And yet, ere William has gone to the silent land, as the

German Salis has it, we shall meet him valiantly doing battle with labour against capital in the metropolis of our country.

CHAPTER IV.

THE BOTHY.

In nothing does Hugh Miller's freshness, strength, and perfect freedom from conventionalism, come more clearly out, than in the unreserved disclosure of all that was really interesting or peculiar in his early career: never do we detect any attempt to dress up the story of his life in a manner that would indicate a wish to leave some other than the actual impression facts would produce. That tendency to shun the homely for the grand (the besetting sin of so many writers), never once seduced him from his simplicity. His experiences of life were occasionally sufficiently humble, and occasionally brought him in contact with the most vicious forms social and domestic existence have assumed in modern times. The bothy may appear to some a very vulgar place, out of which it was by no means likely any man of genius or science should come, and where if unfortunate enough ever to have been, it might just be as well not to shock delicate nerves by saying anything of its rough ways. Hugh Miller had, however, undertaken to give the world a history of his "Schools and Schoolmasters," and had he confined himself to the genteel, we had probably never possessed his autobiography; his experiences of the conventionally genteel, especially in early life, being of the very slenderest kind. All honour to thee, brave one, for thy perfect unreserve on this matter! Now that public attention is being gradually awakened to this colossal social wrong, by which nearly every usage of civilized life is held in abeyance, and man almost reverts to the savage state, thy views are worth a waggon-load of the grandiloquence of sentimental philanthropists, who find in talking about the grievances of labour a cheap mode of establishing a reputation as the poor man's friends. Of old, the workman required to be warned against demagogues of his own order: now he stands in nearly equal, if not greater danger from demagogues of the genteeler sort, who affecting a great interest in his well-being, are in point of fact only making his grievances, real or supposed, the rostrum from which to acquire the little passing personal notoriety they are silly enough to mistake for fame.

We left Hugh Miller enjoying his winter holidays with William Ross. The holiday season is now over. Winter with its moonlight walks and moody reveries is gone, and spring has come again, bringing with it its round of labour—quarrying, building, and stone-cutting. But before midsummer work has failed uncle David, his squad is thrown out of employment, and after a most vexatious interregnum, the old man, now during more than a quarter of a century an employer of labour, is reluctantly compelled to become a journeyman. Misery, it is said, makes man acquainted with strange bed-fellows, and this misfortune of his master, whom Hugh was too loyal to leave in the hour of adversity, first brought him into contact with that degrading form of social life known as the bothy system. It was at some twenty miles' distance on the Conon shore, one of those lovely spots where, as Heber has it, "every prospect pleases, and only man is vile," that he entered this new and noisy school. Despite the criticism of Foster, there is much if there be not even absolute truth in the poet's aphorism, "the proper study of mankind is man;" and here certainly man might be studied to very great advantage by the competent student. In old and settled societies like our own, nearly all of character and peculiarity is either taken out of the mass of the population, or is veiled with so thick a crust of conventionalism that it is well nigh impossible to discover its original features. The liberalizing influence of travel springs mainly from its power to counteract this sinister result of an old civilization. The wanderer in foreign parts gets emancipated from the tyrannic power of custom, the edge is taken off his overweening admiration of the conventional, and he is enabled to contemplate his fellow-man without those accessories through which alone many deign to look at him at all. Very graphically has John Kitto described this influence. "Oh! how it has delighted me," says Kitto, "to take a man distinguished from his brother man by a thousand outward circumstances, which make him appear at the first view almost as another creature; and after knocking off his strange hat, his kullah, or his turban; after helping him off with his broadcloths, his furs, or his muslins; after clipping his beard, his pigtail, or his long hair; after stripping away his white, black, brown, red, or yellow skin, to come at last to the very man, the very son of Adam, and to recognize by one touch of nature, one tear, one laugh, one sigh, one upward or downward look, the same old, universal heart—the same emotions, feelings, passions, which have animated every human being, from the equator to the poles, ever since that day on which the first man was sent forth from Paradise." Hugh Miller had not seen foreign parts, had not mingled with men of many nations, tongues, and peoples; the turbaned and pigtailed sons of the Orient were known to him only by report; but his peculiar experiences in the bye-paths of social life at home, taught him nearly as much as most men learn abroad. The minuteness of his acquaintance with Scottish life, especially in its lowlier forms, was probably never surpassed. In collecting his Border minstrelsy, Scott had indeed made himself pretty familiar with that life in even its humblest walks; its "lights and shadows" have been painted, as Christopher North alone could paint their glory and their gloom. Burns knew its every aspect, from its most exalted to its most abject phase; and whether in the halls of the noble, carrying duchesses off their feet, or careering on the crest of riot in the rag-castle of Poosie Nancy, seemed equally at home. But neither Scott, Wilson, nor Burns, was ever the victim of that most vicious of all social arrangements, the barrack life; in Miller's youth only in its infancy, but unhappily now too generally diffused over Scotland. The impression which that life produced upon the prudent, studious, contemplative youth was far from pleasant; and though the bothy was not destitute of a certain amount of boisterous hilarity, life in such circumstances was in reality sad. May we hope that Hugh Miller's experiences upon this topic will be duly weighed and pondered by the friends of social reform, and that the remembrance of such a man having been for a time the victim of so atrocious a system, will stimulate their efforts in its destruction?

From reason's earliest dawn until reason was no more, Hugh Miller seems to have been encompassed with a strange machinery of the wild and supernatural. Go where he would, he was perpetually meeting some ministrant to that element of the mysterious, which so often sheathes in clouds and darkness the flame of reason, leaving man the prey of gorgons, spectres, and chimeras dire. It might have been supposed that bothy-life was not likely to bring the young mason in contact with anything more than the riotous glee and practical joking of the barrack; but it was not so. He had repaired to a hayloft, the only place of shelter he could find on the first night passed in this new school; and flinging himself down in his clothes on a heap of straw, was soon fast asleep: but unaccustomed to so rough a couch, he awoke about midnight, and took his station at a small window that looked out upon a dreary moor, a ruinous chapel, and solitary burying-ground. The evening was calm and still, but dark for the season; when to the great astonishment of the solitary tenant of the loft, a light flickered among the grave-stones and ruins—now seen—now hid, like the revolving lantern of a light-house; and what seemed a continuous screaming was distinctly heard. The light, quitting the churchyard, came downwards across the moor in a straight line, though tossed with many a wave and flourish. In a moment one of the servant girls of the mansion-house came rushing out half-dressed, and awakening the workmen, summoned them immediately to rise,—"mad Bell had broken out again." The men instantly arose, and as they appeared at the door, were joined by the solitary watcher from above; but on striking out a few paces into the moor, the maniac was found in the custody of a couple of men dragging her to her own cottage, about half a mile away. On entering her hut they proceeded to bind her down to the damp floor. Hugh Miller and a comrade simultaneously and successfully interfered—the maniac was not bound. Her song ceased for a moment; and turning round, presenting full to the light the strongly-marked features of a woman about fifty-five, surveying the youths who had spoken good for her with a keen scrutinizing glance, she emphatically repeated the sacred text, "Blessed are the merciful, for they shall obtain mercy."

Next morning, neatly dressed, and save for her marked features scarcely recognizable, Bell introduced herself to her benefactor—had come to consult him about the deep matters of the soul. The abstruse questions connected with the doctrines of the fall and original sin, at this hour exerting and exhausting the ingenuity and the erudition of the profoundest theologians, had come up before poor Isabel in all their force. The mason and the maniac had both read Flavel, and both appeared to have about equally understood his questionable metaphysics; the former, however, had the important advantage over the latter, of discovering that Flavel was nearly as much in the dark upon the subject as themselves. But though Isabel had not fathomed the doctrines of the fall, or of human depravity, what was capable of being known appears to have been pretty well understood by her. Her knowledge of the highland character, her perception whence sprung the sins and the sorrows of the Celt, was incomparably superior to many much saner people. The ancient highlanders, said mad Bell, were bold faithful dogs, ready to die for their masters, and prepared to do at their bidding, like other dogs, the most cruel and wicked actions, and as dogs often were they treated. The pious martyrs of the south had contended in God's behalf, whereas the poor highlanders of the north had contended in behalf of their chiefs; and so while God had been very kind to the descendants of his servants, the chiefs had been very unkind to the descendants of theirs. Bell's opinion may seem a harsh one; but we do not see that a much different estimate of the Gael is formed by many who affect to mourn the depopulation of the Highlands, but whose sorrow, when analyzed, simply resolves itself into a regret that certain fighting tools are gone from beneath the shadow of their native mountains to hide themselves in the heart of the Australian bush, or the backwoods of Canada. Theology, tradition, social science, political economy, formed the themes of many other conversations between Isabel Lauchlan and Hugh Miller. The mercy shown her in the hour of her distress was never forgotten, and when the mason had gone to the metropolis in the pursuit of his profession, the maniac walked some twenty miles to see his mother in Cromarty. Her end was a melancholy one; fording the Conon in such a mood as that was in which Hugh had first met her, she was swept away by the stream. Thus perished the sister of one of the ablest and most accomplished ministers of the north.

Hugh Miller's speculations upon the peculiarities of professional character, which barrack-life enabled him to study with advantage, are ingenious and interesting, and, so far as concerns the specific profession to which he belonged, just. It is only when he throws his plummet over other branches of labour, and seeks to gauge the *differentia* between them and his own peculiar craft, that the passion for analogical reasoning seduces him into rather imperfect, hasty, and we may add, juvenile generalization. We do not blame him for having cherished the opinion that his own profession is more favourable than any other to the development of genius. We believe that for minds such as his own, it really is so. Had Hugh Miller become a banker's clerk some dozen years before he entered the bank at Cromarty, he would probably not have been so great a man. His was one of those natures that seem rather dwarfed than developed under any specially-forced culture. For those meditative observant powers for which his writings are so pre-eminently distinguished, we should seek in vain a better training than they received amidst those marvels of nature, in whose companionship so much of his life as an operative was passed. But while this peculiar training gave his intellect and character a kind of granitic strength and tenacity on the one side, it left it only partially developed on the other.

A point on which he obviously piqued himself here became his weakness. Indiscriminate eulogists praise Hugh Miller for the resolute way in which he stood aloof from all trades' unions. It is our belief that had he mingled but a little with these associations, instead of standing aside scanning their weaknesses with the most lynx-eyed scrutiny, though he might probably not have reaped much profit as a handicraftsman from descending into the arena where labour and capital waged their all too-unequal strife, he would have taken lessons in a school, the want of whose lessons was a much greater disadvantage in after life than the neglect of that classical lore in which he cut but so sorry a figure in the Grammar School of Cromarty. His general estimate of the worth of trades' unions might not be far from just; but while he would have exhibited more of the temper of the philosopher, had he been a little more tolerant of their failings, and a little more kind to their faults, he would also have enjoyed the opportunity of studying men in masses, and of noting the influence a dominant idea exercises upon a host of minds, each differently constituted from the other, yet all animated by the same potent impulse. The result of such experiences upon a mind so pre-eminently capable of being taught by experience, but so little capable of being taught by aught else, would doubtless have been, that while retaining in undiminished power the capacity for appreciating with admirable precision and comprehensiveness the historic epochs through which a people have passed, he should no longer have failed to comprehend the exigencies of acted history. We do not think he was ever very far astray, in the matter of principle, in any of the conflicts into which he sometimes entered with so much vehemency and maintained with so much ability; but without losing an atom of independence, had Hugh Miller ever been a director, instead of always an opponent of trades' unions, it would have taught him greater tenderness for the exigencies of a church-leader, by enabling him better to comprehend the difficulties of such a position.

Some haughty ecclesiastic may, perchance, be disposed to smile at the comparison of great things with small, implied in the presumption of any analogy between the direction of a trade's union, and the leadership of a clerical confederation. If so, let such remember the historian of "The Decline and Fall of the Roman Empire" was not ashamed to confess, that to his very modest military attainments as a captain of Hampshire militia, he owed a more definite conception of the phalanx and the legion, than to all his reading besides; nor can we doubt that the vividness with which Lord Macaulay has portrayed the growth, struggles, and intrigues of political parties, springs in no small measure from having himself mingled in the strifes of faction. Hugh Miller could study, estimate, comprehend, but could not well co-operate with his compeers. In this primary fact is to be found the key to the partial estrangement that latterly existed between himself and certain leading lights of the Free Church. It was scarcely possible that two so very differently constituted minds as those of Candlish and Miller, should long have been found in harmony with each other. Candlish the man of the hour, always equal to the occasion, ready to grapple with any emergency, the most dexterous tactician Scottish ecclesiastical polemics ever produced,—what had that musing, contemplative, stubborn stonecutter, whom the drift-currents of the moral world had separated from his native North and set down in the editorial chair of the *Witness* newspaper, in common with the agile church leader, skilled in the ways of diplomacy, an adept in "circumlocution and the language of friendly intercourse?" Nothing—absolutely nothing! As speculative writers on church principles, had they compared notes, they might not, indeed, have been found far apart; but upon almost all the modes in which these principles were to be made dominant, their minds were nearly the antipodes of each other. And without robbing either of the guerdon justly due to great talents perseveringly and honourably exerted in a most honourable cause, it may be acknowledged, that while to Miller belongs the credit of that far-reaching sagacity which comprehended at a glance the future of the Free Church, and could define its peculiar sphere with an almost mathematical precision; to Candlish belongs the honour of having breathed into what might else have proved a mere inert mass of pretentious ecclesiastical machinery, the energy and resolution of his own dauntless, and restless as it is dauntless, spirit; and if occasionally, on field days, he boasted a larger muster-roll than was altogether warranted by facts, let men forget his error in his devotion—the ends he sought were at least always noble, if the means by which he sought them were not always equal to the ends. And yet, perhaps, it was well the impetuosity of Candlish was tempered and kept in check by the sagacity of Miller. Through a dearth of men either able or willing, we do not exactly presume to say which, Dr. Candlish has been necessitated to do much of a kind of work in church courts, usually left by a leader to his lieutenants. The consequence has been, that, occasionally forgetting the more exalted in the more subordinate position, he has been seen, as sometimes Napoleon's best generals were seen, compromising the common safety by a special impetuosity. In point of fact, for a commander-in-chief he mingles too much in the ranks, and as a natural consequence, the smoke and tumult of the battle occasionally deprive him of that clearness of vision and serenity of soul so indispensable in the direction of all great contests, whether on the tented field or on the floor of a general assembly.

CHAPTER V.

EDINBURGH.

When just attaining his majority, work failing in the North, Hugh Miller, bidding adieu to his beloved mother and his worthy uncles, sailed from his native town for the south of Scotland. On the evening of the fourth day from losing sight of the hill of Cromarty, he landed at Leith. After a somewhat hasty survey of a small property he was unfortunate enough to possess—a property not of the advantageous sort with which the freehold societies profess to invest the working classes, but a property reminding us rather of Rip Van Winkle's farm, the most pestilent bit of ground in the whole parish—Hugh Miller proceeded at once to the Scottish capital. While sauntering along the streets, admiring with a fresh eye the picturesque groups of ancient buildings with which that most magnificent of cities abounds—as yet looking but little to the population, he was laid hold of by a slim lad in pale moleskins: it was William Ross; and during what remained of that night, the stone-cutter and the house-painter explored the city together. With that true eye for the beautiful and the sublime, whether in art or nature, which never failed him, Hugh Miller at once detected what gives to Edinburgh its peculiar fascination. Like Jerusalem of old, beautiful for situation, that beauty is superlatively enhanced by the circumstance, that to the stranger it discloses at a glance, not one, but two cities, a city of the past and a city of the present. When Hugh Miller first visited Edinburgh, its ancient features were in a state of considerably more perfect preservation than they now are. Many mementos of the renown of centuries have disappeared within the last thirty-five years. No small portion of the old town now exists only in the recollections of the antiquary. As in the country, the small crofting of other days has given place to the large farm, so the memorials of her antiquity with which Edina was erewhile so thickly studded, have, in some of their most interesting features, been swept away by the march of modern improvement, which is yet in many instances not improvement. All old enough to remember the vanished glories, whose places these so-called improvements have usurped, are filled with feelings much akin to those which inspired such of the captivity of Judah as, recollecting the glory of the first temple, lived to witness and to share in the erection of the second.

Through the good offices of a friend, Hugh Miller procured work at a manor-house then being erected in the vicinity of Niddry mill, and beneath the shade of Niddry woods did the Cromarty stone-cutter commence his labours. The squad with which he worked appears to have been tainted in even an extreme degree with the narrowness and exclusiveness common among the more ignorant class of operatives, and to them Miller became an object of undisguised hostility and dislike. The Norlander, in their opinion, if not chased back to his own cold clime, would carry home half the money of the country. This district into which the exigencies of his daily toil had brought him, extended Hugh Miller's acquaintance at once with natural and social phenomena. In the woods of Niddry he discovered not a little that had no existence two degrees farther north, and in the immediate neighbourhood of Niddry mill he met a rude and ignorant race still bearing the stain, if not the brand of slavery.

It will scarcely be believed that so late as 1842, when Parliament issued a commission to inquire into the results of female labour in the coal pits of Scotland, there was a collier, still living, that had never been twenty miles from the metropolis; who could state to the commissioners, that his father, his grandfather, and himself were slaves; and that he had wrought for years in a pit in the neighbourhood of Musselburgh where the majority of the miners were also serfs. How singular the anomalies and contradictions that, even in a period pre-eminent for political and social progression, may yet be permitted to live on uncorrected. Poets, orators, and statesmen were constantly declaiming about how impossible it was for a slave to breathe in England, at a time when the Scotch lairds held the liberties of the poor colliers and salters completely in their iron gripe. That slavery was all the more reprehensible from the circumstance, that it was not a relic of ancient serfdom, but had originated in comparatively recent decisions of the Court of Session. Even the statute passed in 1701, extolled as the Scotch Habeas Corpus Act, brought this pariah race no relief. After reciting the precautions against wrongous imprisonment and undue delays in trials, the statute goes on to say that this act in no way extends to colliers and salters. Even after the first link of their chain had been broken in 1775, their freedom was so clogged with conditions that it was little more than nominal. The eulogists of the Court of Session are constantly declaiming about the immense advantage it has been to Scotland; but with the exception of one brief and brilliant epoch in its history, nearly as little has been done for Scotland by her law-lords as by her land-lords. On almost every critical occasion, ecclesiastical or political, the majority of them has generally been found on the wrong side. As might have been expected, the condition of the inhabitants of the village of Niddry, even of that part of them not belonging to the proscribed race, was of the lowest order; while the colliers themselves carried in their faces the too certain index at once of their social and intellectual condition, being mostly of that type to which a very strong resemblance is found in the prints of savage tribes. The effect of the emancipation of these poor creatures has been, that in less than a quarter of a century this type of face has disappeared throughout Scotland.

With the exception of the foreman and a labourer of the squad in which Hugh Miller worked, and perhaps a couple more who were, however, rather polemical than devotional in their religion; hostility and indifference to Christianity might describe its spiritual condition. Hugh Miller was a churchman, and accordingly was somewhat surprised to find the only religion among his comrades belonged to the dissenters. Like uncle Sandy, some of these men were great readers of the old divines; Durham, Rutherford, Baxter, Boston, old John Brown, and the Erskines, formed their favourite companions; but unlike his uncles, both of whom still retained an unwavering faith in the Establishment, they had begun to question the propriety of such institutions, nay, to hold it might be none the worse, but much the better for religion, that they were uprooted. With the exception of this small fraction of devout men, who, though in it, were not of it, the squad was well represented by its hero Charles, a demoralized, reckless, yet generous-hearted fellow, the only blackguard Hugh Miller ever found possessing magnanimity and generosity.

It was while a stone-cutter beneath the shade of Niddry wood that Hugh Miller first became practically acquainted with combinations. Hallowday had come, and with Hallowday a reduction of wages from twenty-four to fifteen shillings per week; the reduction was, by nearly two shillings, more than it ought to have been; but such were the circumstances of the mass of the masons, that a single fortnight would have more than exhausted their resources. Hugh Miller predicted that the contemplated strike would be a failure, and Charles, the leader of the squad, more than half admitted he was right; but the abandon and glee of a day's fun, and the excitement of a monster meeting on Brunsfield Links, outweighed the dictates of prudence; so the squad marched away from beneath the elms and chestnuts of Niddry to the gathering on the Links, which they joined amidst the cheers of the assembly. After a good deal of speech-making they adjourned, to meet again in the evening in one of the halls of the city of Edinburgh. A low tavern in the upper part of Canongate received the heroes from Niddry; there, amidst the excitement of drinking and the excitement of drawing the badger, the men of the mallet grew deaf to time, and became oblivious to all about the strike. Hugh Miller having left his comrades to their revel, was exploring the trap rocks of King's Park, and instead of attending the evening meeting, he passed the night with his friend William Ross, who, contrary to what might have been expected from his antecedents, took a warm interest in strikes and combinations, officiated as clerk for a combined society of house-painters, and entertained sanguine hopes about the happy influence the principle of union was yet to exercise upon the position of the workman. Amiable dreamer! Stubborn individualist! when last ye met together in your native North, it was not to debate the rights of man, but to hold high fellowship with nature amidst scenes of surpassing beauty and sublimity: then ye were at one; now your sentiments are the antipodes of each other. Shall we mete out indiscriminate approval on the one hand—unqualified censure on the other? We cannot. William Ross was probably too enthusiastic in his expectations; certainly, were we to judge of the power of the principle to which he devoted himself by its operative influence among the painters of Edinburgh, we should be compelled to conclude that it has achieved but little. Yet foolish and futile as the mass of combinations have been, we cannot share Hugh Miller's utter repudiation and total want of sympathy with them, neither can we say they have been wholly useless. Society tolerates many strange abuses, which, so long as they do not touch itself or produce any general inconvenience, are left to right themselves as best they may. But for certain strikes some very clamant evils, now swept away, would still have been left to grind their victims. Is it to be supposed, that had the enslaved colliers and salters been able to give a tongue to their grievances, they would not have been redressed at least half a century before justice was done them? While, therefore, William Ross may have been too much of an enthusiast, there are those who will consider his mingling with his comrades in a common cause, and endeavouring to guide by his superior discretion their general deliberations, a more pleasing trait of character than the Harry-of-the-Wynd style in which Hugh Miller held his own. It is indeed true, that the post of leadership—in nearly all societies a thankless, if in some a brilliant position—is in trades' unions peculiarly critical; and very often what Hugh Miller calls the fluent gabber, is substituted for the man of sense, just as in more important councils; what George Canning called a big voice is mistaken for a genuine statesman. Nevertheless we are reluctant to think them wholly hopeless. The great difficulty they have to contend against is the circumstance, that the men naturally qualified by ability and experience to be the leaders of trades' combinations, seldom remain in the operative ranks, but for the most part step out and step up into the master class.

But though the two friends could not agree in their

opinions of the value of the principle of trades' unions, there were tastes and sympathies which they shared in common, in which they forgot their differences about strikes and combinations. It was, however, with grief and pain of no ordinary kind that Hugh Miller discovered his early companion fast losing confidence in his own powers, and in consequence narrowing the circle of his enjoyments. In reply to an effort to rally him, William Ross, with the characteristic modesty of his nature, exclaimed, "Ah, Miller, what matters it how I amuse myself! You have stamina in you, and will force your way, but I want strength; the world will never hear of me." And so it was; like a flower withered on its stalk, which waited only the visit of the first rough blast to blow it into dust, one after another of his favourite pursuits was discontinued, until at length he quietly dropped into the grave. In his fine, if somewhat circumscribed tastes, delicate constitution, and early death, William Ross reminds us much of the bard of Lochleven, Michael Bruce; and looking at how nearly equally unfit both painter and poet were to endure life's fitful fever, the same epitaph may serve both tombs—"Weep not for the dead; neither bemoan them."

When next the Niddry masons are seen on the march for Edinburgh, it is the great fires of the Parliament Close and the High Street that have summoned them to the city. Graphic pens have described the picturesqueness of these terrible conflagrations. Sir Walter Scott and Lord Cockburn have both recorded their impressions of the sublimity of the spectacle. Over Hugh Miller's soul there swept all the varied feelings the scene was fitted to evoke, and in descriptive power the record of his recollections will bear comparison with even Scott's magic pen, while there is a touch of human interest in Miller's narrative peculiarly his own. He had been surveying, not without some degree of enjoyment, a phlegmatic barber, who, in the very midst of the blazing ruins, was coolly operating upon the face of an immensely fat old fellow, on whose round bald forehead and ruddy cheeks the perspiration was standing out in huge drops, and whose vast mouth was opened to accommodate the man of the razor. Suddenly a poor workman emerged from a close with a favourite piece of furniture, a glass cupboard, evidently snatched not without difficulty from the general wreck of his household gods. The poor fellow, continues Miller, was followed by his wife, and seemingly had got the cherished heir-loom out of the reach of danger, when, striking against some obstacle that lay in his path, he tottered against a projecting corner, and the glazed door was driven in with a crash. There was hopeless misery in the wailing cry of the wife—"O! ruin, ruin; it's lost too!" Nor was his own despairing response less sad, "Ay, ay, puir lassie, it is at an end noo."

When Hugh Miller was quietly working as a stone cutter at Niddry, Dugald Stewart yet lived, Jeffrey and his brilliant staff were in the zenith of their renown, Christopher North and the Blackwood club were enjoying their famous "Noctes Ambrosianæ," the lyre of the mighty minstrel was still unbroken, and the historian of the Reformation yet preached and wrote. Not London itself was the centre of a greater literary activity than was the Scottish capital. Yet, though living in the light of that galaxy of glorious spirits, Hugh Miller was never fortunate enough, with the single exception of Dr. M'Crie, to obtain a sight of any of them; though frequently of a Saturday night, when his comrades were drawing the badger in Canongate, he might be seen lingering in Castle-street, eager to catch a glimpse of the author of "Waverley," but, singularly enough, always unsuccessful. Of Dr. M'Crie alone, therefore, has he been able to give the world any personal recollections that date from this period.

The peculiarly powerful impression made by that able and learned divine upon the mind of the young stone-cutter, is not to be wondered at, when we reflect how essentially manly, and how intensely national were both men. In the substratum of their minds they had much in common, nor had their tastes and reading lain very far apart. Even at that comparatively early period of his career, Hugh Miller was more conversant with

Scottish church history than nine-tenths of her clergy; as a matter not merely of duty but of pleasure, therefore, did he make haste to obey the injunction of his uncles, "Be sure and visit Dr. M'Crie's church when in Edinburgh." That thin, spare, semi-military, semi-ecclesiastical figure, with an air of melancholy spreading its soft shadow over his features, was worthy of the homage even of Hugh Miller. When the humble dissenting minister girt himself for the labour of his life, the names of the Scottish reformers were names of which Scotchmen had become almost ashamed. Historians destitute of all sympathy with the great religious revolution of the sixteenth century, had been left to give the world their estimate of the heroes of the Reformation. The natural result, as might have been anticipated, was, that everywhere the most exaggerated opinions were entertained about their utter want of all delicacy and sensibility of nature. Men looked at their characters through the tears of Mary Stuart. That weeping beauty had so completely fascinated alike the Scottish and the English literati, that neither could see anything good about men whose lives, unfortunately for their fame, though happily for their country, had been spent in resisting her will. The revolution in the public sentiment respecting the real aims and the real characters of the reformers, which has taken place within the last thirty years, is mainly attributable to the influence of the writings of the biographer of Knox and Melville.

What Thomas Carlyle has done for the memory of the hero of the commonwealth of England, that did Thomas M'Crie for the hero of the Scottish reformation. Lamartine's History of the Girondists, it is said, did much to precipitate the revolution of 1848. Scotchmen are not so mercurial as their Gallic neighbours, and are therefore not so easily moved by a book, even though the book should be a very good one. But it is only saying the truth, when we say that the ecclesiastical writings of M'Crie did very much to precipitate the disruption of the Scottish church. He it was who first led the higher and more earnest minds of the Scottish establishment out of that frigid zone of Erastianism, amidst whose wintry influences they threatened to become so miserably dwarfed. What Scotchman who had drunk in the inspiration breathed from the lives of John Knox and Andrew Melville, could fail for evermore to combat for those great principles of spiritual independence for which those heroes contended throughout a lifelong struggle with kings and princes? In point of fact, just to the extent that the leaders of the evangelical party in the Scottish church took these men for their models, did they succeed; and where they failed to do so, either through misapprehension, timidity, or false views, were they unsuccessful. Had they shared as fully the political as the ecclesiastical sentiments of the reformers, there can be no doubt their position would have been less complicated, and their triumph even more complete. We are not making any revelation when we say that the power of the Free Church was not a little crippled in the very hour of its birth, by the attempt of certain leaders to carry into it men who had nothing in common with that noble band, who, esteeming the reproach of Christ greater riches than the treasures of Egypt, left all to follow the fortunes of a sacred principle.

The stone-cutters of the metropolis of Scotland are a short-lived race; the peculiar fineness of the stone amidst which they work brings with it disease of the lungs and chest. Though a temperate mason, Hugh Miller was no exception to the general fate. After about a couple of years' labour, he felt the absolute necessity of relaxation, and resolved to return, for a time at least, to his native town. This visit to Edinburgh, though it introduced him to the acquaintance of none of the lions of the city, furnished him with the opportunity of observing what may be deemed the transition-era of the large towns of Scotland from the proud position which they held as the abodes of learning, piety, and virtue, into the refuges of that pariah race which now nestles in their midst, and whose existence forms so perplexing a problem to modern civilization. The peril with which this large class threatens society is at once apparent, and has often been pointed out. "Let," said Dr. Chalmers, fully a quarter of a century ago—"let but some extraordinary convulsion take place in society, and it will speedily be discovered how feeble a barrier our civilization presents to utter social demoralization." "Dare we," says Isaac Taylor, "had we the infant human race in our arms, dare we turn ourselves to that careworn creature, modern civilization, sitting at her factory gate, and say, Take that child, and nurse it for me?" We are afraid, however, that these authorities, Hugh Miller included, have made a mistake in supposing that the class in question is so peculiarly the growth of modern times and of great cities. Our own opinion is, that all that modern cities have done has been simply to form centres for such a population. So far back as the age of Knox, we find this class in existence under the appellation of "sturdy beggars," and we have the authority of Fletcher of Saltoun for stating, that, at the period of the Revolution, not less than 200,000 of these waifs of society were scattered over Scotland. It is a melancholy reflection that, after all that has been done by the combined exertions of the philanthropists and the religious, this class should continue to outgrow, and seemingly overmaster, all the checks to which it is subjected.

The churches have of late years set about the reclamation of this class, and in the few instances in which superior men have devoted themselves to the work, the success has been most gratifying. Unfortunately, however, these home missions have fallen largely into the hands of preachers who have been unsuccessful in regular charges, and whose general mental power is not such as enables them to exert any salutary influence. Called to combat the dissipation and sensuality of a class in whom dissipation and sensuality have become chronic, it is not to be wondered at, should these intellectual weaklings be unable to effect much amongst a population so degraded. If home missions are ever to be more than a sort of decent house of refuge for those who have broken down in what is deemed the more regular work of the Christian ministry, a totally different class of men must be appointed to labour in that interesting and important sphere of evangelistic effort.

After a tedious voyage, Hugh Miller again set foot on the beach of Cromarty, and was received with the cordial greetings of his two uncles, his cousin George, and other friends and relations; and was soon again in the enjoyment of all the happiness of their united friendship.

CHAPTER VI.

CHRISTIANITY.

When Christianity appeared, it met a world in waiting. The superstitions which had sustained the nations, had degenerated into effete and sterile things long anterior to His coming, to whom the gathering of the people was to be. Even the representative people had done its work—its mission was accomplished—the purposes for which God had selected Israel from amongst all the families of the earth had been fulfilled, and the privileges which had been withdrawn from the race within the circle of the chosen nation were again to encompass a world, and again to infold in their ample embrace all kindreds, and tongues, and peoples, and nations. It was about to be made manifest it was not for themselves alone that Israel's Divine Father had gilded with the sunshine of his favour the hills of their inheritance, but that his way might be known on earth, and his saving health amongst all nations. Such an authoritative and inspired avowal of the cosmopolitan purposes which Judaism was intended to serve, might surely silence the cavils of the sceptic about the narrowness and exclusiveness of the faith of Israel: it was narrow for the wisest of reasons; it was exclusive for the most benignant of objects. And when at length the middle wall of partition fell, which had during so many ages divided mankind; and Jew and Greek, so long severed by antipathies the most inveterate, and by habits the most diverse, met to do homage to a common Master, and to worship one only Lord, it then became apparent what an unspeakable treasure it was which that repellent race who peopled Palestine had conserved for the world. For a time, the new faith went on its way rejoicing; without let or hindrance it sped upon its magnanimous and godlike mission, mingling not with the things of earth. Conscious that the world by wisdom knew not God, the early teachers of Christianity, from the elevation which they had reached, looked down with indifference upon all the philosophy and all the science of heathendom, and eyed with jealousy every attempt to commingle Christianity with the conception of even the loftiest sages of antiquity. Such was the temper of the majority of the first heralds of the gospel; and notwithstanding the censure with which it has been visited by some recent writers who aspire to being considered men of enlarged and liberal thought, we must be permitted to consider that temper a salutary one. It served better than any other course of action could have served, to point out the fact that the new religion was in a high and peculiar sense not of this world,—that amongst all the multifarious forms of worship which had found a shelter and a home beneath the eagles of old Rome, it dwelt apart, and was not to be reckoned as one of them. Humanly speaking, had Christianity in the morning of its existence got entangled in the meshes of a vain philosophy, its power, and consequently its progress, would have been immeasurably crippled. Its capacity to turn the world upside down would have departed from it, and the cross would soon have ceased to be an ensign to the peoples.

There is much that we now know of the scheme of human redemption of which its early teachers probably knew but little. Religion was with them more a thing of the soul, than a thing of system. Their vivid intuitions of divine truth had not yet passed through the alembic of the logical consciousness; many of its heights were left unscaled, and many of its depths unsounded; but the image of the grand leading features of Christianity had been daguerreotyped upon the souls of all of them with an intensity and a faithfulness of which a martyr age can alone furnish us with an adequate conception. Pity it was that that day of glorious action should so soon have been succeeded by a night of gloomy speculation. Within the bosom of the church herself, there speedily arose those who imagined they could lend additional weight and value to the unsearchable riches of Christ, by incorporating with them the treasures of a world's wisdom—that thus the gospel might in this new dress, and clad in this motley robe, gather around it those to whom its unadorned simplicity was repulsive. Full soon, however, did this alliance prove more baneful than beneficial. It speedily became apparent to even the most casual observer, that not a little wood, hay, and stubble, had been mingled with the gold, silver, and precious stones. Christianity gained nothing when it began to flow through the arteries of Grecian philosophy, and the Attic bird, thrilling her thick-warbled notes, marred the melody of the Messianic message. We know it was, in the then circumstances of the world, in the nature of things impossible that Christianity could altogether escape from this comparative contamination. Its heralds announced a message that touched all the deepest problems which philosophy had attempted in vain to solve. The themes Plato had discussed were decided by Paul; the scattered members of truth's lovely form were collected in Christ; and the flickering starlight of philosophy, which men in their darkness had so deified, sank before the majestic sun of eternal truth. All this was no doubt fact, but all this was in the last degree humiliating to men who had so long been gazing upon mere fragments of the truth that they had come at length to regard the *disjecta membra* as more beautiful than the perfect image. Thus arose that opposition which the gospel was fated to encounter, and thus originated that contamination which it was destined to undergo. The reaction of philosophy against Christianity culminated in Julian the Roman emperor, who renouncing the gospel, embraced with all the ardour of a neophyte the outward creed of paganism. Julian did all that a man, and that man an emperer, could do, to restore the ancient mythology to its former place of power; with a zeal worthy of a better cause he laboured to reinvest the gods of Greece with the glory which had departed from amongst them. He was, we believe, a mind peculiarly susceptible to the seductive influence of the old worship; and we can account for his abandonment of Christianity without branding him as an apostate, in the ordinary or odious sense at least in which that word is employed. He had seen little amongst his relations to recommend the new religion. The rulers of Rome who had embraced the gospel were far—very far, from being living epistles of Christ; and that dash of chivalry which was in Julian's nature, combined with his ardent admiration of external beauty, gave the weight of his name and power to the falling faith. It seemed to him a robbing earth of its glory to restrict our conception of God, as revelation does, to an invisible being. He aspired to restore those halcyon days of the world when Grecian mythology, all glorious within, and radiant with the light of the land of the sun, swayed an unchallenged sceptre over the souls of men.

The paganism of Julian was pantheistic in its tendencies, as was indeed all the philosophical idolatry of his age. This fact renders an attentive study of the epoch imperative upon every one who would comprehend aright the present phases of unbelief. However important the question of the evidences and the proof from miracles may be, it is not on these grounds alone that the battle between faith and infidelity must now be fought. It is useless to talk of evidences or of miracles to men who assert that belief in a personal God is "theosophic moonshine," or who look upon the claim for Messiahship set up for Christ as only affording a premium to a crooked and a perverted logic. These men must be encountered with other weapons than those which vanquished the Voltairian school. We must seek in an earlier age than the age of the encyclopædists for the type of their scepticism; we must go back to a time when the young church was contending with the philosophy of the old world, for the rudimentary principles of the unbelief of these latest assailants of our faith. We do not say—we are very far from saying—that either the treatment of the evidences, or the proof from miracles, should even for a moment be lost sight of. Such forgetfulness would be perilous in the extreme. We simply say that it is not enough, and that if we would successfully grapple with the higher forms of scepticism, the old bulwarks must be supplemented with something else, and something more. The difficulty in this matter is to abstract ourselves from our present and Christian modes of thought, for the occupancy of a pagan or Neoplatonic view-point; but until we in some measure accomplish this, we cannot hope to cope successfully with the men who have become fascinated with the one, or are idolaters of the other—men who have even the hardihood to tell us that our Christianity is in the "Phædo."

Efforts have recently been made to show that philosophy was advancing to a solution of some of those abstruse and weighty problems which had so long baffled the utmost efforts of its loftiest sages; and the hymn of Cleanthes, and the dogmas of the Pythagoreans, have been pointed to as proofs that, had time only been granted, they would have accomplished, unaided, what it is the peculiar glory of Christianity to have achieved for man. Nothing so forcibly reminds us that our modern sceptics tread "a land of darkness as darkness itself," as the intense interest with which they gaze upon any gleam of light which may meet them on their pilgrimage. Like the traveller, faint and weary with traversing the trackless wastes of Sahara, they feel more intensely interested with the few stunted shrubs to be found in the oases of the desert, than when embosomed in vegetation "thick as leaves in Vallambrosa."

At the era of the revival of letters, which immediately preceded the Reformation, it was feared by some that the passion for the classics would revive the worship of antiquity. The age of the Medici and Leo X. was unquestionably more pagan than Christian in its tendencies, and the transformation which was feared then, is, to a considerable extent, being realized now through the influence of modern idealism. The men whose dark and lowering crests are to be seen in the van of the scepticism of the age are, for the most part, men who have either lost their way amidst the fogs of German metaphysics, or whose souls have been chilled and frost-bitten by some one or other of the numerous critical systems to which that land of doubters has given birth.

Though not a student of German metaphysics, nor much acquainted with the numerous critical systems, that, like meteors of the night, are ever shooting athwart the intellectual horizon of "the thinkers of Europe," Hugh Miller had not altogether escaped the wintry influences of a sceptical philosophy. Never, indeed, had he at any time made that philosophy a faith; yet its chill had passed over, though it failed to petrify his spirit. A strong dash of hereditary prejudice kept him from being whelmed in its dark and troublous waters, even in the absence of any higher light to guide his steps into the way of peace. The period had, however, now come, when the mists of scepticism are to take themselves off, and religion's tranquil star, which these mists had obscured, is to shed over his soul its selectest influence.

On his return to Cromarty, he found an old companion, one of the band he so long led in days of youthful frolic, relinquishing superior commercial prospects, and entering the curriculum of preparation for the work of the ministry. The two early friends spent much of their time together, and frequently their talk was upon religious topics. The perfect disinterestedness of his companion's abnegation of every worldly advantage under the impulse of religious devotion, brought Christianity as an operative power upon the heart, not a mere system of doctrines, prominently before him. Previous to this period, he seems to have thought Howie's description of that Scottish Ulrich von Hutten, Balfour of Burley's relations to the covenanting cause, would have very well described his own religious condition; and it is with the characteristic reserve of a true Scotchman Hugh Miller tells the story of the great transition-era in his religious history.

Scottish theology, whether in its extreme or moderate form, has unfortunately for the most part presented

Christianity to the people of Scotland rather in the light of a scheme of doctrine to be embraced, than as embodying a being to be loved. The kinsman-redeemer of the "Marrow men" was indeed an exception; but somehow this benignant aspect of the theology of the Bostons and the Erskines was long lost sight of, and not until comparatively recent times did it again, under somewhat altered forms and a modernised nomenclature, emerge from the obscurity into which it had fallen. It was from out the glowing heart of Edward Irving—while yet Edward Irving held fast his integrity—this noblest blossoming of the antique creed of our country again bloomed into beauty. With this theology, one so familiar with the evangelical writers of the Scottish church as was Hugh Miller, could not have been unacquainted; but hitherto it had been to him rather a wandering voice than a thing of power. How his religion became a religion of the heart, as certainly as of the intellect, shall be told in his own words:—"I was," he states, "led to see at this time, through the instrumentality of my friend, that my theological system had previously wanted a central object to which the heart could attach itself; and that the true centre of an efficient Christianity is, as the name ought of itself to import, 'the Word made Flesh.' Around the central sun of the Christian system—appreciated, however, not as an abstraction, but as a divine person—so truly man that the affections of the human heart can lay hold upon him; and so truly God that the mind through faith can at all times and in all places be brought into direct contact with him,—all that is really religious takes its place in a subsidiary and subordinate relation. I say subsidiary and subordinate. The Divine man is the great attractive centre—the sole gravitating point of a system, which owes to him all its cohering, and which would be but chaos were he away. It seems to be the existence of the human nature in this central and paramount object, that imparts to Christianity in its subjective character its peculiar power of influencing and controlling the human mind. There may be men who, through a peculiar idiosyncrasy of constitution, are capable of loving after a sort a mere abstract God, unseen and inconceivable, though, as shown by the air of sickly sentimentality borne by almost all that has been said and written on the subject, the feeling in its true form must be a very rare and exceptional one. In all my experience of men, I never knew a genuine instance of it. The love of an abstract God seems to be as little natural to the ordinary human constitution, as the love of an abstract sun or planet. The true humanity and true divinity of the adorable Saviour, is a truth equally receivable by at once the humblest and the loftiest intellects. Poor dying children, possessed of but a few simple ideas, and men of the most robust intellects, such as the Chalmerses, Fosters, and Halls of the Christian church, find themselves equally able to rest upon the *man* Christ, who is, over all, *God* blessed for ever.

"Of this fundamental truth of the two natures, that condensed enumeration of the gospel which forms the watchword of our faith,—'believe in the Lord Jesus Christ, and thou shalt be saved'—is a direct and palpable embodiment, and Christianity is but a mere name without it. How or on what principle the Father was satisfied I know not, and may never know. The enunciation regarding vicarious satisfaction may be properly received in faith as a fact, but, I suspect, not properly reasoned upon until we shall be able to bring the moral sense of Deity, with its requirements, within the limits of a small and trivial logic. But the thorough adaptation of the scene to man's nature is greatly more appreciable, and lies fully within the reach of observation and experience."

Such is an epitome of Hugh Miller's confession of faith. Its great merit is its harmony with the oracles of divine truth; and, though the doctrine of the incarnation "squares not with the blowing clover nor the falling rain," it is not, therefore, as some of our transcendentalists insist, to be discarded as incredible. Man's relation to the infinite is not to be learned from the book of nature alone, nor is the fatherhood of God to be discovered from the mere material universe. God's creative energy and omnipotent power are, we know, inscribed at once on the curtain of the heavens and the caverns of the earth, but his paternal character is taught elsewhere. It is the lack of any light to disclose the heart of Deity that is the key to the coldness with which the pantheism that has enamoured not a few of the more eminent of our modern litterateurs is so justly charged. The material of which it is made up is perhaps fitted to form that kind of character Campbell has so well hit off in a single line of his "Gertrude of Wyoming,"—

> "A stoic of the woods, a man without a tear."

But it is utterly destitute of all those sympathetic elements which form the peculiar glory of Christianity, and which shall ultimately realize in a higher and holier sense than poet or patriot ever dreamed, that reign of liberty and equality for which the nations thirst.

Pantheism, of old the creed of intellectual and imaginative dreamers,—its resurrection and popularization by great names may, indeed, float it again for a time over the surface of society, but it will bear no higher fruit in modern than in ancient days. It is a system utterly unfit to combat the many evils existing throughout the world: indeed, why should it seek to combat that which it does not recognise in any proper sense as an antagonist force? It has nothing of the Christian sense of evil about it; it sees not that in every garret there is either a "haill Paradise Lost or Paradise Regained;" its ethical theory, notwithstanding the snaky fascination with which the magic of genius and the glitter of antithesis have invested it, is a meagre and jejune substitute for the *morale* of the Sermon on the Mount. That compensatory system with which some of its votaries are so much charmed, and which Emerson has so adorned that the dread bird of destiny which hovers over it is not once perceived by its disciples, was preached of old to that man of Uz, who, perfect and upright, feared God and eschewed evil. The consolation it brought near to Job in the midst of his cumulative calamities, extorted from even his patient spirit the upbraiding cry, "Miserable comforters are ye all." In a certain weakness of the human mind lies the power of the pantheistic system; for that large class who dislike a dogmatic theology, it has a certain nameless attraction and indescribable charm. It is precisely the kind of thing for those who prefer to look at their relations to the infinite through a subdued and coloured medium, rather than in the white light which a definite theology sheds on man's nature and destiny;

and it is only natural the predilections of this class should go with a system which disports itself with the imagination, rather than one that addresses itself to the conscience, and which just sheds over earth enough of the hues of heaven to impart thereto a diviner beauty and more intense fascination.

CHAPTER VII.

POETRY AND A PATRON.

For several months after his return to Cromarty, Hugh Miller continued in a delicate and rather precarious state of health. The stone-cutters' malady had made deeper inroads upon his system than he at first supposed; ultimately, however, his constitution threw off the disease, and he began to experience the quiet and exquisite pleasures of convalescence. An ornate stone dial which he cut for his uncles at this time still exists, a memorial of his superior skill as a workman, even in the more elaborate and ornamental department of the craft. When health had become more fully established, he set about executing sculptured tablets and tombstones in his native town and neighbourhood, becoming, in point of fact, a sort of improved edition of Old Mortality, minus the pony; only that it was for money rather than love he gave what immortality his iron pen could bestow upon many whom, probably, the satiric couplet of Byron might correctly have described,—

> "When all is done, upon their tombs are seen
> Not what they were, but what they should have been."

The style in which this work was executed was of a superior order to any that had been attempted in the North, while the biblical knowledge and literary tastes of the craftsman prevented him from falling into any such mistakes as did an English mason engaged upon the same kind of employment.

A bereaved widower had hired the Englishman to erect a tablet to the wife of his youth, and with great good taste selected for her tombstone one of those aphorisms of the wise king of Israel, which condense into a single sentence what feebler men would require a page to describe: "A virtuous woman is a crown unto her husband." Whether John Bull had been studying Crabbe's synonyms, or from what other cause report sayeth not; but, casting over in his mind what relation a crown bore to the other coin of the realm, with about as little reverence for the authorized translation as any one of the appellants for an improved version, he "gave bond in stone" to this very important announcement—a virtuous woman is five shillings to her husband.

Work failing Hugh Miller in the vicinity of Cromarty, by the advice of a friend whose opinion of his skill as a sculptor was very decided, he visited Inverness, and inserted an advertisement in one of the newspapers soliciting employment. As a voucher for the truth of his advertisement, which described his tablet-cutting as neat and correct, he brought with him a bundle of poetry, and, favoured with a letter of introduction to an influential minister, he repaired without delay to the residence of the reverend gentleman. After waiting some time in the ante-room, amidst a concourse of paupers and intending communicants, he at length obtained audience, and presented the reverend man with his letter, together with an ode to the Ness he had just written. The clergyman belonged to that pretty numerous class of divines who keep "the gloss of the clerical enamel" always peculiarly bright; doubtless, he thought it an act of very great condescension indeed, even to read the verses of the stone-cutter. It was, however, particularly unfortunate that he attempted to criticise them. The solemn shake of the head, in which they are invariably perfect, is the only safety of such men. A shake of the head may mean anything, and, as our Lord Justice Clerk judiciously remarks, cannot be taken down; but, forgetting the aphorism of the royal sage—"even a fool, when he holdeth his peace, is accounted wise"—he unhappily stooped to a verbal dissent, and, to his dismay, instantly found the artizan armed at all points, prepared to dispute, and able to dispute with success, every critical position he assumed, until, hunted out of each successive loophole of retreat, his reverence was fairly at bay. Only the most magnanimous of patrons could have relished such horse-play, and certainly that was the very opposite of the mode in which most men would have expected to interest any patron in their behalf Hugh Miller adopted. Legree, according to Harriet Beecher Stowe, began to look upon the avenger of Uncle Tom with something like consideration, after Master George had laid the ruffian on his back by a well-dealt body blow; but the prompt, and opposite as it was prompt, appeal to a host of the highest authorities in favour of the use of words the clergyman had declared obsolete, awoke in the reverend breast not consideration, but impatience. The result, we need hardly say, led Hugh Miller to determine that henceforth he should try and do without letters of introduction.

Within his own chosen circle, the worthy man who thought *marge* no longer in use among our poets, would no doubt pass for an oracle. Mr. and Mrs. Griffiths, who were wont, as a matter of duty, to revise the manuscripts of Oliver Goldsmith, would most unquestionably appear to the admirers of "gig respectability" every way superior to the erratic Irishman, over whose compositions they exercised so watchful a surveillance. But the rattle of Griffiths' chariot has long since ceased to swell the din of mighty London, while the trumpet of perpetual fame is filled with one long, long echo to the renown of Erin's ill-starred son; and that humble stone-cutter who, in the year of grace 1828, stood cap in hand before official pomposity in the manse of Inverness, lived to see his works the text-books of Oxford, and his name familiar as a household word on the lips of the first savans of Europe. Reader, behold the noble revenge of genius upon the little fantastic tricks which the insolence of office or the accidents of position may have played it, while yet on the bleak side of the hill of life, before success and prosperity sunned its path!

True, it may be answered, as in some sort a defence of the kind of treatment we seek to reprehend, it is not often that genius crosses the path of a parish priest in the disguise of a stone-mason, or comes near the eminent publisher in the form of a bookseller's hack. Within a given range, this defence may be admitted as valid; nay, knowing the evil influences of a too easy or too early triumph, it is perhaps well that, as a general rule, the position of the literary man as one of the forces of society, as a power in the state, can only be attained through much tribulation. Those mighty spirits who yet rule us from their urns, even they were in their time treated with the same indifference and neglect as the struggling genius who but yesterday emerged from obscurity. Go back but a couple of centuries, and we find certain pretentious scribes flippantly talking of "that dull poet, Mr. Milton." To be misunderstood and to be misrepresented seems the fate of all, in every age of the world's history, who have possessed greater intellectual power or greater moral energy than their fellows. And yet it is not to be doubted, even admitting the full force of the considerations we have stated, that a sense of the world's indifference has untoned many a fine spirit, and changed notes that had otherwise been musical as Apollo's lute into harsh and crabbed utterances.

Hugh Miller's skill as a stone-cutter received the promptest recognition in Inverness. His merits as a poet were more slowly acknowledged. Some verses which he had sent to one of the local papers having been rejected, piqued with the disappointment, all the more galling that he had let certain friends into his confidence, led him to resolve on the publication of a volume of poetry. Hugh Miller cannot, indeed, be said to have lisped in numbers, yet at a very early period of his life he must have paid court to the muses, though with what we think but indifferent success; his poetry being, for the most part, only prose in the fetters of verse. Poetry with him was imitation in a balder and more restricted sense than, we presume, Aristotle meant his definition to be understood. We are not, therefore, surprised that even before his volume had issued from the press, he became conscious he had committed a blunder, his thinking faculty having far outgrown the accomplishment of verse. The die was, however, cast, and though the work was by no means hurried through the press, "Poems by a journeyman stone-mason," at length emerged from the printing-office of the *Inverness Courier*; and now the crisis had come when Hugh Miller must run the gauntlet of the critics. The style in which the work was received was characteristic of the ordinary mode of reviewing, which still obtains amongst a large portion of the public press. By some journals he was patronized as a young man of genius; by others he was recommended to rely more on his chisel than his pen. A third class pursued a medium course; and while admitting his volume contained some fair verses, reminded him it was not every man who could expect to reach the high poetic eminence of Charles Doyle Sillerey, a poet now forgotten, but who, if Hugh Miller is to be credited, owed the praise he received to the very substantial pudding he bestowed upon certain members of the metropolitan press. A generous critique by a competent reviewer, the late Dr. Brown, author of a "History of the Highlands and the Highland Clans," more than compensated for any annoyance the curs of criticism let loose at his heels by this poetical adventure had caused. Looking at these poems after the lapse of fully more than a quarter of a century since their publication, during which great modifications of poetic taste have taken place, we cannot say that they furnish any adequate token of the transcendent powers of their author. Hugh Miller, we believe, could at no time write anything very foolish; his volume is therefore, as might be expected, destitute of all that silly sentimentalism which infects with so sickly a hue the major portion of the volumes of verse that in these days issue from the press. But though free from anything very foolish, it contains nothing very fine; a certain massive strength is indeed there, but so totally dissevered from the delicacy and sweetness, which amidst all its strength are the grand characteristics of his prose, that one is very apt to take the poet at his own word when he describes his lays as—

> "Scarce hauflins warmed wi' minstrel fire,
> And little skilled in lear o' ryme."

If poetry be, as Wordsworth asserts it is, the breath and finer spirit of all knowledge, then assuredly Miller's prose is more worthy of the name than any verse he ever wrote; and yet, though relinquishing in set phrase all claims to poetic excellence, it is obvious that to his latest day he never ceased to look back upon the poetic offspring of his youth with all the tenderness of a first love. The very ingenious manner in which he has contrived to introduce so large a portion of them into his "Schools and Schoolmasters," shows the tenacity of this affection; but, though his volume of verse did little for his fame, it had at least this advantage—it brought him in contact with one of the most accomplished of modern journalists and litterateurs, the editor of the *Inverness Courier.* To the columns of that able newspaper Hugh Miller contributed some descriptive sketches, unsurpassed by aught he ever afterwards accomplished. The theme was an humble one, and might seem at first sight rather unpromising—it was the herring fishery; nevertheless, with this comparatively commonplace topic on which to exercise his descriptive powers, his style blossoms into the noblest prose poetry. These papers were reprinted from the *Courier*, so great was the interest they created. This triumph in the treatment of a topic so lowly and unpretentious, at once revealed the man of genius. It is only the mediocre artist who is necessitated to travel into the region of the distant and the unknown for the materials on which to work; the true artist, knowing that all nature is instinct with poetry, seeks and finds it in the men and scenes with which he is surrounded. These literary efforts in prose and poetry had awakened considerable interest in his fortunes among a class that do not usually interest themselves much in the fortunes of the working man. Hugh Miller, in point of fact, now become a local celebrity, was pointed out to strangers as the Cromarty poet. When on a visit to Inverness, the late Principal Baird expressed a great desire to make his acquaintance, and, anticipating it might be of some advantage to bring the two men together, Mr. Carruthers despatched an apprentice from Inverness to Cromarty to intimate the desire of the Principal. The interchange of sentiment between the graduate of the schools and the graduate of labour was both interesting and instructive. Principal Baird was something very different from a monkish scholar who knew nothing save his books; his conversation with Hugh Miller shows him to have been a man of the ripest and most practical wisdom, and to his suggestion do we owe it that his "Schools and Schoolmasters" was written. "The distinction between the educated and uneducated literary man is absurd," said the Rev. Principal; "all are educated in some way, and the more unusual the way, the more interesting its record. Write the history of yours." In these observations lay the germ of the most delightful of all Hugh Miller's works.

About this time also he made the acquaintance of Sir Thomas Dick Lauder. He had likewise got pretty familiar with certain ladies of Cromarty, belonging to a small but select circle, who had cultivated with some success literary tastes and pursuits. Not unfrequently a group of these ladies might be seen in the old burying-ground, where the stone-cutter was at work, discussing topics of the freshest interest in literature and science. During one of these conversations with some rather elderly females, a young lady of very considerable personal attractions, apparently about nineteen, all flurried with running, came hurrying down to bid the group come away, and as instantaneously departed. Hugh Miller did not observe that she had even looked at him, and yet it was for him alone that she had put herself to the trouble of taking so much care of her friends. The young lady's mental powers were equal to her personal charms. She had heard of Hugh Miller as the poet of his native town, and longed to see him; curiosity ripened into love, and, in due time, Lydia Mackenzie Fraser became Mrs. Miller, and has since been known to fame, not only from her relation to the editor of the *Witness*, but as the author of several works of remarkable interest and ability. The family to which Mrs. Miller belonged is a family in which talent seems pretty generally diffused; her brother, the Rev. T. Mackenzie Fraser, late of Yester Free Church, now of Singapore, is known to possess remarkable native powers, and no less remarkable acquirements.

Shortly after the publication of his poetry, a branch of the Commercial Bank was opened in Cromarty; the office of accountant was offered him by the agent, and, after some hesitation, accepted. To gain the necessary experience of the workings of such an establishment, Hugh Miller visited Edinburgh, and was transferred to one of the branches of the Commercial bank at Linlithgow. As might have been anticipated, he looked a little awkward in his new vocation. The same mental peculiarity which made reading so irksome, until he found the secret of reading to lie in the stories it unlocked; which made stone-cutting so irksome that Uncle David despaired of making him a tradesman; now made banking irksome and mysterious, and for a time left an impression upon his superiors of his utter incompetency. But, as in all the other cases, so in this; having mastered the central principle around which the details grouped themselves, he suddenly shot up into an accomplished accountant, was left in charge of the bank during the absence of the manager, and, fortunately enough, did not discount a single bad bill while his superior was away.

After a stay of about two months in Linlithgow, Hugh Miller returned to Cromarty, and was regularly installed accountant of the Commercial Bank now opened in his native town. It was during the first year of his accountantship his "Scenes and Legends of the North of Scotland" appeared, and, during the second, Lydia Mackenzie Fraser became his wife. The spirit in which this important step was taken may be gathered from the following verses inscribed upon the blank pages of a pocket Bible which he presented to Miss Fraser on the eve of their marriage:—

"Lydia, since ill by sordid gift
Were love like mine express'd,

Take Heaven's best boon, this Sacred Book,
From him who loves thee best.
Love strong as that I bear to thee
Were sure unaptly told
By dying flowers, or lifeless gems,
Or soul-ensnaring gold.

"I know 'twas He who formed this heart,
Who seeks this heart to guide;
For why?—He bids me love thee more
Than all on earth beside—
Yes, Lydia, bids me cleave to thee,
As long this heart has cleaved;
Would, dearest, that his other laws
Were half so well received!

"Full many a change, my only love,
On human life attends;
And at the cold sepulchral stone
Th' uncertain vista ends.
How best to bear each various change,
Should weal or woe befall,
To love, live, die, this Sacred Book,
Lydia, it tells us all.

"O, much-beloved, our coming day
To us is all unknown;
But sure we stand a broader mark
Than they who stand alone.
One knows it all: not His an eye,
Like ours, obscured and dim;
And, knowing us, He gives this book,
That we may know of Him.

"His words, my love, are gracious words,
And gracious thoughts express;
He cares e'en for each little bird
That wings the blue abyss.

Of coming wants and woes He thought,
Ere want or woe began;
And took to him a human heart,
That He might feel for man.

"Then, O, my first, my only love,
The kindliest, dearest, best!
On Him may all our hopes repose,—
On Him our wishes rest.
His be the future's doubtful day,
Let joy or grief befall:
In life or death, in weal or woe,
Our God, our guide, our all."

A hundred pounds did not now seem quite so large a sum as Hugh Miller had once imagined, and, to eke out his income, he began to write for the periodicals. The first that came in his way was "Wilson's Tales of the Borders," to which he contributed some of the finest tales that appeared in that popular serial. The remuneration not proving altogether what it ought to have been, the accountant made an offer of his services to Mr. Robert Chambers, and during two years he contributed to his well-known journal, receiving the most liberal remuneration. In his "Schools and Schoolmasters," Hugh Miller takes occasion to acknowledge the kindness of Mr. Chambers, not merely in his own case, but expresses the opinion that perhaps no writer of the present day has done so much to encourage struggling talent as that gentleman. This opinion is one which, we believe, will be endorsed by all who know anything of the genial and benevolent nature of that accomplished man. Some local squibs, written in defence of his favourite minister, Mr. Stewart, who had refused to subordinate his sacramental services to the orgies of a coronation-day, procured Hugh Miller a gentle reprimand from the bank authorities in Edinburgh. This attempt at dictation on the part of the bank, in a matter with which they might seem, on the first blush of the thing, to have no concern, we might be disposed to class in the same category with the dictation to Burns by the excise authorities; but a moment's reflection will show, that, without particularly blaming Hugh Miller, with whom, probably, the offence was a sin of ignorance, his superiors were substantially in the right. The Commercial Bank was meant on its establishment to be quite distinct in its character from the then existing banks, which were all of them political engines. Speaking of their directorates, Lord Cockburn says:—"They were made up of respectable men, but without any talent or general knowledge, and the conspicuous sycophants of existing power." Excluding politics from its trade, the Commercial could not well, in consistency with its character, especially at that early period when party feeling ran so high, even seem to violate its fundamental principle. The reprimand, however, we have said was a slight one, and Mr. Ross, his superior in Cromarty, made it still more mild. Gradually, however, was Hugh Miller drawn into the vortex of a controversy unspeakably more important than any merely local squabble. The battle between the Scottish Church and the Imperial Parliament had convulsed Scotland; Hugh Miller caught the contagion, and plunged with all the earnestness and all the energy of his nature into the thick of the combat.

Though under somewhat modified forms, this battle was essentially the same as that in which the Church of Scotland was engaged, almost from her earliest settlement; it is therefore important that we pause here to take a brief retrospect of the conflicts of the Scottish Church.

CHAPTER VIII.

CHURCH AND STATE.

NOTHING has so much tended to complicate all ecclesiastical movements in Scotland, as the circumstance that the exact relations of the Scottish Kirk have never been accurately defined. The Reformation was consummated during the minority of Mary. When the Scottish queen came from France to Scotland to ascend the throne of her ancestors—apt pupil of the wily Cardinal of Lorraine—she took good care to legalise as little as possible of the doings of the reformers. The voice of the nation was too decidedly in their favour to allow even the queen to set herself in open opposition to what had been done. In these circumstances she very naturally resorted to what is, on almost all occasions, the strategy of the weak—dissembling. When Mary had abdicated the throne, and James VI. reigned in her stead, that amalgam of the pedant and the tyrant, though he blessed God that the Scottish kirk was the purest kirk in Christendom, did not, on that account, leave it to manage its own affairs. It is probable the vain-glorious monarch imagined, that for much of its purity it was indebted to the circumstance that he deigned to lift upon it the light of the royal countenance. And despite his eulogium, no sooner had James succeeded to the throne of "that bright occidental star," Elizabeth, than getting enamoured with the smooth ways of England's bishops, the vigorous self-assertion of the Scottish presbyters became odious in his eyes, and the famous Hampton Court conference was held, to convince Andrew Melville and his coadjutors how antiquated and unscriptural were their ideas. The Scottish clergy, who had been summoned before the king, were a set of stubborn republicans: neither crown nor crosier could induce them to swerve from the simplicity of presbyterial order. The routine and pompous ceremonial of Episcopacy only served as a theme for the satire of the intrepid rector of the university of Glasgow; and after enduring the most humiliating discomfiture, James was obliged to let go the Scottish presbyters, without the gratification of a solitary conversion. Episcopacy being deemed a more pleasant form of faith than the Presbytery, the great object of the Stewarts was to upset, as best they might, the Presbyterian Church. So long as James VI. lived, the scheme was pursued with something like respect for the predilections, and something like consideration for the prejudices of the nation. But, from the moment that his son Charles ascended the throne, the scheme of amalgamation or assimilation was pursued with a hot haste that indicated an utter disregard of the feelings of the country. Happily, Jenny Geddes's cutty-stool cut short the monarch's magnificent plan. "Thou foul loon, wilt thou daur say mass at my lug?" gathered up into a single sentence a nation's idea of Episcopacy. Jenny's stool proved the tocsin which summoned the nation to the conflict with its ancient kings. How that struggle was fought out, need not be here recapitulated. The story of the whole Iliad of woes through which the nation passed, is "familiar in our mouths as household words."

At the Revolution Settlement, unfortunately, what was only a drawn battle was veiled under the semblance of a triumph. The party was undoubtedly defeated who had sought to trample in the dust the "standard of Zion," but the principles of the martyr-heroes did not receive that sanction and that prominence which they were entitled to receive. William, with none of the bigot's zeal which induced his father-in-law, James VII., to forego, as the French sarcastically expressed it, "three kingdoms for a mass," had all the love of power which characterized the Stuarts; and he, more than any other British monarch, is the father of Erastianism in the Scottish Church. Diplomacy did much during his reign to bring to reason the Scottish clergy; and the spirit and temper which William managed to introduce into the Church, rendered the encroachments upon her liberties, which took place under a subsequent sovereign, capable of comparatively easy accomplishment. The Revolution Settlement brought indeed peace, but it did not bring liberty to the Scottish Church. Her spiritual independence, for which on so many a battle-field her sons had contended unto the death, was yet unsecured. To prove this, one has only to listen to the formula with which the General Assemblies of the Scottish Kirk are to this day closed. The first quarrel of the Kirk arose out of the circumstance of the sovereign disputing its right to meet independent of his will. And to this day the Church of Scotland is opened not only by a Royal Commissioner, but, what is more striking and more important, when the Moderator has, in the most solemn manner, and in the name of the Lord Jesus Christ, declared the Assembly dissolved, the Commissioner instantly rises from his chair of state, and, as if in solemn mockery of the Moderator, repeats precisely the same formula, with this slight difference, that the authority under which he declares the Assembly dissolved is not, like the Moderator's, the authority of the Lord Jesus Christ, but his sovereign lady the Queen's.

The scars of the fiery trial through which Scotland had passed, were too deeply imprinted on the heart of the nation to be obliterated even by a change of dynasty.

The product of the persecution was a fierce and defiant fanaticism, ready to dare anything in behalf of ideas for which so much had been suffered; while, by the side of this stoical piety and fortitude, there had gradually grown up, to the great grief of the faithful, a wild and ribald licentiousness both in thought and manners. In their correspondence, the good men among whom there still lingered the last fires of the antique piety of the heroic age which had passed away, are constantly bewailing the heresy and the infidelity of their times. Wodrow's description of the illuminati of his day is by no means exaggerated. "They were born," says the minister of Eastwood, "under the bright light of the gospel, and pains taken in their education, and they want not a certain measure of head knowledge; but their light eats out their exercise, and they rest, I fear, too much on their knowledge, and turn light, airy, and frothy, and woefully evaporate in questions and debates too high for them."

At no former epoch in the history of the Scottish Church, had there been so great a dearth of intellectual power among her clergy. Since the death of Alexander Henderson, so quickly followed by the death of Gillespie, the Church of Scotland produced no leader worthy to be named in the same breath with the three great men, who had in each eventful crisis of her history hitherto guided her destinies. In Knox, Melville, and in Henderson, religion had kindled a bright flame of patriotism: purity of soul, contagious eloquence, and iron strength of will, shone resplendent in them all. But the Revolution of 1688 produced no tribune of the Church. The name of the then principal of Edinburgh University is, perhaps, her highest name; partial historians have, indeed, painted him as a man, the dint of whose pen had been felt by Stillingfleet: but we suspect the polemical bishop was more annoyed with the dint of the pen of John Locke than aught ever written by Gilbert Rule.

In point of fact, the ablest man connected with the Scottish Church at the Revolution had become what no Scottish minister had ever been,—a courtier; and to comprehend exactly the position of the Church of Scotland, and rightly trace the progress of the Erastian element in her constitution, it is necessary that we look for a little at the character of this extraordinary man. William Carstairs was, unquestionably, one of the most remark able men of the Revolution. We may almost say that Glasgow has the honour to have been his birth-place—he was a native of Cathcart. Educated by a most distinguished scholar, an indulged Presbyterian minister, under whom he acquired the most complete mastery of the classics; to save him from embroilment in the politico-religious troubles of the times, under the disguise of a wish still further to perfect his education, his father sent him to Utrecht. On his journey to the continent he carried with him a letter of introduction to an eminent and public-spirited London physician, who happened to be one of those men with whom Flagel, a pensionary of Holland and one of William's agents, carried on an active correspondence. The physician gave young Carstairs a letter of introduction to Flagel, and the pensionary was so much struck with the superior abilities and polished address of the Scotchman, that he at once introduced him to his master, the Prince of Orange. The perfect comprehension of the state of parties in Scotland which Carstairs evinced, won the favour of William, and from that day until the day of his death the great Dutchman and the Scottish divine were fast friends.

Carstairs while in Holland was made chaplain of the Prince of Orange, and minister of the English Protestant congregation at Leyden. On every battle-field he was William's companion; and when the army of the Prince landed at Torbay, as yet it stood along the beach, Carstairs, placing himself at the head of the host that was to deliver England, invoked the divine blessing upon the enterprise; the entire body of the troops uniting in the jubilant notes of that grand old Hebrew song of deliverance and triumph, the 118th Psalm, in that hour consecrated by the biblical genius of our countryman as the Marseillese of the Revolution. Carstairs counselled William to observe the strictest impartiality towards the various parties into which Scotland had been split, and to be very careful to abate nothing of the royal prerogative. He did not wish ill to the Church of Scotland, but he wished her in a greater measure subordinated to the royal will, than the Scottish reformers could ever brook.

Not that in him we detect the full-blown Erastianism which, a little later, characterized the leaders of the Scottish Church. In ecclesiastical politics, Carstairs occupies a position midway between Henderson and Robertson. He did not share the religious enthusiasm of Henderson—he had not stooped to model his church principles upon the philosophy of Hobbes. His name, however, marks the epoch when diplomacy, rather than religious earnestness, became the one thing needful in an ecclesiastical leader. With the last of the Cameronians, the brave Renwick, perishing on the Castle Hill of Edinburgh, religious earnestness was gone from the Scottish Church. The Church did indeed yet struggle for supremacy, but the struggle was continued more in the spirit of a paltry personal egotism, than in the broad and generous spirit that had characterised the contendings of her early reformers. It vindicated its rights with the narrowest bigotry. Patronage was indeed abolished, much against the will of William; once and again had he given it to be understood, it was his wish, that nothing should be done prejudicial to the interests of patrons. Nor were the assemblies of the Church to meet except at his pleasure. "The walls of Jericho," which whoso should attempt to build, Alexander Henderson had cursed with the curse of Heil the Bethelite, were thus again rising all around.

A glance at the muster-roll of the Church at the period of the Revolution Settlement, will enable us to comprehend, not only how it was her liberties were so indifferently secured under William, but also how they were so easily filched from her in the succeeding reign. When the Prince of Orange became king of England, there were three parties in the Scottish Church. First in order and in honour were the aged ministers ejected at the beginning of the persecution—now the representatives proper, the old guard, of the second reformation. Next there were the indulged clergy, and lastly, the unconquered followers of Cargill and Cameron. Of the men who had shared in the work of Alexander Henderson, not more than sixty remained; of the indulged ministers there were at least twice sixty; and of the Cameronians there were but three. With the evangelical and patriotic party so outnumbered, with no commanding mind to direct its energies or shape its policy, it is not wonderful that party should have been unable to make much headway against at once the indifference, if not absolute hostility of the majority of the Church, the king's Erastian policy, and the temporizing management of his adviser Carstairs. Nor, while such was the aspect of its outer, was the Church's inner life greatly more satisfactory. In her best days, the perfection of her government was not more marked than the purity of her doctrine. Now, alas! she had in a great measure become a nest of heresy. In such circumstances it had not been surprising if we found the more earnest minds among the clergy, in an age yet so unenlightened upon the principles of toleration, resorting to rather harsh measures for the conservation of what they esteemed orthodox opinions. Not that we are prepared to justify the narrowness that characterized even the best men of that time. This much only we may state, if not in defence, at least in explanation of their intolerance,—almost all of what is now designated liberality of thought was then, in Scotland at least, associated with principles subversive at once of civil and religious freedom. The dissidents from the confessedly rather stern creed of their country, were generally found on the side of the oppressor.

The case of Greenshields, which has been so often pointed to as a proof of the intolerance of the Presbyterians, doubtless evinces an exhibition of temper with which we are apt to be equally surprised and disgusted. It should be remembered, however, in palliation at least if it do not excuse the spirit of the people, that the episcopal clergyman of that age was not the quiet, gentlemanly, decorous, and polished gentleman of the present times, reading the liturgy unexceptionably on Sunday, and lecturing, mayhap, on poetry or architecture on the Monday to the élite of the population. He was to the Scottish Presbyterians the symbol of thirty years of bloody persecution, and a man more likely, should opportunity offer, to make them acquainted with the merits of the thumb-screw, or the newest improvements on that terrible instrument of torture, "the boots," than the latest advances in æsthetics.

But though jealous, impatient, and intolerant of dissent from her standards, the Scottish Church of this epoch is not guilty of the terrible crime Lord Macaulay has laid to her charge. Her ministers were not the murderers of Thomas Aikenhead. If inquisition is made for the blood of that youth, it is in the Scottish privy council and among the lords of session we must seek the authors of the deed. To prevent any misconception, it may be well to state at once, that we have not one word to utter either in defence or in palliation of the mode in which the poor youth was hurried into eternity. That was doubtless a sad tragedy, and fitted to awaken the saddest emotions, which the authorities of Edinburgh enacted on that gray January morning of 1697. A speculative and studious, if rash youth, not yet major, expiating on a scaffold the crudities of his philosophy and the falsehood of his theology, was a spectacle fitted to kindle the deepest sympathy in all hearts where fanaticism had not frozen the fountains of sensibility; and had Lord Macaulay's withering denunciation been directed against the parties really amenable for the crime, he would have been worthy of all commendation. Unfortunately, however, for the reputation of the Scottish Church, the historian has not given a fair version of the facts of the case.

Lord Macaulay's readers cannot go far without discovering, that among the many excellent qualities he exhibits, not the least conspicuous are the vigour and strength of his hates. The contempt and scorn which he pours upon whole classes, rise at times almost into the sublime. The fate of Thomas Aikenhead presented the historian with a theme on which he could exercise his peculiar talents, and display his peculiar antipathies to the very greatest advantage. While defending religious toleration, and execrating bigotry at the tomb of its unfortunate victim, he was at the same time lashing with the scorpion-like scourge of his stately eloquence a batch of Presbyterian divines, an apostate whig lord advocate, and a brawling republican chancellor of the privy council.

"Aikenhead," says Lord Macaulay, "might undoubtedly have been, by the law of Scotland, punished with imprisonment until he should retract his errors and do penance before the congregation of his parish; and every man of sense and humanity would have thought this a sufficient punishment for the prate of a forward boy. But Stewart, as cruel as he was base, called for blood. There was among the Scottish statutes one which made it a capital crime to rail at or curse the Supreme Being, or any Person of the Trinity. Nothing that Aikenhead had said could, without the most violent straining, be brought within the scope of the statute. But the Lord Advocate exerted all his subtilty. The poor youth had no counsel. He was altogether unable to do justice to his own cause."

One would suppose from this account, that the Lord Advocate had indicted Aikenhead upon the extreme statute alone, and that he thus at once placed himself in a position where, to secure a conviction, it would be necessary to strain every artifice of the special pleader, and also that the form of the indictment placed the jury in the dilemma of either acquitting altogether, or finding guilty of the capital offence. No reader depending upon Lord Macaulay for his information, could ever suppose that the minor statute, to which he refers as one whose penalty would have sufficiently punished the prating of the forward boy, was actually in the indictment as an alternative charge; yet it really was so. The jury were not therefore left, by the subtilty of the Lord Advocate, exactly in the difficulty Lord Macaulay has represented. Nay more; this modified act had only been passed in the session of the then current parliament; and yet the Lord Advocate gives to Aikenhead the benefit conferred upon any one in his position, which was precisely such benefit as is conferred upon a criminal who has been guilty of what the crown, by the exercise of a little dexterity, might easily prove murder, but which they indict as murder or culpable homicide. We know that the effect of such indictments, in the majority of cases, is to acquit the panel of the capital offence. That it failed to do so in the case of Thomas Aikenhead, we must ascribe to some other cause than the subtilty of the Lord Advocate.

That it may not be supposed that we are stretching a point in favour of that functionary, we reproduce the precise words of the Acts under which Thomas Aikenhead was indicted:—"It is statute and ordained that whosoever, not being distracted in his wits, shall rail upon or curse God, or any of the Persons of the blessed Trinity, shall be punished with death." This Act was passed in the reign of Charles II. And by the fourth Act of the fifth session of the current parliament, 1696, ratifying the aforesaid act, it is further enacted, "That whosoever shall by their writing or discourse deny, impugn, or quarrel, or argue, or reason against the being of God, or any of the Persons of the Blessed Trinity, or the authority of the Holy Scriptures of the Old and

New Testaments, or the providence of God for the government of the world, shall, for the first offence, be punished with imprisonment," &c.

No evidence exists to show that the Lord Advocate, although the public prosecutor, took the initiative in this trial; on the contrary, we find it was forced upon him through a minute of the Privy Council, by which Aikenhead was delivered over to Sir James Stewart "to be tried for his life;" such are the precise words of the minute as it stands in the records of the Council. While the only connection of the ministers of Edinburgh with the case, so far as authentic testimony goes, is a connection highly honourable. Lord Macaulay says that the ministers not only desired the death, but they desired the speedy death of the poor youth. The whole evidence for this serious charge is a letter from a member of the Privy Council in which these words occur. It was told that if the ministers would intercede, the youth's life would have been spared. The reader will notice the peculiarity of this testimony or accusation. Lord Anstruther does not say of his own knowledge, that it was the want of intercession on the part of the ministers that was the cause of Aikenhead not receiving a respite; he merely says it was told, that is, he heard somebody say so. Only imagine Lord Macaulay compelled to make good his charge against the ministers of Edinburgh in a place where his sonorous rhetoric would avail him nothing. Suppose him examined by our able but inexorable Lord Justice-Clerk. The colloquy we might imagine to be somewhat as follows:—

You are Thomas B. Macaulay, now commonly called Lord Macaulay?—Yes. You are a literary man of some celebrity?—(The historian modestly bows assent.) You have recently written a "History of England?" —Yes. That book has been fortunate enough to secure a very large circulation?—Yes. As you are so influential and popular a writer, you will of course be very careful to say nothing in your works without good authority?—I am. You will be all the more careful on such a point when character is at stake? —Certainly; the historian who is not so, I regard as a moral assassin. You have made some very serious charges against a class of men whom we cannot suppose a gentleman of your high principle would slander. —I do not exactly comprehend to whom you refer. Is it statesmen or churchmen? It is a charge against churchmen, sir, to which I allude. You have asserted in the fourth volume of your "History of England," that the ministers of Edinburgh were the murderers of an unfortunate youth who was executed for blasphemy in 1697; of course, you would not make such a charge except upon the best authority?—No, my lord; I had the very highest authority for my statement—the letter of a Lord of Session, Anstruther. Did Lord Anstruther make the statement in that letter from his own knowledge, or did he speak upon the authority of another? He wrote what he was told. Is the court, then, to understand it was only a hearsay on the part of Lord Anstruther?—Witness hesitates. Lord Justice-Clerk (gruffly): Show me the letter. (Reads the letter.) I find it is so. The writer of this letter does not know the certainty of what he affirms; he seems only to have been told it. (Turning to Lord Macaulay.) Have you any further evidence to support your charge?—None. The Lord Justice-Clerk: Do you then, sir, deem the record of a hearsay a sufficient basis for the odious charge you have made against the ministers of Edinburgh? (Dead silence—sensation in court.) No answer. Lord Justice-Clerk: You may go down, sir.

There is still another point in connection with this letter to which we wish to direct attention. This Lord of Session, who, at the last moment, indulges in some snivelling sentimentalism about the eminent Christian the youth might have proved, was not only a member of the Privy Council, but formed one of that Council on the day when it delivered up Aikenhead to the tender mercies of the Lord Advocate. No trace of any dissent from the deed of the Privy Council is to be found in its records from the hand of the accuser of the Edinburgh ministers. We must, therefore, be permitted to look upon the evidence of humanity manifested by him at the eleventh hour as somewhat suspicious. It was very natural that a weak man like Anstruther, when seized with remorse for the deed of blood in which he had from the first borne a part, should attempt to throw the odium of that deed upon the shoulders of others; and, if he could persuade himself that the clergy were equally guilty with himself, his superstitions and his fears might be set at rest. We have said that this is all the proof which exists of any participation by the Edinburgh ministers in the guilt of Aikenhead's murder. But even this incidental and second-hand evidence is not left to be confuted by its own improbability and incoherence. We are in a position to confront it with direct counter-testimony given under the hand of one who speaks that which he knows, not simply that which he has heard. Mr. Lorimer, an English minister, though a Scotchman by birth, and a man of some celebrity and talent, was in Edinburgh at the time of the execution; and, in a preface to two discourses, one of which he preached before the authorities of Edinburgh during the period that Aikenhead was under sentence, he states distinctly that the ministers of the city used an affectionate tenderness towards him, and further, that some of the ministers, to his certain knowledge, particularly "the late learned, prudent, peaceable, and pious George Meldrum," then minister of the Tron church, interceded for him with the government, and solicited for his pardon; and when that could not be obtained, he desired a reprieve for him, and he joined with him in it.

Who then, it may be asked, were the parties really guilty? A brief recital of the conduct of the judges of Aikenhead will form the completest and most satisfactory answer to that question. This, we believe, will be admitted to have been peculiarly a trial in which it was the duty of the presiding judge to have given the jury the benefit of his experience. The alternative charge in the indictment was a new act, its limitations and its compass ought to have been distinctly pointed out. Such, at least, is now the custom in our courts of law. But no attempt at either explanation, definition, or restriction was made in the present instance. Nay more, when Aikenhead offered very valid objections to the testimony of Mungo Craig, these objections were repelled by the judges, and Craig's evidence received against him, though that evidence was in the highest degree suspicious—in point of fact, vitiated to a very great extent, by the peculiar relations which had subsisted between himself and the panel. It was not proven on the trial that Aikenhead had been guilty of the higher form of blasphemy, at least directly guilty of it. Craig did certainly swear to the cursing of Christ, but his evidence was not corroborated; the nearest approach to a corroboration being Patrick Middleton's declaration, that he had heard the panel say the authors and propagators of the doctrines of redemption were the damnedest crew in the world. In the very able articles reprinted from the *Witness*, entitled "Macaulay on Scotland," it is indeed stated, that it was distinctly proved upon the trial that Aikenhead had been in the habit of calling Christ a —— impostor, in addition apparently to the evidence of Mungo Craig, which is given on another page, and in addition likewise to the evidence of Patrick Middleton, which is also given. But after examining minutely Cobbett's and Howell's "State Trials," together with the "Records of Justiciary," in the Register-Office, we have not been able to find anything approaching to this dash. In fact, such a thing is an absurdity. Whatever is spoken in evidence is spoken out and recorded—nothing is left to be supplied. Had it been there at all, not the dash, but the word the dash is meant to represent, would have been plainly written down. But such an expression is not to be found in the original manuscript record of the evidence. We notice this fact, because, had the expression existed, in addition to the testimony of the other witnesses, it would have proved the capital charge, and the theory by which we bring home to the judges and the Privy Council the guilt of this murder would have been a groundless theory; Aikenhead would then have fallen with, at least, the forms of justice.

Balloting the jury had not been introduced in those days in Scotland, and, unfortunately, Aikenhead was tried by a batch of Edinburgh bailies. Bailies in those days no doubt represented, as they still represent very well, the respectability, the orthodoxy, and the mediocrity of the population, and, in all that did not demand too great a strain upon their intellectual faculties, were no doubt pretty fair judges; but here was a case in which they were taken at once into a region of speculation altogether foreign to their habits of thought. What the Paternitas-filiatio and Hagio-pneumatos, about which Aikenhead speculated, were, they would have but a very dim conception indeed. Some of them might have heard the expressions uttered occasionally in pulpits by clergymen with a turn for theological controversy and speculation, but these would be the better-informed of the jury; to the others, all such phraseology would remain a mystery. It was, therefore, peculiarly necessary in such a case as Aikenhead's, where justifiable speculation was mixed up with much unjustifiable levity and quibbling dialectics, that the presiding judge should have carefully defined to those who sat upon his trial, and who held his life in their hands, the precise force of the statutes under which he was indicted; pointing out most carefully the distinction between that arguing and reasoning which constituted the lesser offence, and that railing and cursing in which lay the essence of the greater or capital crime. But no such instructions were given, and no such definition was attempted; not the least trouble was taken to enlighten the jury on the point of law. The consequence was, as might have been expected, that, not distinguishing properly between the statutes, they returned a verdict finding the panel guilty of the capital offence. One might have expected that this, if nothing else was able to do so, would have awakened the judges to a sense of their functions as guardians and administrators of justice, especially as the poor youth before them had no counsel: but it was not so. Instead of sending back the jury to reconsider their verdict, that verdict was received by the court without murmur or objection, although only an inferential verdict. Sentence of death was passed by the doomster upon the unhappy youth, and the 9th January, 1697, saw the scholar and speculatist released from all earthly sorrows by the hand of the executioner.

In none of all this procedure do we find any trace of clerical interference. Aikenhead was sent, we have seen, by the Privy Council, "*to be tried for his life*" before the High Court of Justiciary. We have also seen that even the forms of justice were violated against the panel. Upon whom, then, are we to visit the odious charge Lord Macaulay has attempted to fasten upon the ministers of Edinburgh—who were the boy's murderers? Not the clergy, but the Privy Council and the lords of Session. Supposing even the ministers entertained—what it has not been proved they did entertain—revengeful feelings against Aikenhead; supposing it were even proved—though the very opposite has been proved—that they would not intercede for the youth! would that absolve the judicial tribunals from the guilt of immolating the heresiarch contrary to the statute law of the realm? While turning from the deed of blood with shuddering abomination, let us be careful our reprobation falls upon the parties really guilty.

Had Lord Macaulay been half as eager to reprobate the rapacity of the Scottish aristocracy, as he has been to reprobate the intolerance of the Scottish clergy, he could easily have found the amplest materials for his brilliant invective in its sordid bearing to the Church of Scotland. The act of 1690, which abolished patronage, gave patrons a very substantial compensation for their lost patrimony; yet when, in violation of the act of security in 1712, the son of Lord Stormont, inspired by the Scottish Jacobites, introduced the bill restoring church patronage in Scotland, no mention was made of any restoration of the compensation the nobles had received on its abolition. At the period of the Reformation they appropriated fully two-thirds of the Church's revenues. At the period of the Revolution they compounded with the Church for the surrender of a usurped right, and within little more than twenty years of the compound, they resumed the right so definitely resigned. The blow thus aimed at the Church of Scotland was meant as a precursor of the restoration of the exiled family to the throne of their ancestors. It was anticipated the old heroic spirit of the earlier better days would resist the invasion of the Church's rights, and that out of the confusion consequent upon such a conflict, the opportunity of the Jacobites would arise. But a church with the pure gold of Christian principle impregnated with so large an alloy of worldly policy, was no longer a martyr church; and no longer possessing the spiritual might necessary to bear aloft her ancient banner, she bowed ingloriously to the yoke.

Carstairs, though holding no extreme opinions on the subject of popular election, but fully aware of the sinister political bearings of the restoration of patronage at this crisis, exerted himself to the utmost against the act; but all effort was vain. The influence of William's chaplain, so omnipotent with the Prince of Orange, was nearly *nil* with the ministry of Anne. Whatsoever a man soweth that shall he also reap. In the act he now deplored, Carstairs saw the fruits of the *juste milieu* policy to which he had advised his master. King and chaplain were alike afraid of the fanaticism of the Covenanter. Both deemed it the perfection of statecraft to keep in equal countenance prelate and presbyter. But, unfortunately, the perfect equilibrium of parties they had sought to establish, was now somewhat rudely shaken, and the Revolution Settlement itself jeopardized by the fanaticism, not of the Covenanter, but the Jacobite.

From this hour the Church of Scotland, which, notwithstanding her imperfections, had shone so resplendent among the churches of the Reformation, began to feel herself a waning light. There were not indeed wanting, even in the darkest hour of her fortunes, voices calling her up from amidst the toils of statecraft in which she had lost her way, and in which her lamp had well-nigh gone out. These voices, however, though betokening a yet unextinguished vitality, gave little earnest of returning power. But as the darkest hour is the prelude of the dawn, so, from out the all but utter eclipse of the Church's hopes, consequent on the triumph of her enemies, light was seen lacing the lowering clouds that hung bodeful over her future. In a past crisis of her history those solemn words on the lips of the minister of Kinnaird—"He that entereth not in by the door into the sheepfold, but climbeth up some other way, the same is a thief and a robber"—piercing the soul of the minister of Leuchars, had transformed the protégé of Gladstanes into the antagonist of Spottiswoode, and the author of the Covenant. Now another text is about to kindle another flame, destined to burn on even into our own day, not only with undiminished, but with increasing brilliancy.

Some twenty years after the yoke of patronage had been placed anew on the necks of the people of Scotland, it was attempted still more firmly to rivet its chains by a kind of supplemental act, depriving the people of the last vestige of popular privileges they yet enjoyed. The deep undertone of discontent with which this proposition was received, found a tongue in the famous sermon of Ebenezer Erskine, preached before the Synod of Perth and Stirling, October 10, 1732. Devout men inly hailed Erskine on that day as a noble witness for the truth. But, unfortunately, the mass of the ministers of the Church of Scotland were rapidly becoming so deeply leavened with the Erastian spirit of the existing powers, as to be no longer willing "the stone which the builders rejected should be made the headstone of the corner." Light could not any more be borne by ecclesiastical judicatures; and Erskine, Fisher, Wilson, and Moncrieff, bore with them, in their secession, the torch of truth, with which they had sought, but sought in vain, to relume the flickering altar fires of the church of their fathers.

Complaint has been made by ecclesiastical historians entertaining substantially the principles for which the Erskines contended, that they should not rather have stayed within the Church, and endeavoured to turn the tide, then so strongly set in favour of moderatism, into an evangelical channel. Whether this could have been accomplished by some astute tacticians we do not presume to say. But it could not, we think, have been well effected by the fathers of the Secession—men obviously rather evangelical teachers than ecclesiastical leaders. The reluctance of the seceders to return to the bosom of mother church has also, we think, been too harshly dealt with. The Church of Scotland of that day is judged too favourably if judged in the light of the spasmodic efforts made to induce Erskine and his coadjutors to retrace their steps.

In the history of the next twenty years we shall find the amplest material for the corroboration of this opinion. At the close of that period, moderatism has found its true chief. William Robertson, of Gladsmuir, afterwards known as Principal Robertson, inaugurated his accession to the post of leadership by the direction of proceedings issuing in the deposition of the Rev. Thomas Gillespie of Carnock, founder of that branch of the Secession long known as the Relief Church. The manifesto of the moderate party which this case drew forth, (drawn up by Robertson,) seems almost identical in its principles with the principles of Thomas Hobbes of Malmesbury. That a modern sceptic should garnish his philosophy with the maxims of a heathen moralist is not wonderful; but that any Christian minister should have been found virtually asserting "the state is the highest ethics," was surely passing strange. For more than a quarter of a century did Robertson guide the policy of the Scottish Church. When he resigned the reins so long held with so firm a hand, a party had arisen in the Church (his own special friends) demanding that subscription to the Confession of Faith should henceforth be discontinued.

Dr. Hill of St. Andrews, successor of Robertson in the leadership of the Church, pursued the Robertsonian policy; going even a step further than his predecessor. That wary leader had, while supporting to the utmost the rights of patrons, always preserved the form of a call in deference to the traditions of the Church. Hill, bringing a narrower and severer logic to the consideration of the question, seeing, as no doubt Robertson also saw, that patronage and a call were virtually destructive of each other, proposed that the call be abolished. The counsel was not exactly followed, but the fact of it having been given shows the desolate and dangerous coast on which the church was rapidly drifting. Amidst the general unfaithfulness, a bold and energetic voice—the voice of Dr. Thomas Hardy—is heard, honestly declaring that the experience of seventy years, and the revolt of one hundred thousand of her people, are proofs that absolute patronage is irreconcilable with the genius of presbytery.

What a man so honest and so able as Hardy might have done for the church, had life been given him, we cannot tell; as it was, he had little more than time to lift the trumpet to his mouth, and to sound this jarring and dolorous blast in the ears of the moderates of his day, ere death summoned him from the church militant to the church triumphant. At this epoch moderatism may be considered to have fully developed itself as a system within the Church of Scotland. How far it had deflected from the doctrines and the spirit of the Reformers may be learned from two facts,—its leading lights had been the friends of Hume—their followers were the tools of Dundas.

CHAPTER IX.

NON-INTRUSION.

SINGULARLY enough, to the pecuniary difficulties of the Edinburgh Town Council does Scotland owe it, that the dreary and leaden reign of moderatism was first broken. In 1810, Dr. Andrew Thomson was brought to Edinburgh; in 1814, he became minister of St. George's. His popularity was unbounded; he filled the coffers of the Town Council, and he destroyed the prestige of the moderates, who up to that hour had numbered in their ranks the leading intellect of the Church. This tribune of the people clothed himself with a threefold power; from the pulpit, the platform, and the press he assailed, with all the energy of his intensely-earnest nature, whatever opposed itself to the purity of God's truth, or the freedom of God's children. Five years after Thomson is settled in Edinburgh, Chalmers is settled in Kilmany—like stars in the horizon, one by one the evangelical leaders of the Scottish Church are appearing. From Kilmany Chalmers went to Glasgow; from Glasgow to St. Andrews; from St.

Andrews to Edinburgh. In Edinburgh, he was surrounded with a group of coadjutors worthy of himself, of whom he was the central figure. The "voluntary controversy," the elements of which had been gathering for nearly half a century, now burst forth over Scotland with the fury of a tornado. Soon the leading men, alike of the Establishment and Dissent; were drawn into its vortex. A spirit of the most rigorous inquiry and investigation was abroad, searching, as with a lighted candle, the corruptions, real or supposed, of the Scottish Church. In the pictures which the leading voluntary agitators drew of the Kirk of Scotland, her sons scorned to recognize their mother; denouncing their representations as caricatures, but conscious of the power they wielded over the popular mind. Dr. Chalmers,—irritated that the popular feeling threatened to leave the evangelical party

> "Like some gallant bark,
> Well built and tall, which angry tides have left
> To rot and moulder in the winds and rains
> Of heaven,"

—exclaimed, "The Voluntaries have taken the platform, we must follow them there." They did follow them. The voluntary controversy merged in the non-intrusion controversy. The leaders of the evangelical section of the Scottish Church carried into her courts the sentiments to which they had given utterance from the platform. These sentiments, acted out, speedily brought them into conflict with the Court of Session and the Imperial Parliament. It was in the crisis of the struggle the quondam stone-cutter's voice was first heard as a controvertist. A sleepless night passed by Mr. Miller, after learning the decision of the House of Lords in the Auchterarder case, resulted in "A Letter from one of the Scotch people to the Right Hon. Lord Brougham." This letter was despatched from Cromarty, so soon as finished, to the manager of the Commercial Bank, Mr. Robert Paul, a gentleman who had shown Mr. Miller no small kindness. Mr. Paul carried the pamphlet to his minister, then the Rev. Mr. Candlish of St. George's. On perusing it in manuscript, the keen eye of the leader of the Free Church detected in its writer the man his party had been looking out for to edit their contemplated organ. At once, in the extent of its popularity, and in the circles into which it found its way, this first *brochure* was a successful hit. It was read by most of the members of the ministry of the day, including the late Lord Melbourne. Daniel O'Connell enjoyed its racy English, and Mr. Gladstone noticed it with approval in that elaborate work on "Church Principles," which Lord Macaulay subjected to such a trenchant criticism.

Thus does the Cromarty-bank clerk address the ex-Lord Chancellor of England:—

"With many thousands of my countrymen, I have waited in deep anxiety for your lordship's opinion on the Auchterarder case. Aware that what may seem clear as a matter of right, may be yet exceedingly doubtful as a question of law,—aware, too, that your lordship had to decide in this matter, not as a legislator, but as a judge, I was afraid, that though you yourself might be our friend, you might yet have to pronounce the law our enemy. And yet, the bare majority by which the case had been carried against us in the Court of Session,—the consideration, too, that the judges who had declared in our favour, rank among the ablest lawyers and most accomplished men that our country has ever produced, had inclined me to hope that the statute-book, as interpreted by your lordship, might not be found very decidedly against us. But of you yourself, my lord, I could entertain no doubt. You had exerted all your energies in sweeping away the Old Sarums and East Retfords of the constitution. Could I once harbor the suspicion that you had become tolerant of the Old Sarums and East Retfords of the church! You had declared, whether wisely or otherwise, that men possessed of no property qualification, and as humble and as little taught as the individual who now addresses you, should be admitted, on the strength of their moral and intellectual qualities alone, to exercise a voice in the legislature of the country. Could I suppose for a moment that you deemed that portion of these very men which falls to the share of Scotland, unfitted to exercise a voice in the election of a parish minister!—or rather, for I understate the case, that you held them unworthy of being emancipated from the thraldom of a degrading law,—the remnant of a barbarous code, which conveys them over by thousands and miles square, to the charge of patronage-courting clergymen, practically unacquainted with the religion they profess to teach. Surely the people of Scotland are not so changed, but that they know at least as much of the doctrines of the New Testament, as of the principles of civil government,—and of the requisites of a gospel minister, as of the qualifications of a member of Parliament!

"You have decided against us, my lord. You have even said that we had better rest contented with the existing statutes, as interpreted by your lordship, than involve ourselves in the dangers and difficulties of a new enactment! Nay, more wonderful still! all your sympathies on the occasion seemed to have been reserved for the times and the memory of men who first imparted its practical efficiency to a law under which we and our fathers have groaned, and which we have ever regarded as not only subversive of our natural rights as men, but of our well-being as Christians. Highly as your lordship estimates our political wisdom, you have no opinion whatever of our religious taste and knowledge. Is it at all possible, that you, my lord, a native of Scotland, and possessed of more general information than perhaps any other man living, can have yet to learn that we have thought long and deeply of our religion,—whereas our political speculations began but yesterday; that our popular struggles have been struggles for the right of worshipping God according to the dictates of our conscience, and under the guidance of ministers of our own choice; and that when anxiously employed in finding arguments by which rights so dear to us might be rationally defended, our discovery of the principles of civil liberty was merely a sort of chance-consequence of the search. Examine yourself, my lord. Is your mind free from all bias in this matter? Are you quite assured that your admiration of an illustrious relative, at a period when your judgment was comparatively uninformed, has not had the effect of rendering *his* opinions *your* prejudices? Principal Robertson was unquestionably a great man,—but consider in what way. Great as a leader, —not as a "Father in the Church;" it is not to ministers such as the Principal that the excellent among my countrymen look up for spiritual guidance amid the temptations and difficulties of life, or for comfort at its close. Great in literature,—not, like Timothy of old, great in his knowledge of the scriptures; aged men who sat under his ministry have assured me, that in hurrying over the New Testament, he had missed the doctrine of the atonement. Great as an author and a man of genius,—great in his enduring labors as a historian,—great in the sense in which Hume, and Gibbon, and Voltaire were great. But who can regard the greatness of such men as a sufficient guarantee for the soundness of the opinions which they have held, or the justice or wisdom of the measures which they have recommended? The law of patronage is in no degree the less cruel or absurd from its having owed its re-enactment to so great a statesman and so ingenious a writer as Bolingbroke;—nor yet from its having received its full and practical efficiency from so masterly a historian, and so thorough a judge of human affairs as Robertson;—nor yet, my lord, from the new vigour which it has received from the decision of so profound a philosopher, and so accomplished an orator as Brougham."

Roused by his labours, even while yet unaware of the success of his first effort in defence of just principles of ecclesiastical polity, Mr. Miller had begun a second pamphlet. About the year 1820 a remarkable case of intrusion had occurred in a neighbouring parish. Lapse of time had rendered the people indifferent or forgetful of the violence that had been done to their Christian rights, and probably, like his neighbours, Mr. Miller had not hitherto thought much over the matter; but Lethendy, Marnock, and Auchterarder had now thoroughly awakened the more earnest portion of the membership of the Scottish Church. Mr. Miller's zeal was at white heat, and on a Saturday evening he set out for the house of a friend, that he might attend the deserted church on the following Sabbath, to glean from actual observation the materials of a truthful description, which, he trusted, would tell in the controversy. That description Mr. Miller has given entire in his "Schools and Schoolmasters," nor shall we mutilate the passage:—

"There are associations of a high and peculiar character connected with this northern parish. For more than a thousand years it has formed part of the patrimony of a truly noble family, celebrated by

Philip Doddridge for its great moral worth; and by Sir Walter Scott for its high military genius; and through whose influence, the light of Reformation had been introduced into this remote corner, at a period when all the neighbouring districts were enveloped in the original darkness. In a later age it had been honoured by the fines and proscriptions of Charles II.; and its minister, one of those men of God whose names still live in the memory of the country, and whose biography occupies no small space in the recorded history of her 'worthies'—had rendered himself so obnoxious to the tyranny and irreligion of the time, that he was ejected from his charge more than a year before any of the other non-conforming clergymen of the Church. I approached the parish from the east. The day was warm and pleasant; the scenery through which I passed, some of the finest in Scotland. The mountains rose on the right, in huge Titanic masses, that seemed to soften their purple and blue in the clear sunshine to the delicate tone of the deep sky beyond; and I could see the yet unwasted snows of summer, glittering in little detached masses, along their summits; the hills of the middle region were feathered with wood; a forest of mingled oaks and larches, which still blended the tender softness of spring with the full foliage of summer, swept down to the path; the wide undulating plain below, was laid out into fields mottled with cottages, and waving with the yet unshot corn; and a noble arm of the sea winded along the lower edge for nearly twenty miles, losing itself to the west, among blue hills and jutting headlands, and opening in the east, to the main ocean, through a magnificent gateway of rock. But the little groups which I encountered at every turning of the path, as they journeyed with all the sober, well-marked decency of a Scottish Sabbath morning, towards the church of a neighbouring parish, interested me more than even the scenery. The clan which inhabited this part of the country had borne a well-marked character in Scottish story. Buchanan has described it as one of the most fearless and warlike in the north. It served under the Bruce at Bannockburn. It was the first to rise in arms to protect Queen Mary, on her visit to Inverness, from the intended violence of Huntly. It fought the battles of Protestantism in Germany, under Gustavus Adolphus. It covered the retreat of the English at Fontenoy; and presented an unbroken front to the enemy after all the other allied troops had quitted the field. And it was the descendants of these very men who were now passing me on the road. The rugged robust form, half bone, half muscle; the springy firmness of the tread; the grave manly countenance;—all gave indication that the original characteristics survived in their full strength; and it was a strength that inspired confidence, not fear. There were grey-haired, patriarchal-looking men among the groups, whose very air seemed impressed by a sense of the duties of the day; nor was there aught that did not agree with the object of the journey, in the appearance of even the youngest and least thoughtful.

"As I proceeded I came up with a few people who were travelling in a contrary direction. A Secession meeting-house has lately sprung up in the parish, and these formed part of the congregation. A path nearly obscured by grass and weeds leads from the main road to the parish church. It was with difficulty I could trace it, and there were none to direct me, for I was now walking alone. The parish burying-ground, thickly sprinkled with graves and tombstones, surrounds the church. It is a quiet solitary spot of great beauty, lying beside the sea-shore; and, as service had not yet commenced, I whiled away half an hour in sauntering among the stones, and deciphering the inscriptions. I could trace in the rude monuments of this retired little spot a brief but impressive history of the district. The older tablets, grey and shaggy with the mosses and lichens of three centuries, bear, in their uncouth semblances of the unwieldy battle-axe and double-handed sword of ancient warfare, the meet and appropriate symbols of the earlier time. But the more modern testify to the introduction of a humanizing influence. They speak of a life after death in the 'holy texts' described by the poet; or certify, in a quiet humility of style, which almost vouches for their truth, that the sleepers below were 'honest men, of blameless character, and who feared God.' There is one tombstone, however, more remarkable than all the others. It lies beside the church door, and testifies, in an antique inscription, that it covers the remains of the 'GREAT . MAN . OF . GOD . AND . FAITHFVL . MINISTER . OF . IESVS . CHRIST,' who had endured persecution for the truth in the dark days of Charles and his brother. He had outlived the tyranny of the Stuarts, and, though worn by years and sufferings, had returned to his parish on the Revolution, to end his course as it had begun. He saw, ere his death, the law of patronage abolished, and the popular right virtually secured; and, fearing lest his people might be led to abuse the important privilege conferred on them, and calculating aright on the abiding influence of his own character among them, he gave charge on his death-bed to dig his grave in the threshold of the church, that they might regard him as a sentinel placed at the door, and that his tombstone might speak to them as they passed out and in. The inscription which after the lapse of nearly a century and a half, is still perfectly legible, concludes with the following remarkable words:—'THIS. STONE. SHALL. BEAR. WITNESS. AGAINST. THE. PARISHIONERS. OF. * * * * * * * * * IF. THEY. BRING. ANE. UNGODLY. MINISTER. IN. HERE.' Could the imagination of a poet have originated a more striking conception in connection with a church deserted by all its better people, and whose minister fattens on his hire, useless and contented!

"I entered the church, for the clergyman had just gone in. There were from eight to ten persons scattered over the pews below, and seven in the galleries above; and these, as there were no more '*John Clerks*' and '*Michael Tods*' in the parish, composed the entire congregation. I wrapped myself up in my plaid and sat down, and the service went on in the usual course; but it sounded in my ears like a miserable mockery. The precentor sung almost alone; and ere the clergyman had reached the middle of his discourse, which he read in an unimpassioned monotonous tone, nearly one-half his skeleton congregation had fallen asleep, and the drowsy listless expression of the others showed, that, for every good purpose, they might have been asleep too. And Sabbath after Sabbath has this unfortunate man gone the same tiresome round, and with exactly the same effects, for the last twenty-three years;—at no time regarded by the better clergymen of the district as really their brother,—on no occasion recognized by the parish as virtually its minister;—with a dreary vacancy, and a few indifferent hearts inside his church, and the stone of the Covenanter at the door! Against whom does the inscription testify?—for the people have escaped. Against the patron, the intruder, and the law of Bolingbroke,—the Dr. Robertsons of the last age, and the Dr. Cooks of the present. It is well to learn, from this hapless parish, the exact sense in which, in a different state of matters, the Rev. Mr.

Young would have been constituted minister of Auchterarder. It is well too to learn that there may be vacancies in the church where no blank appears in the Almanac."

It would have been marvellous indeed, if writing like this, and the appearance of such an ally at so critical a juncture, had not created a sensation. The non-intrusion party powerful in the church courts; victorious over the moderates in every General Assembly; proudly elate with its triumphant position, had yet one sad drawback to its popularity;—it was but feebly supported by the press of Scotland. Whig journalists could not aid a movement which threatened to overthrow that peculiar subordination of the church to the state, with which the traditions of their party had immemorially associated a regulated liberty. It was also somewhat unfortunate, and contributed not a little to a misconception of the real aims of the non-intrusionists, that many occupying advanced positions in the movement-party of the church, had, during the great political struggles through which the nation had then but recently passed, been found ranged on the side of toryism. Suspected of sinister aims by their political antagonists, they naturally enough expected some assistance from their political friends; but, despite the utmost finesse and management by certain ecclesiastics noted for their diplomatic adroitness, political toryism recoiled from even seeming to support a cause which it deemed the cause of spiritual republicanism.

The non-intrusion leaders were thus left to seek their allies among those devout men, of all shades of political opinions, in whom religious earnestness rose superior to all political considerations. It is not wonderful that the anomalous position in which they found themselves towards both sections of the great parties in the state, induced them to consider the propriety of establishing a journal devoted to the advocacy of those principles the evangelical party in the Scottish Church were known to represent. To start a party organ was a comparatively easy matter. The peculiar difficulty was to find an editor, able to make such an organ respected. Hugh Miller's pamphlets at once proved his passport to the office. No sooner had Dr. Candlish read the first of those rare tractates, than with characteristic promptitude and acuteness he exclaimed, "Here is an editor for our *Witness*."

A letter was despatched to Cromarty inviting the bank clerk to meet the leading non-intrusionists in Edinburgh. In obedience to the invitation, Hugh Miller repaired to the Scottish capital, met the men so soon to be the heroes of the Disruption, in the manse of Liberton, (the Rev. Dr. Begg's,) accepted the editorship of their projected organ, arranged to enter upon his duties, and, returning to Cromarty, terminated his engagement with the Commercial Bank.

CHAPTER X.

THE WITNESS.

It was on the 15th January, 1840, that the first number of the *Witness* newspaper appeared. At the call of duty, not the mere whim of either taste or temperament, its editor flung himself into the stormy ecclesiastical controversy then raging in Scotland. It had been his ambition to leave the world a something it would not willingly let lie. He knew well how much of newspaper-writing must necessarily be of comparatively temporary interest, and above all, he knew how ephemeral and short-lived papers on ecclesiastical controversy, however well written, invariably prove. Such work was felt by Hugh Miller, as John Milton felt the controversies of the evil times on which he had fallen, to be a kind of writing to which he brought, as the poet expresses it, "at best only his left hand." And yet such had been his peculiar training, and his peculiar reading, that it may be questioned, even laying the matter of genius out of consideration, and looking at Hugh Miller merely as an accomplished *litterateur*, if another man could have been found in all Scotland so well fitted for the task for which he had now girt himself.

The moderate section of the Scottish Church had somehow, up to a very recent period, embraced within its pale all—at least almost all—the literary talent of the Church. The representatives of evangelical truth, though unspeakably more powerful as preachers than any men the moderate party could show, were utterly unable to cope in the field of general literature with the Robertsons, the Blairs, the Homes, and the Logans on the Erastian side of the Scottish Establishment. Not until Thomson and Chalmers rose, did that reputation for comparative illiteracy, which had become inseparably associated with the idea of an evangelical Scottish minister, begin to break up and pass away. As the mists of morning are lost in the rays of the rising sun, so this unfortunate misconception, to which accident had given a colouring of probability, disappeared in the blaze of the blended literary and scientific glory which the Astronomical Discourses of Chalmers shed over evangelical truth. Henceforth it was felt that not alone the genuine piety, but the genuine ability and genius of the Church, would gravitate rather to the doctrines of the modern "Marrow-men" than to the clay-clad creed of men who had transformed the Scottish Church from a genuine Christian institute into a mere State machine. Still, notwithstanding this conviction, shared by all the earnest men of the Establishment—a conviction which the events of the Disruption proved to be well-grounded—the representatives of that old party mustered strong in the Church; some of them possessing genuine ability, of a peculiar order it is true, but yet not to be despised or under-estimated. The literary man on the evangelical side, who should combat this party successfully, must needs be a man who understood it thoroughly, possessing an intimate acquaintance with its history, its traditions, and its literature. In all these respects Hugh Miller was amply endowed for the work he was called to perform. Perfectly acquainted with not the acts alone, but also the aims of the founders of the Scottish Church—having a most accurate conception of the ground-plan, so to speak, of the Scottish Reformation—able to put his finger at once upon all those points which indicated how widely the moderates had deflected from the ecclesiastical polity of Knox and Melville—at home in their favourite literature—knowing its excellencies no less than its defects—he entered upon his duties, a workman needing not to be ashamed, and descended into the arena of ecclesiastical conflict, armed at all points, so far as the discussion of principles was concerned.

Without being justly chargeable with any undue proneness to moralizing, we cannot contemplate Hugh Miller in the position he was now called to occupy, without feeling how peculiar are the leadings of Providence. He who in early life felt no call to become a minister of the church, in the maturity of his powers voluntarily assumes the onerous position of defender of that church's most sacred spiritual privileges. And, though certain histories of the Ten Years' Conflict are strangely oblivious of the advent of the *Witness*, thousands will peruse with interest those words of greeting with which its editor addressed his readers on the threshold of his mighty toils:—

"We enter upon our labours at a period emphatically momentous—at the commencement, it is probable, of one of those important eras never forgotten by a country, which influences for ages the condition and character of the people, and from which the events of their future history take colour and form. We enter, too, upon them at a time when, with few exceptions, our Scottish contemporaries in the same field—unable, it would seem, to lead, and unwilling to follow—neither guide the opinions of the great bulk of their countrymen, nor yet echo their sentiments. Strange as it may seem, it is a certain fact, which in the nature of things must every day be coming more and more obvious, that on one of the most important questions ever agitated in Scotland, the public and the newspapers have taken different sides.

"A few simple remarks on the point at issue may show more conclusively than any direct avowal, the part which we ourselves deem it our duty to take. There are parties which continue to wear their first names long after they have abandoned their original principles; and the historian, in tracing their progress, has to regulate his definitions by his dates. There are parties, on the contrary, which remain unchanged for years. The followers of Werter are in every respect, in the present day, what they were when their extraordinary leader first organized their society. There is, on the other hand, a section of our Scotch Seceders who see nothing to fear from the counsels or the increase of Popery, and who can compliment the Gowdies and the Simpsons of the time on the policy which drove the Fishers and the Erskines out of the Church. But the remark is exemplified at least equally well by two antagonistic bodies which, for the last century and a half, have composed the same corporation. The differences of the contending parties within the Church of Scotland arise solely from the circumstance, that the one retains its original principles, and that the other has given them up: nor is it at all improbable, that it shall be decided by the issue of the present conflict, whether the Church shall continue to unite its old character to its old name, or whether for the future it shall retain the name only. . . . . . .

"The cause of the unchanged party in the Church is that of the Church itself; it is that of the people of Scotland, and the people know it; it was the cause of their fathers, and the fathers of the Reformation;—it is the cause of a pure, efficient, unmodified Christianity. And the cause opposed to it is exactly the reverse of all this. We appeal to even our opponents. We urge them to say whether, in the expressive language of Dr. M'Crie, the cry which now echoes throughout the country be not the identical 'cry which has not ceased to be heard in Scotland for nearly three hundred years?' We request them sincerely to consider their present position, as illustrated and determined by the history of the Church. Among what party (in the pages of Calderwood and Wodrow, for instance) do they recognize their types and representatives of the body to which they are opposed? History is more than usually clear and definite on the point—it is one of those, regarding which the testimony of the present age regarding the past, anticipates that of the future regarding the present. It would be no overbold matter to class the John Frosts of our times with the Jack Cades of the times of Henry VI., or to compare the part taken by the mayor of Newport in the late riots, to that taken by the mayor of London in the disturbances of Wat Tyler. There are general similarities of conduct and circumstances which occur to every one, and which constitute the simpler parallelisms of history. But there are also cases that are more than parallel, and circumstances that are more than similar. It was identically the same, not a similar Christianity, which was denounced by the Sanhedrim, and which suffered in the Ten Persecutions. It was identically the same Protestantism for which John Huss endured martyrdom on the Continent, and George Wishart in our own country. It was identically the same Presbyterianism for which Melville died in exile, and Guthrie on the scaffold. Is there no such well-marked identity of principle between the churchmen on whom the fires of Middleton and Lauderdale fell heaviest, and the churchmen exposed in the present conflict to the still more merciless exactions of the Court of Session? and would not such of our bitter opponents as profess a high respect for the fathers of our Church, do well to remember, that what has already occurred may possibly occur again, and that there once flourished a very respectable party, who, when busied in persecuting the prophets of their own times, were engaged also in building tombs to the memory of the prophets slain by their fathers?"

In this preface to his great work, one knows not whether more to admire the calmness of statement, or the precision of definition by which it is distinguished. To some, indeed, it may seem in certain passages breathing only the egotism of the partisan, the sectary, and fanatic, ever ready to identify his own crotchet with a national cause. But that surely must be acknowledged to have been something nobler than a crotchet, which shook Scottish society to its foundations, brought a national Church into deadly antagonism with the highest courts of the realm, and ultimately, in obedience to the behests of a great truth, led hundreds of the noblest of the Scottish clergy—men pre-eminent in learning, eloquence, and piety, to abandon the church of their fathers. A great logician has, we know, described the Disruptionists as "martyrs by mistake." Posterity, we suspect, will pronounce the mistake to have been all on the right side. No student of Scottish ecclesiastical history can for a moment fail to perceive, that the principles the party represented by the *Witness* asserted, were substantially the principles for which "Melville died in exile and Guthrie on the scaffold." And had the logical position of that party, then the majority in the General Assembly of the Church of Scotland, been equally invulnerable with its historic position, the Disruption-ministers had this day been the Scottish Church. It was the flaw in the logical position of the evangelical, as opposed to the moderate party in the Establishment, that precipitated the crisis of 1843. In ascertaining the exact nature of that flaw, we shall best comprehend the somewhat anomalous position from which the descendants of the Erskines looked down upon the Ten Years' Conflict; and also discover how far the Scotch Seceders, on whom Hugh Miller has here cast a rather suspicious glance, and to whom he has assigned a somewhat questionable position, were justified in the attitude they assumed.

The founders of the Scottish Church, in common with the men of their time, had obviously but very ill-defined ideas of the distinction between the temporal and the spiritual powers. The sanguine anticipation, that Scotland "under an opened gospel" was immediately to become as one of the kingdoms of Messiah, naturally enough led the framers of the "First Book of Discipline" to assign to the civil magistrate "the conservation and purgation of religion." Should any doubt be entertained whether in the opinion of Knox such was the duty of that functionary, his "Letters from Geneva" will at once dissipate that doubt. In these letters the Reformer distinctly states, that "to the civil magistrate specially appertains the ordering and reformation of religion." In the enunciation of such a sentiment, Knox may seem to some little less than the patron of a full-blown Erastianism. But those ready to leap to this conclusion forget a very fundamental distinction between the sentiments of Knox at this early epoch, and the sentiments of those who, to adopt the phraseology of a later period, sought to set "the power of the sword" above "the power of the keys." That distinction lies in the oft unremembered fact, that with Knox, as with Calvin, the idea of a Christian Church and a Christian Commonwealth were identical, each being commensurate with, and involving the other. The theocratic thought of the heroes of the Reformation has, unfortunately for the world, never been realised. Not until His coming whose right it is to reign, may men behold the kingdoms of this world become the kingdoms of our Lord and of his Christ. But in the year of grace 1560, the year that gave to Scotland its First Book of Discipline, such a transformation was still with the Reformers a glorious possibility. A quarter of a century of conflict between the spiritualism of these Christian confessors and the secularism of the Scottish aristocracy, sufficed to turn this bright hope, then robed in the most celestial light and putting forth its noblest blossoming, into darkness and dust.

The results of that mournful conflict are to be found embodied in the Second Book of Discipline. In that book the distinction between the ecclesiastical and the civil government is stated at length. In that statement we find the Church—the reformed Church of Scotland —entrenching itself behind positions which had served of old to set the tiara of the Roman pontiff above the crown of the Cæsars. In vindication of the leaders of the Scottish Church, it must, however, be borne in mind, they took refuge in these principles, not as Rome had taken refuge, in the interests of priestly caste and for the advancement of priestly ambition, but solely as a means through which to conserve the spirituality of the Church of Christ, perpetually menaced by those they had fondly dreamed would have been nursing-fathers and nursing-mothers to the nascent reform. The exigencies of their position had taught the framers of the Second Book of Discipline, that the civil and the sacred powers were in their natures distinct. But the legitimate corollary to that proposition, viz., that things thus radically distinct in their natures could not safely be incorporated, had not yet dawned upon them. Not even the fierce and prolonged persecution which so soon enwrapt the Church, brought near to her sons a conviction of this salutary truth. And, when persecution no longer raged—when the Revolution of 1688 was a fact accomplished, and the tyrant who had so "persecuted the Church of God and wasted it" had become a fugitive and a vagabond on the face of the earth—when all this was done, and when under another *régime* those encroachments of the civil powers were renewed, which separated the fathers of the Secession from the National Church, the calamity was attributed rather to accidental circumstances, than to any flaw in fundamental principles. A century's experience taught the descendants of the Erskines, that the combination of secular prestige and spiritual power their ancestors had sought in vain to realize in the Establishment, and to which the evangelical section of the Scottish Church still clung so tenaciously, was utterly incompatible. When, therefore, almost in the very hour this light dawned upon them, they found a formula of spiritual independence—the watchword of a martyr age, once again "in bannered bloom unfurled," was it wonderful that, undazzled by the glorious souvenirs under which the non-intrusion, now the dominant party in the Establishment, combated, they estimated its battle-cry by the light of the logic of events, as developed in some three centuries of the history of the Scottish Church, rather than in the lustre with which, in the enthusiasm of the hour, the conflict stood invested? Long, very long, had they themselves clung to the day-dream that now fascinated their evangelical friends; and with the blinding mirage, which throughout a hundred years had veiled the stern facts of the case, just fallen from their eyes, it would have been too much to have expected they would do more than just endeavour to laugh those friends out of their delusion. Such a temper, it may be granted, was not the most Christian that might have been manifested in the circumstances. But while making this acknowledgment, a sense of justice compels us to add, that neither was the attitude of the leading advocates of the spiritual independence of the Church of Scotland towards Scottish Dissent, the attitude best fitted to evoke its brotherly kindness and charity. But, as it is altogether foreign to our purpose to revive the memory of mutual wrongs, perpetrated in the excitement of controversy, we refrain from any more specific allusion to the unseemly antagonism between evangelical churchism and evangelical dissent, too often manifested throughout the non-intrusion and voluntary controversies. Before, however, passing from this topic, a word, partly in vindication, and partly in reprehension of the Scotch Seceders, is necessary. There is no denying, it was one of the delusions with which a newly-discovered principle is so often found to intoxicate its votaries, that induced the Seceders to assert, "Popery is no longer Popery when it declares on the side of voluntaryism." There was just that infinitesimal amount of truth about the proposition which served to veil its hollowness and utter falsity from men panting to right all that was wrong, whether in Church or State, and inspired with the conviction that society had only to be conditioned by their own narrow formula, and the mighty transformation was accomplished. Alas! the "mystery of iniquity" was too profound to be fully fathomed by unsophisticated Scottish voluntaries. The phase through which Roman Catholicism was then passing, rendered it politic for it to assume the garb, and echo the accents of an extreme liberalism. We need not say how very completely subsequent events have shown how miserable a phosphorescent meteoric light, gleaming its brief hour above the Pontine marshes, that was, the Dissenters of Scotland mistook for the godlike radiance of a star of heaven. The shallowness of the logic is now transparent, which induced Scotch Seceders to listen even for a moment to the syren song of liberty on the lips of representatives of a church, whose policy and whose ritual are a device against the civil and religious freedom of man. On this point, then, we freely concede, that the representatives of the Fishers and the Erskines amply merited the censure Hugh Miller has meted out to them, in what may be regarded as the prolegomena of the *Witness*.

On the second count of their indictment, however, we cannot say Guilty. The light in which they looked upon the moderate party in the Establishment, does not seem to us open to rebuke. Making legitimate deduction for the asperities of controversy, the dispassionate reviewer of their position must pronounce them to have been here from the first, as they were proved at the last, right. It was made matter of bitter reproach, that they were honest enough to assert the moderates held the only position compatible with remaining an established church. Non-intrusionists indignantly resented the idea, that because connected with the state, they were thereby fettered. But did not the Disruption demonstrate the stern verity of that proposition, with a power transcending even mathematical certitude? The great truth with which that exodus of the *élite* of the clergy of the Church of Scotland is at this hour silently leavening their flocks, is precisely the truth for maintaining which Scotch Seceders were not unfrequently stigmatized as atheistical voluntaries.

But while asserting that the moderate party in the Scottish Church occupied the more logical position, the Seceders were under no delusion about which of the great sections of the Church of Scotland was inspired with the nobler instincts; none knew better to whom they were indebted, within the pale of the Establishment, for that revival of evangelical religion by which a large portion of its ministry had latterly been distinguished. It was indeed felt to be a little irritating, and somewhat unfortunate, that the vision of these good men in the Scottish Church was generally so circumscribed, that they saw only the good themselves had done, and seldom remembered, in estimating the religious agency and religious influence at work upon the nation, to estimate aught else than the agency they employed and the influence they exerted. While ignoring a century of effort on the part of others, is it marvellous that those whose efforts were thus lightly esteemed should have failed to proclaim, as if from the house-tops, this new-born zeal? Veterans who had borne the burden and heat of the day in the Master's work, might be pardoned when pausing to discover, if from being as tumultuous, the zeal of these neophytes was likely to prove as evanescent, as the mountain torrent, which, leaping from ledge to ledge of the spray-clad rock, bounding over every barrier, and bearing down all opposition, is yet, at the terminus of its headlong and agonizing descent, found altogether lost in the sands of the valley.

But those slight deductions which Scotchmen who had renounced the establishment-principle might be disposed to make, in their general estimate of Hugh Miller's acceptability as the editor of an ecclesiastical journal, arose out of tendencies and opinions which qualified him only all the more completely for the task he had assumed. A brief glance at the nature of that task, and at the circumstances in which it was entered upon, will enable us to form something like an adequate conception at once of the very critical position Hugh Miller was called to occupy, and the very great services he rendered to a cause with which his name must henceforth for ever remain so indissolubly associated. The first difficulty the *Witness* had to contend with, was the fact that, originated by a clerical conclave, it might not unnaturally be assumed to be a merely clerical organ. Scotchmen have ever cherished a jealous dread of ecclesiastical influence upon journalism. Nor have those portions of the press that have fallen under its control been at all calculated to dissipate that dislike, or lay their vigilance asleep. Abhorred for its truculence and mendacity, or pitied for its inanity and senility, the religious newspaper has been by turns detested or despised; but respected—never. We believe we shall not be contradicted in asserting, that the *Witness* is the only journal, avowedly originated to represent an ecclesiastical party, that has courageously kept itself aloof from the sin that so easily besets all ecclesiastical organs. It is no secret, that the maintenance of this independent position cost its original editor much sacrifice of feeling. He had undertaken the duties and the responsibility which his onerous position imposed, from deeply conscientious motives. He was ready to do battle with all comers in behalf of those principles upon which he believed the historic and national Church of the country based, and the herculean efforts made in their defence in the earlier years of the existence of the *Witness*, prove, beyond all controversy, his devotion to the principles of the Free Church. But when the battle was hottest, Hugh Miller was a loyal combatant, not a free lance; and no man could more promptly resent dictation and interference, even when that dictation and that interference came from those he otherwise honoured. When a certain eminent ecclesiastic proposed to secure uniformity in the utterances of Free Church journalism, by appointing something like a censorship over the editorial columns of the newspapers supposed to be in its interest; careless how others might think, feel, or act in the matter; with the spirit of a man zealous to uphold the independence of the profession he had chosen, Mr. Miller resented the attempted dictation, although in resenting he forfeited for a time the good opinion of those hitherto most highly esteemed. It was, no doubt, painful to break with some who had first pointed him out as fit to fill the editorial chair; but with a conscientious man all things cease to be painful, when supported by the consciousness that he has discharged his duty.

CHAPTER XI.

POPULAR DISTRUST.

SUCH, then, were the powers, the tastes, and the temper of the man the non-intrusion leaders selected to popularise their movement among the people of Scotland. Hitherto, despite their utmost efforts to dislodge from the popular mind all suspicion of sinister aims, they continued to be everywhere looked upon with the greatest distrust. Their zeal for the people's rights, it was feared, only veiled the intrigues of priestly ambition. Never before had a nation been so disposed to accept as accurate Milton's aphorism,—"New presbyter is old priest writ large." What the state of feeling among the community generally was, even after seven years' agitation, down to almost the very hour the *Witness* took the field, may be gathered from the following passage in a private note, addressed by Hugh Miller to Mr. Paul, Edinburgh, in 1839, when forwarding to him from Cromarty the manuscript of his letter to Lord Brougham:—"The question which at present agitates the country is a vital one, and unless the people can be roused to take part in it (and they seem wofully indifferent as yet) the worst must inevi tably prevail." That was a modest, and, as the sequel has shown, a not ill-grounded hope, to which in the same letter the writer ventured to give expression in these words—"The people may perhaps listen to one of their own body who combines the principles of the old with the opinions of the modern Whig; and who, though he feels strongly upon the question, has no secular interest involved in it." Mainly to the establishment of the *Witness* may be attributed the rapid awakening of the people of Scotland to the real import of the non-intrusion controversy, by which the years 1840 and 1841 were so peculiarly distinguished. Even so late as 1839, Dr. George Cook could state, without fear of contradiction, that he could scarce enter an inn or a stage-coach, without finding respectable men inveighing against the utter folly of the non-intrusionists, and the worse than madness of the Church courts.

Nor are the concurrent testimonies of a sanguine non-intrusionist and a veteran moderate the only sources from which we are left to form our opinion of the true state of public sentiment at this critical juncture. The Veto act was passed in 1834. The decision of the House of Lords in the Auchterarder case was given in 1839. During all the intervening years, petitions in favour of the independence of the Church had been presented to Parliament; but the paucity of the signatures obtained had been most marked. Even in the metropolis of Scotland, the chosen home of the non-intrusion leaders, the scene of the labours of Chalmers and Welsh, Gordon and Cunningham, Candlish and Begg, not more than from 4000 to 5000 was the average number of signatures these petitions received. The appeals of an eloquence such as had not been heard in the assemblies of the Scottish Church since the days of Knox and Henderson, so far from setting the soul of the nation on fire, had proved but as water spilt upon the ground. To their dubious antecedents did these orators owe the scepticism with which their efforts on behalf of spiritual independence were almost everywhere received. People had a difficulty in believing men the sincere friends of sacred liberty, who so very recently were such indifferent friends to civil freedom. It was peculiarly fortunate for this party, that the editor of the *Witness* was above suspicion; no souvenirs of a sinister career were associated with his name, or beclouded his character. His antecedents were hostages for his perfect independence. The result of his labours in dispelling the distrust with which non-intrusion principles had been hitherto viewed, was apparent in the fact, that in 1840, the first year of the existence of the *Witness*, the petition sent from Edinburgh to Parliament, in their behalf, contained some

13,000 signatures, being more than double the number a kindred petition had obtained in the previous year Already had the *Witness* disabused a large section of the public of the fatal suspicion that it was for clerical power, not popular rights, the non-intrusion leaders so earnestly contended.

Nor while thus eminently successful in his peculiar mission as an ecclesiastical polemic, was it merely from his efforts as a controvertist that his countrymen were left to gather their impression of his powers. It is seldom, indeed, that a man of high faculty is not also many-sided. The old divines were wont to represent man as a microcosm of the universe; and it would seem that, just in proportion to his intellectual development, is the degree of ease with which he intermeddles with all knowledge.

Whether in science, literature, or criticism, Hugh Miller seemed equally at home. From out the stormy arena of ecclesiastical controversy, he turned at will into the peaceful region of æsthetics. With nature's self an old acquaintance, we are not surprised to find him, even so early as the second month of his connection with the *Witness*, indulging his readers with certain glorious recollections of the beautiful and the sublime, awakened by the contemplation of the triumphs of art in the annual exhibition of the Royal Scottish Academy. Few first visits to that exhibition ever produced such "criticism for the uninitiated" as this delicately beautiful description of a northern dell suggested to Hugh Miller while lingering in the presence, and under the spell of one of the richest landscapes of the exhibition:—

"In this solitary dell the banks, which, on either hand, at every angle and indentation, advance their grassy ridges, or retire in long sloping hollows, partake perhaps rather of the picturesque than of the magnificent; but the trees which rise along their sides, and which for the last century have been slowly lifting themselves to the freer air of the upper region, look down from more than the higher altitude instanced by Rousseau. Often when the evening sun was casting its slant red beams athwart their topmost branches, and all beneath was brown in the shade, we have sauntered along this little stream, lost in delicious musings, whose intermingled train of thought and feeling we have no language to convey. We have felt that the cogitative faculty in these woods had not much of activity; but then, though it wrought slowly, it wrought willingly and unbidden; and around, every minute thing would swell and expand an atmosphere of delightful feeling, which somehow seemed to owe its origin as much to the magnitude as to the quiet beauty of the surrounding objects; and which has reminded us fancifully, but strongly, of the minutest of all the planets—of the Asteroids rather—whose atmosphere rises over it more than ten times the height of the atmosphere of our own planet. We have looked up to the branches that twisted and interlaced themselves so high over our head, and the leaves that seemed sleeping in the light; we have seen the deep blue sky far beyond; we have caught glimpses through the chance vistas of little open spaces, shaggy with a rank vegetation, and which we have loved to deem the haunts of a solitude still deeper than that which surrounded us; we have marked the varieties of beauty which distinguish the several denizens of the forest—the ash with his long massy arms that shoot off from the trunk at such acute angles, and his sooty blossoms spread over him as if he were mourning—the elm with his trunk gnarled and furrowed like an Egyptian column, and his flake-like foliage laid on in strips that lie nearly parallel to the horizon—the plane, with his dark green leaves and dense heavy outline, like that of a thunder-cloud—the birch, too, a tree evidently of the gentler sex, with her long flowing tresses falling down to her knee; and as we have looked above and around, we have felt our heart swelling within us with an exquisite emotion that feasts on the grand and the beautiful as its proper food; and surely that mind must be chilled and darkened by the pall of a deathlike scepticism, that does not expand with love and gratitude, under the influence of so exquisite a feeling, to the great and wonderful Being who has imparted so much of good and fair to the forms of inanimate nature, and has bestowed on the creature such a capacity of enjoying them."

Nor is the following ought less grand:—

"When standing in front of M'Culloch's exquisite landscape—'Deer Startled'—we were enabled to call up some of our own moonlight scenes of quiet and soothing beauty, or of wild and lonely grandeur. We stood on a solitary shore. A broken wall of cliffs, more than a hundred yards in height, rose abruptly—here advancing in huge craggy towers, tapestried with ivy, and crowned with wood—there receding into deep gloomy hollows; the sea, calm and dark, stretched away, league after league in front, to the far horizon. The moon had just risen, and threw its long fiery gleam of red light across the waters to the shore. A solitary vessel lay far away, becalmed in its wake; we could see the sail flapping idly against the mast, as she slowly rose and sank to the swell. The light gradually strengthened—the dark bars of cloud, that had shown like the grate of a dungeon, wore slowly away—the white sea birds, perched on the shelves, became visible along the cliffs—the advancing crags stood out from the darkness—the recesses within seemed, from the force of contrast, to deepen their shades—the isolated spirelike crags that rise thick along the coast, half on the shore, half in the sea, flung each its line of darkness inward along the beach. A wide cavern yawned behind us, rugged with spiracles of stalactites, that hung bristling from the roof like the icicles at the edge of a waterfall, and a long rule of light that penetrated into the innermost wall, leaving the sides enveloped in thick obscurity, fell full on what seemed an ancient tomb and a reclining figure in white—sports of nature in this lonely cave. There was an awful grandeur in the scene—the deep solitude, the calm still night, the huge cliffs, the vast sea, the sublime heavens, the slowly rising moon with its broad cold face!—we felt a half-superstitious feeling creep over us, mingled with a too oppressive sense of the weakness and littleness of man. Pride is not one of the vices of solitude—it grows upon us among our fellows; but alone and at midnight, amid the sublime of nature, we must feel, if we feel at all, that we ourselves are little, and that God only is great.

"The scene passed, and there straightway arose another.' We stood high in an open space, on a thickly-wooded terrace, that stretched into an undulating plain, bounded with hills. The moon at full looked down from the middle heavens, undimmed by a single cloud; but far to the west there was a gathering wreath of vapour, and a lunar rainbow stretched its arch in pale beauty across a secluded Highland valley. A wide river rolled at the foot of the wooded terrace, but a low silvery fog had risen over it, bounded on both sides by the line of water and bank, and we could see it stretching its huge snakelike length a-down the hollow, winding with the stream, and diminishing in the distance. The frosts of autumn had dyed the foliage of the wood—the trees rose around us in their winding-sheets of brown and crimson, and yellow, or stretched in the more exposed openings their naked arms to the sky. There was a dark moor beyond the fog-covered river, that seemed to absorb the light, but directly under the nearest hill, which rose like a pyramid, there was a tall solitary ruin, standing out from the darkness, like the sheeted spectre of a giant. The distant glens glimmered indistinct to the eye, but the first snows of the season had tipped the upper eminence with white, and they stood out in bold and prominent relief—nearer apparently than even the middle ground of the landscape. The whole was exquisitely beautiful—a scene to be once seen and ever remembered."

On the last day of February, 1840, Hugh Miller's first geological contribution to the columns of the *Witness* appeared. Its subject was "The Chaotic Period." The paper embodies certain opinions and conjectures upon the order of creation which, in "The

Testimony of the Rocks," he saw fit considerably tc modify. In little more than a month later, the opening chapter of "Old Red Sandstone" was published. Twc years before the advent of the *Witness*, the substance of this chapter appeared in "Chambers's Edinburgh Journal," to which, on abandoning "Wilson's Tales of the Borders," he had become a pretty regular, and always a welcome contributor. Even thus early, one knows not whether to admire more the catholicity of taste and the versatility of talent, displayed in the marvellous diversity of topics on which he lavished the riches of his intellectual and imaginative powers, or the profundity with which all he touched was treated. Now he is instinct with the enthusiasm of the hour combating for non-intrusion principles with a zeal worthy of a Cameron or a Renwick, mayhap mauling, with all the gusto of a Junius, some unfortunate apostate from the good cause; and now, withdrawn from the strife of tongues—a sojourner in the city of the dead, "the skeletons of nations around the lonely man," his sole companions the representatives of the vanished ages, slowly and laboriously gathering up, by the most painstaking induction of facts, the materials out of which his imperial imagination has set as in a hall of mirrors the glories of the primitive world. Other men of science might be able—some probably more able—to read the story of the fragmentary fossil skeleton imbedded in the strata of mother earth; but no one of them all was so capable of realizing a life-like picture, at once of the plants that adorned, and the living things that peopled an earlier world. In breadth and picturesqueness of description, no writer of this age has surpassed the author of the "Stones of Venice;" but Ruskin, we suspect, would find even his powers paralysed on the pavement of the primitive world. Not so Hugh Miller. Long study of its extinct organisms had given him a familiarity with its every feature, which it only required his powerful imagination to set free from the fossilized condition in which, like some imperial taskmaster, nature's mighty forces had through æons of ages remorsely bound them. Nay, we question if it will not be found that, though in the gorgeousness of diction Ruskin has surpassed our great countryman, for pre-Raphaelite-like accuracy of minute detail and severe truthfulness to nature the guerdon must be awarded to Hugh Miller. His geological studies were to him what the study of anatomy is to the painter; they enabled him to present, not merely a boldly delineated image of the thing or the scene described, but they also enabled him to preserve, amidst the utmost boldness and vigour of outline, the minutest verisimility.

In literature and in science, as in all else he did, Hugh Miller worked from a centre outwards. Given the nature of the rocks of a country, and Hugh Miller would describe its scenery; but to describe its scenery as he deemed description, such knowledge was necessary. From a peculiarity of his mental nature, manifested from the very earliest epoch, and not, as some have alleged, from an overweening fondness for those scientific pursuits with which his name has become so honourably associated, is he found so frequently treating literary questions in a semi-geological strain. His was pre-eminently a pictorial and analogical, rather than analytical mind; and being so, his geological studies were on all occasions of pre-eminent service, furnishing him with a perennial source of fresh and apposite illustration. In this pecular idiosyncrasy, we apprehend, is to be sought the wholeness of Hugh Miller's scientific speculations. With the positive school of philosophy he had no sympathy, being, in point of fact, the most conspicuous illustration of its falsity modern times have furnished. Instead of finding in Hugh Miller's works a winnowing of science from those philosophical and theological puzzles with which in earlier ages it was laden,—on the contrary, we find it oppressed with the same problems which, from the remotest antiquity, have engaged and exhausted the ingenuity of man—problems which baffled the acumen of the sages of Arabia thousands of years before they tasked the acumen of the doctors of the Sorbonne, or exercised the wits of the *illuminati* of our own age—

while the positive philosophy does not encounter those difficulties, only because it wants courage to come abreast with them. It had been the dread of Hugh Miller, in entering upon his editorial duties, that he might possibly be deprived of the opportunities he had formerly enjoyed of prosecuting his favourite geological investigations. The first year of his connection with the *Witness* set these fears at rest. The brilliant success of his papers on the "Old Red Sandstone" showed how compatible, in his case at least, are the duties of the journalist with the tastes of the man of science.

Some, we know, for whom the records of the rocks have no charm, have lamented that so much of his time should have been given up to the stony science, thinking it might have been better spent upon topics of the day. In reply to such fault-finders, we have only to say, that on looking over that large mass of controversy upon questions of the hour which the *Witness* contains, and on which its editor long so freely lavished the opulence of his intellectual powers, he surely must have a most unhealthy relish for polemics, who would have desired any greater attention to them than they seem to have received. There is, however, a class of persons who, because the editor of the *Witness* was something more than the echo of the opinions of a coterie of Church leaders, a presbytery, or an assembly, see in that fact a want of interest in the pet schemes of his party. Such is ever the fate of the man of superior powers. He is not absorbed by a special pursuit. A cause which has swallowed up the entire energies of the ordinary man, can have justice done it by the extraordinary, and yet leave him leisure for devotion to other themes, which it may be supposed by the fanatic bear no relation to what should have been the absorbing passion of his life. But so far, therefore, from lamenting Hugh Miller's devotion to science, we believe mainly to that devotion we owe it, that the magnificent powers with which he was gifted budded and bloomed to the last. Had it been possible for him to have lost that taste for those studies nursed in his many wanderings, until it had become an overmastering passion, and sunk down into the mere party leader—the fighting man of his Church—he might indeed oftener have received the bigot's huzza, but he would have dwarfed his highest endowments. Operating under such conditions, that purely illustrative and beautifully analogical power which he possessed, would have borne no more likeness to the native faculty, than the stunted and doddered oak upon the blasted heath bears to the monarch of the forest in his pristine glory;

> "The form of beauty smiling at his heart,"

must have drooped and withered beneath that wintry sky.

CHAPTER XII.

STATE CARPENTERS.

"THE quarrel among the Scotch parsons," which English statesmen expected the decision of the House of Lords in the Auchterarder case would effectually set at rest, after a brief breathing-time became only all the more portentous in consequence of that decision. It had not been anticipated the judgment of the Court of Session would have been affirmed in the face of so influential a dissent as Lords Fullarton, Glenlee, Moncrieff, Cockburn, and Jeffrey. And though anticipation was disappointed by a tribunal from whose decision there lay no appeal, the Church was not disposed to accept either Lords Brougham or Cottenham as true exponents of the polity of the Scottish Establishment. In point of fact, the evangelical party looked upon Lord Brougham, whose lead Lord Cottenham seemed implicitly to have followed, as not an independent exponent of the principles of their Church, but simply the echo of the policy of his great relative, Principal Robertson. To them it seemed the historian's literary eminence veiled the odiousness of his ecclesiastical policy, and in the shadow of a great name the ex-chancellor forgot his own brilliant antecedents. Long years of earnest toil in behalf of popular rights, it was thought, might have inspired some other feeling than hostility to a principle that aimed to carry into the Church a measure of that liberal policy of which, in other days, Harry Brougham's name had been the symbol. Much of the power of Hugh Miller's first pamphlet springs from the dexterity and adroitness with which his lordship's political and ecclesiastical opinions are pitted against each other. With the more logical, or the more earnest of the whig school of politicians, such considerations would doubtless have their force.

It was, however, the misfortune of the evangelical section of the Establishment, that it should have entered upon its crusade in behalf of spiritual independence while its political antagonists were in power. Fully more than three-fourths of the movement party in the Church of Scotland belonged to the conservative camp. The government of Lord Melbourne looked upon Dr. Chalmers as not merely a political, but almost a personal foe. Animated by such feelings, mutual distrust was inevitable. It was no secret to the whig cabinet, that the party which now approached the treasury in behalf of their favourite schemes of Church extension and spiritual independence, sighed for the hour that would dismiss those now besought to redress their grievances to the cold shade of the opposition benches. The pressure from without was, however, great; and the whig government, after most protracted negotiations, at length announced a measure was in preparation that would solve the difficulties of the Scottish Church. But the hope kindled by the announcement was soon extinguished. The enemy had gained the ear of government. Small as was the political influence of the Voluntaries in the House of Commons, the whig cabinet could not venture upon an act which would most inevitably have alienated them. Government, therefore, deeming discretion the better part of valour, resolved to do nothing, and in answer to the expectations of the friends of the spiritual independence of the Church, they at length stated, that opinions were so conflicting, they were unable to devise a measure that would be at all satisfactory to the varied interests it was necessary to consult.

The peculiar character of the claim for spiritual independence now put forth by the evangelical party, unquestionably renders it less surprising that the whigs should have declined to help the majority in the Church into the position it sought to occupy. In point of fact, that party scarcely deserved to succeed in the policy which, in this emergency, it made its own. Severing the question of spiritual independence from the question of popular rights, the evangelical was seen invoking the aid of the moderate side of the house to protect the authority of the Church. Without doubt the two questions were theoretically distinct, and circumstances might be imagined in which they could also be practically separated. But unfortunately for the success of this appeal, the position of the Church was such it was impossible to look upon the one as aught else than the complement of the other. Indeed, an impartial retrospect of Scottish ecclesiastical history can hardly fail to carry conviction to all minds, that there has ever existed a pre-established harmony between the principles. Unquestionably the spiritual independence of the Church was menaced by the decisions of the Court of Session and the House of Lords; but, in the opinion of the moderates, it was so menaced because the evangelical majority had done what, so long as patronage existed, was an illegal act. It was not therefore wonderful, that moderatism—cool, logical moderatism, essentially of the earth earthy—turned a deaf ear to evangelical enthusiasm. By running counter to its *canny* creed the evangelicals had got into difficulties, and the only deliverance it could offer was based upon unhesitating acquiescence in its own erastian policy. Not in this way was deliverance to arise; rest in such circumstances had not been good. It is only when the battle is fought, when the victory is won, the good soldier can honourably lay up his arms.

Might we not imagine the defender of the Church's spiritual independence in this crisis, thus apostrophizing his moderate brother, as he declines the last call to enter the battle-field :—"Well, be it so; perhaps thy outward life shall be peacefuller. But thou shalt at best abide by the stuff—like some cherished house-dog, guard the stuff,—perhaps with enormous gold collar and provender; but the battle, and the hero's death, and the victory's fire-chariot carrying man to the immortals, shall never be thine."

And yet, despite their heroism, never, perhaps, did any body of sincere and earnest men occupy a more anomalous or indifferently defined position, than did the evangelical party in the Scottish Church at this crisis. So far back as 1833, the historian of Knox and Melville had publicly denounced any paltering with the rights of the people by peddling half-measures. Dr. M'Crie was aware, that not a few of the leading lights of the evangelical party in the Scottish Church, much as they disliked patronage, yet "feared the people." That visionary fear he addressed himself to rebuke in a vein of caustic irony. "But the people, the people," he exclaimed, assuming for the nonce the attitude of alarmist—"if we expel the patrons, the people will rush in like air into a vacuum, and raise such a storm, tempest, and hurricane as will root up and scatter everything precious and venerable in our Church.

Good friends, be not so much alarmed. The period of ecclesiastical agitation is past. The popular current is changed. The current has turned from religion to politics. Instead of rushing in, the people have been rushing out from you. You have told them that it is a delusion to think that the Christian people have an inherent right to choose their own minister. But to pacify them you have added, that every man has the right of choosing what minister he shall hear,—and they have learned the lesson. The time may come when you will need all the assistance the people can give—when you will be fain to stimulate instead of stifling their voice, and to ask their suffrages instead of telling them they are incapable of anything but dumb and dogged resistance, without the assignment of a reason." When giving utterance to these sentiments in 1833, Dr. M'Crie was naturally enough esteemed a man of extreme opinions. Events had now shown it was sagacity, not rashness, that guided the speaker upon that day. The period was rapidly approaching when his counsel was to become the policy of the Church. Before, however, adopting the simple course to which such high authority had beckoned them in the initial stage of the controversy, the leaders of the evangelical party must once more turn their eyes to the government of the day. The fate of the whigs was now sealed. The conservatives filled the treasury benches.

Sir Robert Peel and Dr. Chalmers were friends. When on the shady side of those benches, Sir Robert has said some very amiable things about the Church—nay, in 1835, he had seized the opportunity his brief tenure of office bestowed, to embody certain important principles Dr. Chalmers first enunciated in a funeral sermon on the death of the Princess Charlotte, in his "king's speech." All this Peel had done. What then more natural than the expectation that Peel should now do something more substantial? Unfortunately it was on fiscal questions, not questions of faith, that Sir Robert was great.

The Scottish Church was therefore handed over to the Earl of Aberdeen, to be dealt with as the noble earl saw meet. This state carpenter, by profession a diplomatist, entered upon negotiations with the evangelical leaders of the Scottish Church, with all the finesse of the professional red-tapist. In a correspondence with Dr. Chalmers, a misunderstanding speedily arose. The statesman got sulky—got angry with the ecclesiastic, and Dr. Chalmers ultimately discovered that he had about as little to expect from toryism as from whiggery—that, in fact, the sole difference between whig and tory on the question was, that while the whig cared little for an establishment at all, the tory appeared nearly equally indifferent if the establishment was not the mere creature of the state.

Probably no man of all the Scottish clergy, whether moderate or evangelical, was inspired with a more chivalrous reverence for aristocracy than Thomas Chalmers. He loved to think of it, he loved to speak of it as the Corinthian capital of society, giving grace and polish to British manners republics could never possess; and though the feeling was sentimental, not pusillanimous, there can be no doubt to some extent it unfitted him for the rough work and plain speaking the exigencies of the Church rendered necessary. How different in this respect was the church leader of the nineteenth from the church leader of the sixteenth century! Knox stood unawed in the presence of the feudal barons of Scotland, a veritable king of men among the proudest of earth's nobility. Chalmers was ever somewhat unmanned in the company of a lord. With such a native tendency, we all the more admire the vigour of the principle that rose superior to its subtile and ensnaring power. Indeed, nothing is more marked or more honourable, as exhibiting the depth of vital principle in the mass of the evangelical party, than the unwavering constancy with which they battled on in behalf of the principles of the Church. "No weakness, Danton," said the revolutionary demigod, when face to face with death; and in the most private and confidential correspondence of the heroes of the Disruption even in the darkest hour of their fortunes, they maintain a calmness and serenity of soul worthy of a martyr age. Realizing at length, in the entanglements of their position, the faithfulness and sagacity of M'Crie's voice of warning, the Veto act was abandoned. They had found that, so far from being muzzled by that act, the monster with which it sought to grapple had not been even muffled. A more definite policy was now adopted. Finding it impossible to regulate patronage, they declared for its abolition.

But just in proportion as the Church awoke to a conception of what was necessary to protect and insure her independence, in a like proportion did the State become reluctant to do her justice. The intrigue of "the forty," so hopeful in the eyes of temporising politicians, had utterly failed to break down the evangelical majority in the General Assembly. The ministry could not, therefore, any longer continue to give no sign. Accordingly in June, 1842, Sir Robert Peel announced in the House of Commons, that after a full consideration of the subject, her Majesty's government had abandoned all hope of settling the question in a satisfactory manner, or of effecting any good by introducing a measure relative to it. This declaration, so rapidly following the second decision of the House of Lords in the Auchterarder case—a decision in which Lords Lyndhurst and Campbell acquiesced with Cottenham and Brougham—rendered the path of duty plain. "Unto the upright there ariseth light in the darkness." That light now pointed in but one direction. Within the Establishment there was now henceforth for them only darkness and the shadow of death. The intrigue and management by which statesmen had sought, during the "Ten Years' Conflict," to fritter into nothingness a great principle, are described by Hugh Miller with the most withering sarcasm.

"It has been remarked, that in proportion as our English dramatists sank in the genius of their profession, they made amends, in some sort, by becoming adepts in all the merely mechanical parts of it. If they could no longer attain to the sublime in their poetry, they at least succeeded in making unexceptionable thunder. If their dialogues were no longer easy and natural, no one could say the same of their side-scenes of painted canvas, or their snow showers of white paper. If wit no longer flashed athwart the scenes, never in any former time were their flashes of ground rosin equally vivid. If their descriptions were tame, so were not their draperies and drop-curtains. Their plots might be unskilfully managed, but their trap-doors were wrought to admiration. They were masters of costume, if not of character; and ghosts, lions, and tempests, Nahum Tates and Elkanah Settles, amply occupied the place of truth, power, and nature—William Shakspeare and Philip Massinger. The poets disappeared, but their successors, the playwrights, were ingenious after their kind.

"We live in an age in which, apparently for some purpose of judgment, the more prominent actors on the political stage are but a kind of mechanists and playwrights—men that bear the same sort of relation to true statesmen that the Shadwells and Littles of the English drama bore to its Jonsons and Fletchers of an earlier period. There is this difference, however, that whereas the playwrights were skilful after their kind, our mechanical statesmen are not. They are by no means mechanical statesmen of a high degree of skill. Their trap-doors creak in the opening—their ghosts awkwardly drop the winding-sheet in the rising—their lions betray the pasteboard—when they thunder, we detect the roll of the rusted shot in the iron kettle—and when they lighten, the rosin puffs unkindled in a cloud of white dust athwart the stage. They are statewrights of an inferior grade.

"Has the reader ever seen a nervous gentleman running on tiptoe with his coat-tails tucked up under his arm, magnanimously resolved on clearing at a leap some formidable five-feet ditch, but stopping abruptly short at the edge, at once panic-struck and angry, and merely gazing across for lack of courage to do more? Have they seen him repeat and repeat the vast effort, and bring it in every instance to the same grave conclusion? If so, they will find it no easy matter to fall on a fitter emblem of my Lord Aberdeen and his coadjutors than the nervous gentleman. Ever and anon his lordship tucks up his coat-tails, and, taking a last run, to clear at a bound the Church question, gets panic-struck just as he reaches its nearer edge, and, standing stock-still, grins angrily across. His last exhibition of the kind our readers will find recorded in our parliamentary report, and they would do well to cast an attentive eye over it. His lordship and his lordship's coadjutors have not yet felt what it is they have to deal with. The steam of their ministerial Sunday dinners so obscures their dining-room panes, that they fail to see through them the religious beliefs of the country. They mark on the dimmed glass what they deem impalpable shadows stalking past, and as impalpable shadows they persist in treating them. Fools, and slow of heart, who have failed utterly to know the day of their visitation, do they not even yet see, that it is not with a handful of clergymen, but with the deeply-based religion of Scotland, that they have to do?—that they have come in rude collision, in their blindness, with a principle which, in its long struggles, has been often overborne and grievously oppressed, but never eventually overcome, and whose battles, once begun, never terminate till opposition dies?"

Written on the eve of the Disruption, now that the passions of the hour are hushed, this satire upon our "state carpenters" might have been pardoned if found to contain even more than the wonted amalgam of intolerance and enthusiasm, common to controvertists.

But events have since transpired England was more capable of comprehending than ought connected with Scottish ecclesiastical controversy, that have left an impression respecting the general character of these statesmen, not materially different from the opinion Hugh Miller has expressed in his trenchant criticism. In the attitude of Aberdeen, on the eve of the Russian war, men discovered the same nervous gentleman of the "Ten Years' Conflict," with coat-tails tucked up, and seemingly ready to take the desperate plunge; but somehow much to the chagrin of the spectators, just at the moment they expected the thing done, and the ditch cleared, the earl's courage, like the courage of Bob Acres, "oozed out at the finger-ends."

A second-rate diplomatist inveterately wedded to the tactics of his profession, but destitute of the intellectual sagacity that enables diplomatists of the first order almost intuitively to discover when their craft can no longer avail; in a season of calm weather, such a state pilot may not be very unsafe, though even then likely to be perpetually overreached in countless small matters; but the utter feebleness of such a guide only comes fully out in a period of internal or external tempest. This want of perspicacity it was, that in both the critical and stormy epochs alluded to, wrecked Aberdeen's reputation as a statesman. Sir Robert Peel had, perhaps, as little native capacity for comprehending the operative power of an abstract principle. But the hour struck when the abstract principle must, for the safety of the state, assume a concrete form, and be incorporated with the British constitution: no statesman was so ready to bow to the inexorable necessity. It was unfortunate for the Church of Scotland that when Sir Robert Peel was premier of England, the laird of Haddo House held a chief seat in the cabinet. Had the son of the Lancashire cotton-spinner bent his eminently practical understanding to the comprehension of the ecclesiastical polity of the evangelical party in Scotland, he might not indeed have fully mastered the principles it maintained, but he would have better appreciated the exigencies of its position than the Scottish lord. Eminent statesmen have, we know, sketched the character of Aberdeen in more flattering colours than it has been painted in the columns of the *Witness.* Guizot has described him as a man of "unfettered, yet judicious mind, as just as delicate, always ready to understand and admit the changes of time, the motives and merits of men." But it must be remembered as some abatement of this very favourable portrait, that in Tahiti, in Morocco, and in Spain, Lord Aberdeen had quietly acquiesced in the dominance of French over English policy. It would, therefore, have been in the last degree ungraceful had the great *doctrinaire* failed to pay a fitting tribute to that readiness "to understand, and admit the motives and merits of men," which so often and so signally served his interests when first minister of the Citizen King.

In point of fact, remembering the antecedents of Byron's "travelled thane, Athenian Aberdeen," had Hugh Miller sat down to write a historical sketch rather than to pen a stinging article, he could scarcely have drawn the portrait in other colours. George Hamilton Gordon belongs to that tribe of mediocrities, who, on the death of Pitt, parted the mantle of the "heaven-born minister" amongst themselves, and down to the period of the Reform Bill misgoverned England. For the genuine power of that great, if erring, statesman, his pseudo-successors had substituted the basest prejudices and passions of the times. Their policy was a pandering to popular ignorance; exclusion was the principle of their political constitution, and restriction the genius of their commercial system.

Reasons of state induced them to cast their blandishments upon the Scottish Church, especially upon the evangelical section of that Church; and in an evil hour did the evangelicals give to it their political allegiance, flattered by being esteemed a bulwark of British institutions. When the manly heart of Chalmers at length discovered that it was a tool, not an ally, the State sought in the Church, we can easily understand the utter revulsion of soul with which he recoiled from contact with so much gartered and coroneted meanness, found where he had expected to find only the soul of chivalry. The Earl of Aberdeen did, indeed, affect to have been made the victim of misrepresentation by Dr. Chalmers, and most solemnly asserted he had acted throughout in the most perfect good faith. But Chalmers and his coadjutors were in no mood to accept fair words as an atonement for foul acts. They knew what he had done; what his intentions might originally have been they could not so well compute; and to all assurances of purity of aim and rectitude of purpose, were disposed to reply much after the manner Mary Stewart once addressed a time-serving friend. Lords Ruthven and Lindsay, in conjunction with Lord Melville, had borne to the queen a somewhat unwelcome message. Melville turned, as they retired, to assure her Majesty that his loyalty and truth were still unchanged. "*Tush!* Melville, *tush!*" said Mary, "what signifies the truth that walks hand in hand with mine enemy—falsehood?"

CHAPTER XIII.

THE DISRUPTION.

The "Ten Years' Conflict" had now brought the leaders of the evangelical party in the Scottish Church face to face with the Disruption. The first five years had been years of effort; the latter, years of negotiation. All had been done human ingenuity could do, short of dereliction of highest duty, to turn aside the blow about to be dealt to the religious interests of Scotland. In vain had Chalmers elaborately demonstrated to the great ones of the earth, that the principles he had given his imprimatur had really nothing in common with the vulgar radicalism of the day. With a few honourable exceptions, the aristocracy of Scotland continued impervious to every appeal on behalf of the independence of the Scottish Church, and the foe, though vanquished in the field of reason, took refuge in the strong tower of self-interest, whence he looked forth in laughter at the shaking of the spear.

"By their fruits ye shall know them," is the test the highest authority has left us for the trial of men and of systems; and on the threshold of the catastrophe of the Church of Scotland we pause to ask, what had Chalmers and his coadjutors done that they were doomed to such an alternative? The Church at the period the men ultimately its evangelical leaders became connected themselves with it, was in what may be regarded as the normal condition of an establishment. The majority of its ministers were "at ease in Zion," loving more the comfortable independence a benefice conferred, than the work for which that independence was bestowed. As an illustration of by no means the worst class the Robertsonian policy had given the Church, a Buteshire clergyman, whose acquaintance the late Dr. Jamieson, author of the Scottish Dictionary, made when a probationer, may be given. The young dissenting licentiate had received appointments as a preacher in the parish of this clergyman. Fortunately for Mr. Jamieson, the man, though fully sharing the irreligion, was free from the intolerance of his class. The young preacher had not been many days in the locality, when the parish minister called and intimated, that as there was plenty of room in the manse, it was useless being at the expense of separate apartments; he might therefore just leave his lodgings and live with him. After some further conversation, the clergyman began to make inquiry about Mr. Jamieson's habits of study, and his intentions as to sermon-writing. "Do you," he said—

"do you mean to prepare fresh sermons for your people every week?" Jamieson assenting, the veteran moderate burst out into a fit of laughter at the simplicity of the young seceder, and narrating his own practice, said —"I have only preached four sermons during all the time I have been here. I deliver them every month. I always take care to change the texts, and I believe, that, with the exception of blind David, not one of my parishioners has found me out."

In the best days of the Church's history, among her more earnest ministry, diets of visitation, especially in country parishes, were understood to be most powerful instrumentalities for diffusing and elevating the religious knowledge of the peasantry of Scotland. This fox-hunting Buteshire parson had improved upon the ancient system. "I make intimation," said he to Mr. Jamieson, "that the people of a given district are to meet me at a particular public-house, where I have dinner prepared for them. I go gradually round my parish in this way. And I believe," he added in a tone of quiet satire—"I believe the people relish my visitations much better than they are likely to do yours." "This," says Dr. Jamieson in his Autobiography, "was one of the most kindly-hearted men I ever met." And, compared with certain of the moderate clergy of his time, he was indeed quite a model minister. He at least cared for the bodies of his parishioners, and was not more indifferent to *their* spiritual weal than to his own. Jamieson's visit to the scene of his labours he deemed quite superfluous; not that he had any jealousy in the matter; he simply believed that the commodity he brought with him was not wanted.

The growth of religious earnestness amongst the people in after years had so multiplied the "blind Davids" throughout the parishes of Scotland, that clergymen of the class to which the Buteshire parson belonged were everywhere found out. The nation would have none of them. The whole aim of the evangelical majority in the General Assembly had been to give effect to the convictions of this class. Already, during the brief period of its ascendancy, it had produced some of the ablest and most earnest men that ever graced the pulpits of an establishment. Not satisfied even with what could be done within the pale of the National Church, or with the ecclesiastical machinery at its command as a State-endowed institution, it had gone forth on a vigorously-aggressive crusade against that mass of irreligion and immorality, which nestles in our midst "without God and without hope in the world." During the ten years preceding the Disruption, not less than two hundred additional churches had been built for what Dr. Chalmers called the "unexcavated heathen of our country."

Such great things accomplished by the unaided efforts

of the friends of church extension, it might have been supposed would have proved a pledge for the purely religious aims of the movement-party in the Establishment. But it was not so. All who reasoned after this manner forgot that an establishment may possibly become too much in earnest to be any longer serviceable for the purposes of statesmen. Sir Robert Peel was the Church's friend so long as he expected a substantial *quid pro quo* for that friendship; but so soon as it was discovered the Scottish Church could no longer be calculated upon as a political engine, the premier proved a very candid friend indeed.

Through life Dr. Chalmers had been haunted with a dread of the spectre of democracy. On him, as on Edmund Burke, the atrocities and excesses of the first French Revolution had exerted a most obnoxious influence. It is scarcely possible now to account for the excess of terror which that event very generally inspired. Even the most robust understandings recoiled with aversion from contemplating the principles of liberty, by reason of the excesses wrought in its name. Once and again throughout his works has Dr. Chalmers depicted, in his own fervidly eloquent diction, the ruin the dreaded triumph of democracy would inevitably inflict upon general society. Alas! it was not democracy that was to deal the most terrible blow to his most cherished schemes. From that body with which politically he had been through life associated, was the thunderbolt launched that hurled in the dust the dreams of his ardent, his holiest ambition. It was a tory majority in the Court of Session, and a tory ministry in the houses of Parliament, that upset the Revolution-settlement, and sealed with its imprimatur the derelictions of moderatism from the principles the Church had received a heritage from its confessors.

When we look at the roll of illustrious names that at this crisis led the evangelical party, it seems almost marvellous how it was they were even politically vanquished. Not only was there one man towering above the mass of the ministers of the Church, whether moderate or evangelical, at once in native genius and established fame, but there was a legion of younger men whom the "Ten Years' Conflict" had brought upon the scene—lieutenants scarcely inferior to their chief as ecclesiastical combatants. The eloquence and influence of Chalmers were supplemented by the subtlety and logical acumen of Candlish, the massive power and surpassing erudition of Cunningham, the strong common sense of Begg, the transcendent pictorial power of Guthrie, the historic lore of Welsh and Hetherington, the character of Gordon, to say nothing of a host little inferior to these foremost men. The moderate party had really no men, with the exception of Dr. Cooke, Robertson of Ellon, and Dr. Robert Lee, capable of being pitted against these illustrious names. It has been remarked, however, and the history of nearly every revolution is a signal illustration of the justness of the remark, that in all great conflicts the victory remains, not so much with the party possessing the greatest genius, as with the party possessing the strongest will. The Girondists—the noble, the eloquent, the magnanimous Girondists—full of the fire of genius and imagination, were all reaped away by the sickle of death, while "pale sea-green Robespierre" remained master of the republic. The parties which in turn that dictator conquered, had among them men infinitely his superiors in genuine power and breadth of intellect; but none of them produced a man with the same strength of will and stern vigour of character.

It was the fortune of the moderate party in the Establishment to possess, not indeed in its clerical ranks, but in a quarter where more service could be done by a good servant than in any of the courts of the Church, a defender uniting qualities rarely found united —the most passionate vehemence of temperament with the most indomitable resolution. The head of the Scottish bar at this period belonged to an ancient tory family in which force of character appears hereditary; and in John Hope, the dean of faculty, now lord-justice clerk, the evangelical section of the Scottish Church encountered its most redoubtable antagonist. In the council chamber, at the bar, through the press, and by correspondence with her Majesty's ministers in every emergency of the "Ten Years' Conflict," from the day he broke with Chalmers until the day that sealed the fate of the Church, did he labour to defeat the purposes of the evangelical majority. This antagonist, at once by his influential position, vigorous intellectual powers and dauntless perseverance, succeeded in accomplishing what had never before been accomplished; establishing by legal decisions the Erastian character of the Scottish Church.

From the first hour of its existence as an establishment, there had been a conflict of wills respecting the scope of the Church's jurisdiction, the ecclesiastical power ever seeking to establish the utmost freedom of action for itself. And, in direct antagonism to the Church, the State was ever ready to circumscribe her authority, and reduce within the narrowest limits the rights she claimed. Yet notwithstanding the prolonged antagonism between the party esteeming itself heir of the aims of the founders of the Scottish Church and the representatives of Erastianism, not until the 8th March, 1843, was a final legal form given to an idea from which Knox, Melville, and Henderson would have alike turned in shuddering abomination. When on that day the motion of the right honourable Fox Maule, that the House of Commons should go into a committee to take into consideration the claims of the Church of Scotland, was rejected, honest men could no longer doubt either their position or their duty.

We can indeed easily understand the difficulty English statesmen had in comprehending the theory of co-ordinate jurisdiction, by which the position of the evangelical party had been defended. Lord Jeffrey had justified his vote in the Court of Session in its favour upon that principle, and it formed the basis of the legal argument by which Mr. Rutherford had supported the claims of the majority in the Assembly before the Imperial Parliament. Nevertheless it was not the theory upon which the Church of Scotland was founded. The truth was, that though deflecting in many points from its original platform, it was still a Church altogether unique in Christendom; and to comprehend aright what its founders contemplated it should become, we must transport ourselves from Scotland to Geneva.

In days when that city-state was the refuge of the proscribed of Europe, Knox and Melville had successively enjoyed its generous hospitality. Knox had seen the gospel as freely preached elsewhere; but in Geneva alone had he seen truth taught and practised with nearly equal purity. John Calvin was the soul of that system of government which had so fascinated in exile our great reformer. What that system was may be better learned from Ranke than, perhaps, any other historian. With all the peculiar philosophic precision and comprehensiveness of the higher order of German thinkers, has he delineated the Calvinian system of government. "Calvin's deviation from Catholicism," says Ranke, "did not consist by any means in a desire to render life independent of the authority of the Church. On the contrary, whilst he rejected the decrees of the Latin Church, he adopted it the more strongly as taught in the original records of Christianity, the harmony of whose doctrines he was pre-eminently qualified to comprehend. Whilst with a powerful congregation separated from the hierarchial corporation that dominated Europe, he sought to realize the most perfect communion which lies at the foundation of the idea of a church; under his guidance—for he also took part in the temporal legislation—the strongest fetters of discipline were laid upon outward conduct. The expenses of clothing and of the table were confined within certain limits; dancing was prohibited, and the reading of certain books, such as "Amadis," forbidden; gamblers were seen in the pillory with the cards in their hands; once a year an examination took place in every house, to ascertain whether the religious precepts were known and observed; mutual imputations of failings which the members of the council observed in one another, were permitted at their sittings. No indulgence was known for transgression; a woman was burned for having sung immodest songs; one of the most distinguished of the citizens was compelled to kneel in the great square with an inverted torch in his hand, and publicly to entreat forgiveness, because he had mocked the doctrine of salvation and personally insulted the great preacher."

Though not by any means a slavish copyist, it was very much a transcript of this stern system, found bearing the fairest fruits by the banks of the Leman lake, Knox took with him from Geneva to Scotland. And however modified by time and circumstance it might have become during the lapse of centuries, it requires but little sagacity to discover, that to make the civil power dominate such a system, was to annihilate it. When, therefore, by the most deliberate and solemn decisions of both houses of Parliament, the Scottish Church, originally thus theocratic in it's basis, was declared a mere creature of the civil power, nothing remained for the evangelical party save to sever its connection with an institution so utterly "fallen from its high estate." Drs. Hanna, Hetherington, and Buchanan have each in turn, and each after his peculiar manner, described that remarkable exodus. Hugh Miller shall describe it for us. In the *Witness* of the 18th May, 1843, he thus wrote:—

"How woefully different the state of matters with regard to the governing powers at the present day! One is continually reminded of the complaint of the kelpie in the old legend—the hour is come, but not the man. Great exigencies have found little men to grapple with them, and in a style, of course, that exhibits the character of the men, not the exigencies. The stratagems by which chamber-maids out-manœuvre one another in the graces of their mistresses, have been substituted for the large principles by which the guidance of great affairs should be invariably regulated; and questions that affect the deepest feelings, and involve the vastest consequences—questions that can rest only on the basis of eternal truth and justice, have been attempted to be settled through the exercise of exactly the same kind of arts as are employed by jockies when they sell horses at fairs. We are reminded of the text in which God represents himself as taking away, for the sins of a people, the prudent and the councillor, the captain and the honourable, the judge and the prophet, and appointing children to be their princes, and babes to have rule over them.

"The fatal die has been cast. On Thursday last the religion of Scotland was disestablished, and a principle recognized in its stead which has often served to check and modify the religious influences, but which in no age or country ever yet existed as a religion. Not but that it has performed an important part, even in Scotland. It has served hitherto to control the Christianity of the Establishment—to dilute it to such a degree, if we may so speak, as to render it bearable to statesmen without God. And now its appointed work seems over. It constituted at the best but the drag-chain and the hook—things that have no vocation apart from the chariot. But the time has at length arrived, in which the state will bear with but the hook and the drag apart from that which they checked—with but the diluting pabulum apart from that which it diluted. An antagonist force to the religious power has been virtually recognized as exclusively the principle which is to be entrenched in the parish churches of Scotland. The day that witnessed a transaction so momentous can be a day of no slight mark in modern history. It stands between two distinct states of things, a signal to Christendom. It holds out its sign to these latter times, that God and the world have drawn off their forces to opposite sides, and that His sore and great battle is soon to begin

"The future can alone adequately develope the more important consequences of the event:—at present we shall merely attempt presenting the reader with a few brief notes of the aspect which it exhibited. The early part of Thursday had its periods of fitful cloud and sunshine, and the tall picturesque tenements of the old town now lay dim and indistinct in shadow, now stood prominently out in the light. There was an unusual throng and bustle in the streets at a comparatively early hour, which increased greatly as the morning wore on towards noon. We marked, in especial, several knots of moderate clergy hurrying along to the levee, laughing and chatting with a vivacity that reminded one rather of French than of Scotch character, and evidently in that state of nervous excitement which, in a certain order of minds, the near approach of some very great event, indeterminate and unappreciable in its bearings, is sure always to occasion.

"As the morning wore on, the crowds thickened in the streets, and the military took their places. The principles involved in the anticipated disruption, gave to many a spectator a new association with the long double line of dragoons that stretched adown the High Street, as far as the eye could reach, from the venerable St. Giles, famous in Scottish story, to the humbler Tron. The light flashed fitfully on their long swords and helmets, and the light scarlet of their uniforms contrasted strongly with the dingier vestments of the masses, in which they seemed as if more than half engulfed. When the sun glanced out, the eye caught something peculiarly picturesque in the aspect of the Calton Hill, with its imposing masses of precipices, overtopped by towers and monuments, and its intermingling bushes and trees, now green with the soft delicate foliage of May. Between its upper and under line of rock, a dense living belt of human beings girdled it round, sweeping gradually downwards from shoulder to base, like the sash of his order on the breast of a nobleman. The commissioners' procession passed, with the sound of trumpet and drum, and marked by rather more than the usual splendour. There was much bravery and glitter—satin and embroidery, varnish and gold lace—no lack, in fact, of that cheap and vulgar magnificence, which can be got up to order by the tailor and the upholsterer for carnivals and Lord Mayor's days. But it was felt by the assembled thousands, as the pageant swept past, that the real spectacle of the day was a spectacle of a different character."

The Assembly opened, the protest read, and the protestors gone, Hugh Miller lingers a moment to mark the effect of the desertion:—

"The empty vacated benches stretched away from the Moderator's seat, in the centre of the building, to the distant wall. There suddenly glided into the front rows a small party of men whom no one knew—obscure, mediocre, blighted-looking men, that contrasted with the well-known forms of our Chalmerses and Gordons, Candlishes and Cunninghams, M'Farlanes, Brewsters, and Dunlops, reminded one of the thin and blasted corn ears of Pharaoh's vision, and, like them too, seemed typical of a time of famine and destitution. Who are these? was the general inquiry; but no one seemed to know. At length the significant whisper ran along the house—'The Forty.'* There was a grin of mingled contempt and compassion visible on many a broad moderate face, and a too audible titter shook the gallery. There seemed a degree of incongruity in the sight that partook highly of the ludicrous. For our own part, we were so carried away by a vagrant association—and so missed Ali Baba, the oil kettle, and the forty jars, as to forget for a time, that at the doors of these unfortunate men, lies the ruin of the Scottish Establishment."

The march of the disruptionists from St. Andrew's to Tanfield need not be dwelt upon. A single incident of the exodus hitherto unchronicled, and not unworthy to be recorded, we had the pleasure to hear narrated by

* "The Forty," we may explain, was a middle party mainly composed of recreant non-intrusionists, who, satisfied in a certain sense with the vague assurances of statesmen, deemed it their duty, when the hour of trial came, to keep what they had got. The sobriquet took its rise at a meeting of the synod of Glasgow and Ayr, held some time previous to the disruption. One of the number, intending to herald the importance of the party, said, "There are forty of us in the synod." The worthy man was not a wit, and therefore did not perceive the ridicule he had brought on his associates. Guthrie and Miller had, however, too keen a sense of the humorous to let it pass. The phrase daguerreotyped the faction.

the learned principal of New College, at the jubilee of the venerable professor of exegetical theology to the United Presbyterian Church. When the noble army of Christian heroes entered Tanfield Hall, as the Moderator, Dr. Welsh, ascended the platform, Dr. Brown rose and greeted with the right hand of fellowship the Free Church of Scotland. The glad all-hail with which the chief of the old saluted the new secession, looked at in the light of events transpiring in connection with both these influential sections of the Church of Christ, almost appears to have possessed an element of the symbolical and prophetic. In the heat of the voluntary controversy, Hugh Miller and others had deplored, what they deemed the aberration of the minister of Broughton from the hereditary faith of his family. But on the platform in Tanfield Hall, on the 18th day of May, 1843, even the most cynical would recognise the grandson of the author of the Self-interpreting Bible, in his proper sphere, and doing his proper work.

For twelve days two assemblies have now held their sittings in the metropolis. In describing the close of these ecclesiastical congresses, the writer has perhaps dipped his pen a little too freely in "dyes of earthquake and eclipse." Nevertheless, though strongly coloured, the picture as a whole is just. Such as may consider there is in it rather more than is meet of the alarmist, should remember that at that hour the general aspect of society, political and religious, seemed peculiarly portentous. The clouds which then hung the heavens with blackness have since *dislimned;* but let us not forget Hugh Miller wrote within the shadow of their gigantic glooms.

"The Free and Residuary Assemblies have closed their sittings—the over-strung mind of the Scottish public demands its interval of rest; and thrilling excitement and incessant labour give place, for a brief period, to comparative quiescence and repose. For our own part, for at least a few months to come, we shall see the sun rise less frequently than we have done of late, and miss oftener the earliest chirp of the birds that welcome the first gray of morning from among the old trees of Heriot's and the Meadows. The chapter added to the history of the Church of Scotland has just been completed—the concluding page presents the usual blank interval; and we feel inclined to lay down the volume for a space, and ponder over its contents.

"How very brief a period has elapsed since the government of this country could have settled at small expense the Church question! and how entirely has it passed beyond the reach of human adjustment now! In disestablishing the religion of Scotland, there has been a breach made in the very foundations of national security, which can never be adequately filled up. The yawning chasm is crowded with phantoms of terror;—there are the forms of an infidel Erastianism in front, and surplices, crosses, and triple crowns in the rear; while deep from the darkness comes a voice, as of many waters, the roar of infuriated multitudes broken loose from religion, and thirsting for blood. May God avert the omen! That man must have studied to but little purpose the events of the last twelve days who does not see that there is a guiding hand ordering and regulating all. The pawns in this great game do not move of themselves;—the adorable Being who has 'foreordained whatsoever cometh to pass' is working out his own designs in his own way;—the usurpations of the civil magistrates,—the treachery of unfaithful ministers,—the errors and mistakes of blind-hearted and incompetent statesmen,—all tend to accomplish his decrees; and it would be well, surely, since in one way or other all must forward his purposes, to be made to forward them rather as his fellow-workers than as his blind insensible tools. Let the disestablished Church take courage—there is a time of severe conflict before her, but the result of the battle is certain."

How genuine a touch of human interest is that folded up in these so felicitous allusions to the glory of the dawn—the music of the minstrels of the grove "warbling their wood notes wild," regaling eye and ear and soul of the jaded journalist, as he retires from his desk to his home. At such an hour, and with such surroundings, the overtasked intellectual toiler forgets all lassitude and exhaustion. In the bosom of nature "dress'd in earliest light," and amidst the blended repose and enjoyment of the good and fair, the perturbed spirit that for a little while has left behind a thousand anxieties, a thousand earth-born cares, almost seems already to taste the happiness of the contrast of the tumult and the unrest of earth with the rest of heaven.

CHAPTER XIV.

A RETROSPECT.

NOTHING is more noteworthy about the "Ten Years' Conflict," than the revival of all the old traditions and memories whose spell was still upon the peasantry of Scotland, by which the movement was distinguished. From the period of the enactment of the Veto law, until the catastrophe of 1843, how marvellous was the resurrection of ancient Scottish worthies! Every remarkable pamphlet, every remarkable biography that yet had power to charm, was sought out and reproduced. No doubt men, even good men, sometimes relaxed into a smile at the parallel attempted to be instituted between their own times and times when

> "The standard of Zion
> All bloody and torn 'mong the heather was lying;"

but the success of the effort redeemed it from sneers. It appealed to certain strongly-marked features of the national character. A Scotchman ever manifests a peculiar aptitude for grappling with those ecclesiastical and religious questions, in which the historical and the logical elements are nearly equally blended. The patristic lore in which so many graduates of Oxford have lost their way, has no seductions for him. The most elaborate historical argument the profoundest erudition could construct, if logically vitiated, he spontaneously scouts. But let the logical demonstration and the historical be equally valid in his eyes, instantaneously the Scotchman stands forth, fired not only with the consciousness that he battles for the right; his faith is in that moment sublimed—risen into the transcendent by the thought that the voice of centuries ratifies his own convictions.

A most singular sagacity was therefore, as we think, manifested in that scattering broad cast over Scotland, during the "Ten Years' Conflict," the antique literature of the Covenant.

Long contact with the grandees of the empire had corrupted the simplicity and purity of state-endowed presbyterianism. The brilliancy of the evangelical pearl had been stained by the pollutions of earth. The patronage the Church of Scotland received from the Scottish nobles, while bringing with it the minimum of worldly prestige, brought with it the maximum of spiritual thraldom. During all the years of contest that preceded the Disruption, the evangelical section of the Church was gradually shaking itself loose from these fetters; and just as it struck its roots deeper in the hearts of the people, in a similar proportion did it recede from contact with the noblesse.

Admirably supplementary of these efforts to popularise the principles of the Church made by its evangelical friends, were the labours of the editor of the *Witness*, and the epoch the Disruption marks in Hugh Miller's literary history, seems a not inappropriate point at which to pause to contemplate for a moment the service he had already rendered the cause the *Witness* represented. The schools in which its editor had been trained, were schools in which he had become familiar with the inner life of the peasantry of the northern counties of Scotland. The west and south have been pretty well explored, but the north is yet almost virgin soil. Glimpses of its condition may be caught in the biographies of its great men; but hitherto no effective or comprehensive estimate has been attempted of the peculiar character of the Highlands during that great transition-era, when all the old forms of hereditary chieftainship were broken up to make way for a more modern civilization and a more centralized authority. It is, therefore, not the least of the services Hugh Miller has rendered to literature, that he should have left, even though scattered throughout the columns of the *Witness*, so many mementos of that epoch, which, but for his pen, must in all probability have perished with the present generation. From these reminiscences we gather, that somewhere about the period of the Revolution settlement, a remarkable development of religious earnestness was manifest in not a few northern counties. A race of men arose representatives of that movement, who cannot be better described than by saying they very much resembled the men of the Covenant. They came a generation or two later than the covenanters, and probably their ancestry, in not a few instances, might have been found in that "Highland host" erewhile so terrible to the Lowlands of Scotland. But now the sons had become obedient to the faith the fathers destroyed.

The more eminent of those thus won to the evangelical cause occupied a peculiar position among their countrymen. Known throughout the north as "the men," and found in nearly all the Gaelic-speaking districts of Scotland, they exercised a most potent influence among their countrymen. On more than one occasion had moderatism essayed the difficult task of controlling their fanaticism. It may be acknowledged, indeed, that in some instances this might have been done beneficially; but the material on which moderatism worked was a material of which it could make exceedingly little. Seeing only the eccentricities, not the excellencies of "the men," it was incapable of dealing effectively even with their faults. The position they occupied in the

Church, though perfectly in accordance with the genius of presbytery, was somewhat anomalous when compared with the general practice of presbyterian churches. They bore to the regular ministry much the same relation which the local preacher among the Methodists bears to the ordained clergyman. But the power they wielded over their unlettered countrymen, resembled more the power with which "the man of God" of the ancient Hebrew theocracy was clothed, than aught in modern times with which it may be compared. Mighty in the Scriptures, the Bible their only book, when possessing strong natural powers—and many of them did possess superior native capacity—the effect of their religious addresses was superb.

Not long was the *Witness* newspaper established, when Hugh Miller, with the intuition of genius discerning the important aid "the men" were capable of rendering to the evangelical cause, commenced a series of papers illustrative at once of their genuine worth and historic position. Won to the side of non-intrusion, they were all of them faithful in the hour of trial. Not the utmost vindictiveness of the Highland lairds could shake their allegiance to the good cause. They rallied round the leaders of the Disruption with the heroic devotion their ancestors rallied for the Stuarts.

This triumph of the Free Church in the highlands and islands of Scotland speedily brought her into sternest conflict with the Scottish nobles. That the peasantry of Scotland should have dared to think for themselves, and dared to spurn the spiritual fetters the peers of Britain had sought to forge for them, was not to be borne. The peasantry must be put down. There is incipient rebellion in the attitude they have assumed, which it is imperative to suppress at all hazards. Out of these feelings arose the great site-controversy, and for a considerable period that controversy formed a leading feature in Hugh Miller's labours. Without having adopted any peculiar theory, or homologating any extreme political views, the editor of the *Witness* was precisely the man to hold his own in a contest with even the aristocracy of Scotland. Where principle was at stake he spared none. From the question of sites he naturally turned to the discussion of the question of clearances, and not even the proudest nobles of the realm escaped castigation. His appeals to the Duke of Sutherland are models of controversial writing, blending faithfulness with dignity, doing justice to the man while condemning his policy. The most notable, however, of his efforts at his epoch, if not in intrinsic worth, certainly in its immense popularity, was "Lochiel's Warning." The descendant of that historic house, in answer to the petition of his tenantry for sites, had counselled them to stick by the old ship. To him, accordingly, Hugh Miller addressed the following faithful monition:—

"Of all his many square miles of bleak moor and barren hill-side, mottled over with cottages, the homes of a religious people attached, in the proportion of ten to one, to the Protesting Church, he cannot spare so much as a single useless rood, on which the children of the soil may meet under cover to worship God agreeably to the dictates of their conscience. And, inditing a very neat letter to say so, he sends it to the newspapers, that the public may see in what well-turned sentences a highland chieftain can cast himself loose for ever from the affections of his clan. Surely it needs no wizard on this occasion to warn Lochiel of the peril which he is so wantonly incurring. He lives in an unsettled time, destined apparently to witness the fall of more than one institution. The formidable masses of the country, maddened by suffering and broke loose from all moral restraint, bid fair to possess themselves by and by of a charter admirably fitted to disannul and abrogate all the charters of Lochiel. 'The Lowlands shall meet him in battle array.' And amid all the various signs of change that are starting up thick and portentous on the darkening horizon, we scarce know a sign more ominous than that Lochiel, regarded as the representative of his order, should be thus throwing loose from him his people, by coming between them and their God in the spirit of wanton persecution, and compelling them to detest and renounce him. His gallant ancestor was a wiser man. The letters of our intolerant proprietors, of which we have already furnished so many specimens to our readers, form documents of strange significancy. It was the shrewd remark of a writer of the last century, that no author was ever effectually written down save by himself. Nor are we at all sure that the truth which the remark embodies should be restricted in its application to a single class. It may refer to our men of land as certainly as to our men of literature. Our lords of the soil, after catching no harm from the pens of levellers and ten-acre men, seem now in a fair way of writing themselves down by their own.

"Be this as it may, however, it is properly a concern of neither the Free Church nor of the people of Scotland, but of the proprietors themselves. The question which concerns the Church and the people is simply this, How are these hostile proprietors to be dealt with? They have unquestionably great power in their hands. Lochiel virtually possesses power enough to prevent the people of a wide district from meeting for purposes of public worship under the cover of a roof, and this, be it remembered, in a severe and weeping climate. He has virtually power enough to prevent the minister of their choice from residing within many miles of them. He has power enough, if not to exclude the gospel from his bounds, in its character as a wayfarer, who takes up lodgings for a night and then passes on,—to exclude it as a permanent resident. It may be a foreigner travelling on his lands despite of him; but he can effectually prevent its naturalization, and declare it incompetent to have a holding on the soil. And all this he can do in virtue of the legal powers in which he is vested as a proprietor. Our intolerant proprietary take their stand on their legal rights; and nothing surely can be more obvious, than that in order adequately to meet with them in the contest, the people must be enabled to take up legal ground also. It would never do for the Highlanders of Lochiel to precipitate themselves on their chief now, as they used to precipitate themselves on his enemies a century ago. The attempt would involve both themselves and the Free Church in ruin. In refusing them a site for their place of worship, Lochiel stands on ground as perfectly legal as that on which *they* would stand, were they, if urged in some hour of extremity to rise and fight for him, to content themselves by just asking in reply, *what he had left them to fight for*. His right must be recognised as entirely legal, however oppressively exercised.

"Be it remarked, however, that legal means may be employed for the furtherance of illegal ends. A man may set himself to attain some definite object, protected at every step of his progress by some sanction of law, and yet the object itself may have no sanction of law whatever. Though the way be a well-defended covered-way, if we may so speak, the position to which it leads may lie unwalled and open. And well it is for the Church that this is specially the case at present with the hostile proprietary of Scotland. They have set themselves to effect a determinate object, through the employment of certain legal means; but though the means be legal, the proposed object is utterly unprotected by any legal line of circumvallation; and so the true way for the people to meet with them is to take up a determined position, not against their well-defended means, but against their ill-defended end—not against their covered-way, but against the unwalled and open position to which the way leads. And thus, in carrying on the war, the people and the proprietary of the country shall stand so far on equal ground, that the position of both will be perfectly legal.

"Let us explain. The marksman must be enabled to see the butt ere he can take aim at it with any fair chance of success; and it is of importance, in present circumstances, that the people should have a clear *sight* of the object at which they are to level. What do our proprietors purpose to themselves by refusing sites on their grounds for the erection of Free presbyterian churches, or of dwelling-houses for the accommodation of Free presbyterian ministers? We do not think they are at all mysterious on the point. Sir James M'Kenzie tells the eldership of Avoch, in answer to their application, 'that though a member of the Church of England himself, he is nevertheless proud to avow that, for the Church *as by law established* in Scotland, he entertains feelings of high respect and veneration,' and that, therefore, he will 'certainly not lend *his* aid either to mar its usefulness or tarnish its reputation.' 'I love and respect the Church of Scotland as by law established,' says another very great proprietor of the north, in reply to a similar requisition. Lochiel echoes the sentiment in all its fulness. Even the philosophic baronet of Coul, though not quite satisfied with the craniology of the State institution, prefers her mightily to the Free Church. She has, he thinks, a much smaller development of the organs of *Wonder* and of *Hope*, and her *Veneration* is a vast deal more moderate; and though miserably flat in the coronal region, 'with a forehead villainously low,' and a huge mass of propensity behind, he is determined to back her at all hazards against the tall-headed church of the people.

"Thus the palpable, nay the broadly avowed object of all these proprietors, is to bolster up the Erastian institution. They lay the Free Church under strict embargo, that the chartered corporation may trade meanwhile without danger of rivalship, and vend its damaged and unwholesome wares with complete command of the market. They employ the legal means which the rights of property put at their disposal, to accomplish the illegal end of forcing the people into the communion of a Church which they detest and abhor. We say illegal end. There are rights of toleration as certainly as rights of property; both are equally embodied in the laws of the country; and if violently to force from a proprietor, against his will, a portion of his lands, be an offence against the law of property,—to force a people into a communion which they abhor, is as certainly an offence against the law of toleration. The proprietor's means are legal, we repeat, but the end for which he employs them is grossly the reverse; and the people, in order adequately to meet with him, must take up their position, not against his legal means, but against his illegal end. They must determine *not* to be forced into the communion of the residuary Church. If the landlord and his factor sit down on legal ground to invest their religion, if we may so speak, and put it in a state of blockade, then must they sit down on ground equally legal, to invest the residuary clergyman's religion, and put *it* in a state of blockade. In every case let the person and property of the hireling be sacred—whether he occupy the pulpit of Dr. M'Donald of Urquhart, or of Dr. Burns of Kilsyth,—of Mr. M'Leod of Snizort, or of Mr. Stewart of Cromarty;—let his person be as sacred as if the Court of Session had presented to the charge one of its red-nosed macers, or as if he were not the Erastian parson, but the constable, or sheriff-officer, or thief-catcher of the district. But to his safety and his property let this sense of sacredness be restricted. Let it on no occasion be forgotten, that he is the person on whose behalf the proprietor is flagrantly oppressive and unjust. Let him be regarded as virtually the one excommunicated man of the district,—the man with whom no one is to join in prayer,—whose church is to be avoided as an impure and unholy place,—whose addresses are not to be listened to,—whose visits are not to be received,—who is to be everywhere put under the ban of the community; and until the proprietor raises the siege of the Free Church on his part, let it be held imperative by the people that the siege of the residuary clergyman and the residuary church be kept up on theirs. There is to be a contest of wills in this matter; and there is standing equally legal for both the antagonist parties engaged in it. But while the people have justice as well as law on their side, our hostile proprietary have law only; and so, if the Scottish character has not lost its old characteristic firmness,—if our Whiggism of the old school be still the old *dour* Whiggism,—the Whiggism that has been rarely broken, and never once bent, the better cause in the end must infallibly prevail."

The London press, religious and secular, was alike indignant at the boldness of this attack. It formed a standard topic of controversy with the *Witness* in the *Record* newspaper for weeks afterwards. The *Globe* asserted that its sentiments might have well enough suited the gloom of the sixteenth or seventeenth century, but the writer had mistaken the clock. Hugh Miller answered his assailants in an article entitled the "Position of the Scottish lairds." We extract the concluding paragraphs. By a dexterous use of the *argumentum ad hominem*, he very successfully turns to foolishness the counsel of Lochiel:—

"There is," says Hugh Miller, "one point in the letters of our hostile proprietors which we have not yet directly adverted to, but which strikes us as tolerably rich in the ludicrous. Nothing can be more natural to men than the proselytizing spirit. It extends not only to all modes of religious belief, but to almost all the various negations of religious belief. It possesses not only the bosoms of fanatics, but of atheists also. But there is one specific form in which it has begun to manifest itself in these latter times, in which it does not seem to have existed before. The fanatic has striven to make men fanatics after his own type. The atheist has laboured to make them atheists. It has been reserved for our Scottish proprietors to exert themselves in behalf of a religion not their own. They recommend to others what they reject for themselves, as if to realize to the letter, and that after a very striking mode, Voltaire's remark, that the princes who protect or change the religion of a country seldom have any religion themselves. I am not a member of the Church of Scotland, says Lochiel. I am myself, you know, a member of the Church of England, says Sir James of Roseavoch. Thus runs the general preamble, and yet in every case the advice is in effect the same—We pray you hold fast by the establishment we ourselves have left, or, as Lochiel pithily ex presses it, 'stick to the ship.' Does it not seem exceedingly natural to ask in reply, 'Then pray, gentlemen, why have you not stuck to the ship? If desertion be at all a bad thing in us, pray what must it have been in you? We quit the vessel because the pest has broken out in her—because the plague flag of the Court of Session floats portentously at her mast-head. We feel it would be death for us to remain in her longer. And therefore do we betake ourselves to the long-boat, determined to effect a landing, let you frame your quarantine laws as you may.'"

That the opinions expressed by the editor of the *Witness* on the question of sites, should have been neither very palatable to whig journalists nor tory lairds, was to be anticipated. It may be granted the articles in question were not the most mannerly that could be addressed to a Highland chieftain; but it should be remembered, that men bereft of their rights are rarely in a mannerly mood. Even though gaining nothing by it, they like to have out their growl; and for any exaggeration of tone into which, in the passion of the hour, Hugh Miller may have been hurried, the men he lifted his pen to denounce are infinitely more censurable than he. Flippant journalists, with the jargon of the progress school on their lips, might talk of the editor of the *Witness* having "mistaken the clock;" the truth was he had only too accurately gauged the influences of the age. So far from deeming the opinions embodied in these memorable articles at all extreme, we deem them moderation itself. Perhaps he would have appeared less vindictive had he taken higher ground. We suspect it would be difficult to maintain, that any Celtic chief acted legally in refusing sites to his clan. To legalise such a course, clanship must give place to feudalism. The law of gavelkind, under which these chiefs held their lands, rendered the conduct of Lochiel as illegal as it was vexatious.

The only point in which we might not be disposed altogether to coincide with Lochiel's reviewer is in urging the concentration of the hate and scorn of the people upon the residuary clergyman, the fact being that the clergyman was only the representative of the opinions of the lord of the soil—a mere cipher in himself. Dr. Chalmers was right in characterizing the Establishment, such as the Disruption left it, a "moral nullity;" and such a rigorous spiritual quarantine as Hugh Miller sought to establish, implied a greater power of mischief than, except in singularly rare instances, belonged to any of the residuary clergy. He has also, as we think, attributed rather too great generosity to the Scottish lairds, in supposing it was in the interests of the residuary clergy they assumed so hostile an attitude to the Free Church. Except in so far as the residuaries served their purposes, they cared for them as little, and probably respected them less than the "outed ministers." They had, however, proved supple instruments, and it was necessary the instruments should not be left to perish in the storm of popular indignation then sweeping over Scotland. They knew that storm, if not exactly uprooting the goodly tree the Scottish reformers planted, had stripped it of its umbrageous foliage, leaving nought save a sapless trunk and withered branches—the memento of its vanished glory. It was therefore imperative, to prevent its utter disappearance from the scene, that a strong fence of intolerance be raised all around. The winds of heaven must not be permitted to visit it too roughly; their serfs must see that this shrivelled and sapless thing is the object of their peculiar care.

All but fifteen years have passed away since the Disruption; and though the results of that event have not yet fully developed themselves, enough has transpired to show that Hugh Miller's vaticinations were neither the offspring of an unbridled hate nor a misguided fancy. At this hour the Church of Scotland represents nothing Scottish. Her ministers, with a few honourable and highly-redeeming exceptions, cannot be said to be zealous for ought save the maintenance of their own status. With all changed around them, they continue to cling tenaciously to the relics of a buried past; and on everything bearing the semblance of advancement, the general assemblies of the Scottish Kirk are ready to put their most resolute veto. To borrow a homely illustration, the State Church at this moment very much resembles a carriage broken down in the centre of a crowded thoroughfare; making no progress itself, and as far as possible preventing all progress on the part of others. The prolonged existence of such an institution cannot be other than intensely pernicious to the spiritual interests of the nation.

It is matter of deep regret that for what of seeming strength she has been able to gather into herself since the Disruption, she is mainly indebted to the mistakes of the Free Church. Had that church, on the threshold of its otherwise brilliant career, seen its real position and discovered its true policy, even the very slender hold the creature of the Court of Sessions yet retains of the people of Scotland, would now have been altogether gone. The unseemly and ostentatious repudiation of voluntaryism with which Dr. Chalmers inaugurated its first General Assembly, gave a kind of galvanic life to the only embodiment of the antagonistic principle Scotland possessed. Mankind are not logicians, and the excellencies and superiorities ascribed to the abstract principle of an establishment were naturally enough transferred to its concrete form. In this way it came to pass, that what the leader of the Disruption meant only as a middle wall of partition hastily thrown up between the Free Church and Scottish Dissent, became a buttress of the residuary and Erastian Church.

We do not attribute voluntary principles to Free-churchmen, because we do not believe any great number of them have even yet adopted those principles. But without going that length, it will be conceded pretty generally that at least a more common-sense view of matters is beginning to be entertained. The Free Church is gradually discovering that an establishment after its model is a hope not to be realized; and coincident with this conviction on the one side, voluntary churches have discovered that the principle of which they are so enamoured, is not the alpha and the omega of Christianity. In this somewhat modified attitude of both the great sections of Scottish Dissent towards each other, is folded up the germ of a future union. Should the movement for that object, already so auspiciously inaugurated, go steadily onward to its consummation, we may anticipate some very important political changes in the position of ecclesiastical parties. Ireland has permitted the church of a minority to become the Church of Ireland. But we greatly mistake the temper of our countrymen, if Scotchmen would continue any longer to tolerate an establishment so vastly outnumbered by a single dissenting communion, as in the event of such a fusion the Church of Scotland would inevitably become. The zeal with which certain eminent statesmen have flung themselves into the movement for the union of the Free and the United Presbyterian churches, foreshadows the hour when the present Erastian institution will be disestablished, her revenues secularized for educational purposes, religion liberated from all state-control, and Scotland enjoying an educational system surpassing the most ardent dreams of the most sanguine educational reformers.

CHAPTER XV.

HERO-WORSHIP.

"The worship of great men is now the only possible religion," is the oracular utterance of one of the leading lights of our day. Multitudes not yet perhaps prepared to subscribe his formula, hold substantially his faith. There is a something about the creed that synchronizes with "the spirit of the age." It has nothing of the dogmatic narrowness that belonged to what in other times "was most surely believed among us." With the hero-worshipper, devotion to a principle as such is bigotry. Men of the most opposite convictions, and the most conflicting practices, receive from him the same meed of approbation. The mission of Mahomet and the mission of Moses are looked upon with equal favour. Moral excellence is forgotten in mere energy of character. That an ethical theory so bald and so palpably unsound should ever have gathered around it any disciples worthy of the name, is not a little surprising. With its votaries, sincerity is the primordial and crowning virtue of man.

Like most other errors, the now fashionable faith has seized a fragment of the truth, and it is that fragment which floats it. Sincerity as a basis of all true nobility of character is unquestionably indispensable. In every age of the world's history, hollow-heartedness has been held in nearly equal abhorrence. The hero-worshipper has not therefore discovered any latent excellence in this virtue not formerly perceived by man. All he has done has been simply to exaggerate it into an importance not its own, making its shadow fall upon every other grace and every other virtue of the soul. In acting thus it has forgotten, that sincerity, to be really worthy of our homage, must be guided by another power than its own, and in itself considered, is blind. Men of the most diverse sentiments and the most antagonistic practices, may be equally sincere. This creed, therefore, requires qualification, limitation. It is only the man whose earnestness is under the guidance of just principles, whom we can truly venerate. Earnestness is a noble quality when nobly directed; directed otherwise, it may be terrible, but noble it cannot be. John Graham of Claverhouse, and John Brown of Priesthill, were both earnest men, but whether do the accents of heavenly resignation which fall from the lips of the doomed Covenanter, or the fiendish execrations of the brutal cavalier, sound sweetest in the ear; or shall we admire both, simply because both were equally sincere?

The scourges of the earth, who have waded through slaughter to thrones, were no doubt earnest men, but are not their deeds the severest satire on the virtue which forms the life's essence of this pretentious moral code?

It is scarcely possible even to think of hero-worship, without the name of Thomas Carlyle spontaneously suggesting itself. Nor, while dissenting from much he may have taught on the subject, can any lover of England's great ones withhold a tribute, however feeble, to the superlative service he has rendered their memories. His biography of Cromwell solved the mystery which, from the days of the English Commonwealth to our own days, hung around the character of the Protector. And it is with something like proud satisfaction we reflect, that while British statesmen, in the genuine spirit of *flunkeyism*, were refusing England's greatest sovereign *a niche* in the new palace of Westminster, a countryman of our own should have been quietly and unostentatiously, in his modest mansion at Chelsea, laboriously building up from out "the authentic utterances of the man Oliver," a monument more enduring than ought the sculptor's utmost art could bestow. In the depth and comprehensiveness of his intellectual insight into the real essence of the Cromwellian era, Carlyle stands unequalled and unapproached.

Other writers are, indeed, quite as eulogistic, but

none so appreciative. Macaulay has exhausted upon it nearly every epithet of praise his very comprehensive vocabulary could furnish. Vaughan and Forster are elaborately minute in chronicling its excellencies. But the works of these writers, though manifestly the fruits of solid studies, are all of them wanting in some element more or less essential. Macaulay wants sympathy for the intense spirituality which distinguished the statesmen of the Commonwealth, and distinguished none of these statesmen more than Cromwell. Vaughan, though possessing perhaps even a still more perfect comprehension than Carlyle of the religious life of the Protector, is destitute of Carlyle's pictorial power. He reasons—he argues about, rather than portrays character. Forster's enthusiasm for the Long Parliament has made him unjust to Oliver. Guizot's "Cromwell and the English Commonwealth," reproduces most of the prejudices that, despite its excellencies, disfigure his History of the Revolution. Thirty years ago, Guizot gave the world his opinion of England's uncrowned king, and early prepossessions have so incorporated themselves with the texture of his mind, that all after effort to dislodge them would appear to have proved abortive.

It is, indeed, true, long before the publication of those "Letters and Speeches of Oliver Cromwell," ample justice had been done the merely intellectual qualities of the hero of the Commonwealth. The most inveterate supporter of church and king was ready to concede his possession of powerful intellect and imperial will. Not his intellectual, but his moral qualities, were questioned. It is the crowning glory of Carlyle that he has for ever dissipated the tissue of calumny which, from the Restoration downwards, veiled the transparent integrity of purpose by which the career of Cromwell had been distinguished.

But while readily acknowledging it is no vulgar greatness at whose shrine the sage of Chelsea prostrates himself; aware that Carlyle is dowered with "a hate of hate, a scorn of scorn," for much before which the world is ever forward to kneel; and conscious "the idols of the tribe" are not the idols before which he bows: it may yet be questioned if that "hero-worship" over which he has flung the meteoric splendour of his brilliant genius anchors itself in ought really different from the old worship of force, which, ere the dayspring from on high dissipated the darkness in which they dwelt, was the religion of our Pagan ancestry. The Norseman was a hero-worshipper of the most genuine type. How far that worship was from conducting him to an adequate conception of the perfections of Deity, a comparison of the ideas of our Scandinavian ancestors with those of the most unlettered peasant of our own day will at once discover.

The great gulf which separates Pagan from Christian

thought, is created by Christianity taking off the human mind from the overweening contemplation and admiration of all those modes of man's activity, in which mere force of intellect or energy of will exhibit themselves. The race, under the potent influence of this spiritual magnet, is being gradually lifted into a loftier region of thought and feeling. "The earthly guest breathes imperial air" when taught to seek, not in intellect or energy *per se*, but in intellect and energy as the handmaids of moral excellence, the highest style of man.

The revolutions of the last sixty years have, we believe, mainly contributed to the creation of a literature so largely impregnated with the doctrine of hero-worship, as is British literature at this hour. Naturally enough, perhaps, amidst the numerous schemes of social regeneration, which, in endless succession, have risen to the surface of society, only to fall even more quickly than they rose, our more energetic *litterateurs* have turned in disgust from so much froth and feebleness, to call the world to worship at the shrines of those heroes whom fame has eternized, and to whom ordinary mortals look up as to a race of superior beings. According to Carlyle, perhaps the truest representative of the disturbing forces of this revolutionary epoch, the hero is hardly any longer possible; the association has taken the place of the individual, the dynamical has been superseded by the mechanical, and by no possibility can any tone of the eternal melodies be heard in our times.

As the antithesis of all this, Carlyle calls us to note the silent steps by which Christianity, while the dew of its youth was yet fresh upon it, took its way to the dominion of the world; and passing from the rise and progress of Christianity, to the crusades, to the Reformation, to the English and French revolutions, he asks triumphantly, how immeasurably superior is the dynamical to the mechanical. Doubtless, there is a large amount of truth in Carlyle's somewhat cynical estimate of the age. It has too much faith in systems and organizations, and too little faith in individual effort; it does not recognize sufficiently the potentiality of man as man. Men are so massed, they have lost the sturdy individuality wont to characterize them. Mechanicism takes off the edge of all those angularities and peculiarities which give picturesqueness to national character. But while admitting so much against mechanicism as exhibits a beautiful principle pervading all things, which serves to check the pride of man, even in his loftiest efforts, by revealing that his most splendid attainments in one department are often followed by loss in another, thus serving to keep in something like equation the sum of the happiness of the race in all ages of the world's history—we have to ask, is the mechanical so completely the antipodes of the dynamical that there is no possibility of making the one subservient to the other? Cannot the lesser principle become the auxiliary of the greater, or must they for ever wage an internecine war? Can we not put soul into machinery? Is not machinery only bad, and only degrading when it is made the substitute for that which it can never replace—the living, breathing, energizing spirit of man?

Carlyle's own illustrations furnish the refutation of the theory they are adduced to support? Had not the apostles the key to all the languages of the nations which then dwelt upon the face of the earth? Was there not a universal empire, which facilitated in a remarkable manner the mission of the first heralds of the cross? And with respect to the myriads who flocked to the standard Peter the Hermit unfurled in the face of Europe, and took their way to Palestine to combat for the Holy Sepulchre, will it be maintained that it was better that crusading host had to make the tour of Europe before setting foot upon the soil of the Saracen, than that it should, like our own braves, have been transported to the scene of its operations in comfortable ships? From the want of mechanicism, these crusaders, notwithstanding all their enthusiasm, perished by thousands and tens of thousands ere they caught a glimpse of the land of Israel. With respect to the Reformation, it is true the central force was dynamical; the Reformation lay in the soul of Luther—but how vain had been

Luther's efforts, as were indeed the efforts of many of his precursors, had the printing-press not come to his aid, putting him in possession of a power more than match for the combined efforts of crook and crown to crush the nascent reform.

In point of fact, the Reformation owed its success mainly to the harmony between the dynamical and the mechanical forces employed in its furtherance; and though Carlyle sneers at the universities, it should not be forgotten that it was from the universities principally the light of a Protestant Christianity radiated over the surrounding darkness. A reference to the leading men who filled their chairs at that epoch in Europe's history, when the sleep of ages was broken, would effectually prove that at best it was only a half-truth Carlyle uttered concerning the Reformation in the sixteenth century. With respect to the English and French revolutions, 'tis true they were dynamical, but precisely because they were too purely dynamical were they unenduring. If the letters and speeches of Oliver Cromwell prove anything, they prove that, so soon as the strong common sense of Cromwell failed England, so soon did anarchy once more lift its head; and France, unhappy France, could embody its aspirations after liberty, equality, fraternity, in nothing better than a reign of terror. The revolutionary government of France fell to pieces, because it wanted mechanism, or perhaps, to speak more correctly, because its only mechanism was the guillotine.

It is to be regretted that the teaching of that school of which Carlyle is the *facile princeps*, is in so great a degree illusory. Modern hero-worshippers, like the ancient artificers in wood, in stone, in iron, and in brass, have not a little to do with the creation of the objects of their adoration. And if not the work of their own hands, at least the creatures of their own fancy, veil from them a grander ideal, and an infinitely nobler type of humanity, than is embodied in the highest earthborn heroism. There is a something deeply mournful about the ceaseless oscillations of human opinion respecting not what may be called subsidiary, but essential truth—truth that must ever form the central principle and motive power of all moral government. Now, perhaps, we may find not a few speculative thinkers, peculiarly enamoured with a creed, which, if generally accepted, would convert mankind into a herd of slobbering sentimentalists. Love, without any element of order or authority, is their ideal of infinite perfection. With them "God is love," in a sense that excludes infinite holiness and infinite justice, and no interpretation of the sterner facts of Divine moral government can be accepted that does not square with this benevolent theory; "nature red, in tooth and claw," must be ignored in presence of these sentimental philosophers. Anon, it is discovered, that whatever root in feeling the theory possessed, it had no existence in fact. The eternal verities of the universe are arrayed in serried phalanx against it, and like the gourd of the prophet which sprung up in a night, it withers in as brief a period. But, alas! the false philosophy is abandoned only to rush into falsehood's opposite extreme. The still small voice of love is hushed; nothing is heard save the menace of authority; and man, hitherto the creature of infinite tenderness, he whose eye, wherever it wandered, turned on smiles, has become the sport and plaything of "the necessities and the destinies," and grim fate, like some Giant Despair, holds his future in his inexorable gripe. Nowhere shall we find, within the whole circle of modern writers, a more perfect antithesis to that class of *litterateurs*—

"The magnet of whose course is gone, or only points in vain,
The shore to which their shivered sail shall never stretch again"—

than in the writings of Hugh Miller. The influences that for the last sixty years have been streaming in upon modern thought, if they did not leave his thinking altogether untouched, never drove him from his early moorings. Happily withdrawn, during that season when the human spirit is so peculiarly impressionable, from the malign influences which, during his morn of life, were pouring themselves over society, the storms of that great revolutionary epoch, so fatal to many a fine spirit, never once untoned his. It was, indeed, known that a mighty conflict was being fought out between the antagonistic forces, the hostile camps of Europe; but the great depths of his being were not broken up by the tumult of a battle thus only heard from afar. Had the self-reliant stone-cutter been thrown, at a favourable conjuncture of circumstances, into the vortex of the politico-philosophical speculation with which, ever since the French Revolution, Europe has teemed, the whole after life of the editor of the *Witness* might have been something widely different. As it was in that boreal region, in which childhood, youth, and early manhood were passed, his spirit was nursed amidst infinitely gentler influences than the influences of the age. His living teachers, his literature, his theology, all belonged to an earlier epoch.

No one who has more than the most superficial acquaintance with his writings, can have failed to perceive how deep, how wide, how accurate is his acquaintance with the writers that immediately preceded the revolutionary epoch. With the wits and humourists of the eighteenth century, Hugh Miller was quite as familiar as Thackeray, admiring with an equal admiration Addison and Swift. Hardly any of his works are wanting in frequent reference to Goldsmith; often indeed does he turn aside to pay a touching tribute to one whose genius he admired and appreciated, better, perhaps, than any man since the days of Johnson. Thackeray, in his own style, has hit off the piquant peculiarities of poor Goldy, but the portrait is marred by mannerism. Macaulay, the lucky, the successful Macaulay, has little sympathy with the luckless, imprudent son of Erin. Goldsmith's mind did not move on a scale sufficiently grand fully to awaken the sympathies of De Quincy. After his inimitable biographer, Forster, Hugh Miller alone, of all our modern *litterateurs*, seems inspired with that genuine affection for the warm-hearted author of the Vicar of Wakefield, which his many virtues and fine genius might be expected to evoke. It was this perfect familiarity with those great masters, who in other days had imparted so much grace and symmetry to our land's language, that gave to Hugh Miller's works that style which the late Baron Hume had begun to regard as one of the lost arts, until, no less surprised than gratified, he discovered the joy of his youth untouched by any shade of years in "Scenes and Legends of the North of Scotland."

The literati of Edinburgh made an immense cackling about the testimonial to the purity of Principal Robertson's style, which Walpole furnished. In these Scenes and Legends, written, not within the shadow of the metropolis, but in a distant and sequestered nook of Scotland, there is not only all the purity, there is what

Robertson never attained, all the flexibility of the best English writers. Nay, we venture to claim for Hugh Miller's style still higher praise. The grace and beauty of the classics of the eighteenth century are due, not more to innate taste, than to the scrupulous avoidance of all those topics which, by demanding deeper thinking, would have left less leisure to study mere polish of expression. Hugh Miller is the first English writer who found, in the style of the eighteenth century essayists, a vehicle for thoughts that touch the human soul at infinitely profounder depths than any Addison or Goldsmith, Swift or Steele, Richardson or Fielding ever reached.

Precluded almost equally by the precepts of religion, and the principles of taste, from elevating to the throne of his intellect or affections, any one of the gods of that literary pantheon in which so many men of letters offered their homage and adoration, Hugh Miller's heroes were his companions; a genuinely human and brotherly sympathy existed between them. He had seen enough of the realities of life, to dissipate the illusion with which the greatest of the sons of men are invested, and even by the grave of Shakspeare, could speak as a man should speak.

"How would this master of human nature have judged of the homage that has now been paid him for these two centuries? and what would have been *his* theory of 'hero worship?' Many a bygone service of this inverted religion has Stratford-on-Avon witnessed. The jubilee devised by Garrick had no doubt much of the player in it; but it possessed also the real devotional substratum, and formed the type, on a splendid scale, not less in its hollownesses than in its ground-work of real feeling, of those countless acts of devotion of which the poet's birth and burial places have been the scene. 'Man praises man;' Garrick, as became his occupation, was a little more ostentatious and formal in his jubilee services,—more studious of rich ceremonial and striking forms,—more *High Church* in spirit,—than the simpler class of hero-devotees who are content to worship extempore; but that was just all.

"'He drew the liturgy and framed the rites
And solemn ceremonial of the day,
And called the world to worship on the banks
Of Avon, famed in song. Ah! pleasant proof
That piety has still in human hearts
Some place, a spark or two not yet extinct.
The mulberry-tree was hung with blooming wreaths;
The mulberry-tree stood centre of the dance;
The mulberry-tree was hymned with dulcet airs;
And from his touchwood trunk the mulberry-tree
Supplied such relics as devotion holds
Still sacred, and preserves with pious care.
So 'twas a hallowed time; decorum reigned,
And mirth without offence. No few returned
Doubtless much edified, and all refreshed.'

"Such was Cowper's estimate,—to be sure, somewhat sarcastically expressed,—of the services of the jubilee. What would Shakspeare's have been of the deeply-based sentiment, inherent, it would seem, in human nature, in which the jubilee originated? An instinct so widely diffused and so deeply implanted cannot surely be a mere accident; it must form, however far astray of the proper mark it may wander, one of the original components of the mental constitution, which we have not given ourselves. What would it be in its integrity? It must, it would appear, have humanity on which to rest,—a nature identical with our own; and yet, when it finds nothing higher than mere humanity, it is continually running, as in the case of the Stratford Jubilee, into grotesque idolatry. Did Shakspeare, with all his vast knowledge, know where its aspirations could be directed aright? The knowledge seems to have got, somehow, into his family; nay, she who appears to have possessed it was the much-loved daughter on whom his affections mainly rested,—

> 'Witty above her sexe; but that's not all,—
> Wise to salvation was good Mistress Hall.'

So says her epitaph in the chancel, where she sleeps at the feet of her father. There is a passage in the poet's will, too, written about a month ere his death, which may be, it is true, a piece of mere form, but which may possibly be something better. 'I commend my soul into the hands of God my Creator, hoping, and assuredly believing, through the only merits of Jesus Christ, my Saviour, to be made partaker of life everlasting.' It is, besides, at least something, that this play-writer and play-actor, with wit at will, and a shrewd appreciation of the likes and dislikes of the courts and monarchs he had to please, drew for their amusement no Mause Headriggs or Gabriel Kettledrummies. Puritanism could have been no patronizer of the Globe Theatre. Both Elizabeth and James hated the principle with a perfect hatred, and strove hard to trample it out of existence; and such a laugh at its expense as a Shakspeare could have raised, would have been doubtless a high luxury; nay, Puritanism itself was somewhat sharp and provoking in those days, and just a little coarse in its jokes, as the Martin Mar-Prelate tracts survive to testify; but the dramatist, who grew wealthy under the favour of Puritan-detesting monarchs, was, it would seem, not the man to make reprisals. There are scenes in his earlier dramas, from which, as eternity neared upon his view, he could have derived little satisfaction; but there is no 'Old Mortality' among them. Had the poor player some sense of what his beloved daughter seems to have clearly discovered,—the true 'hero worship?' In his broad survey of nature and of man, did he mark one solitary character standing erect amid the moral waste of creation, untouched by taint of evil or weakness,—a character infinitely too high for even his vast genius to conceive, or his profound comprehension to fathom? Did he draw near to inquire, and to wonder, and then fall down humbly to adore?"

He who could thus gaze with undazzled eye upon the

splendour of that mighty orb of song, was, in his tastes and sympathies, something very different from an echo of the general trump of fame. For an obscure minister of his native village, who "died and made no sign," he asks our homage as for one of the greatest of Scotch theologians. Others might ransack the rolls of continental, of English, or of Scottish ecclesiastical history for the chief of sacred orators. Hugh Miller found that chief in the friend of his youth. In after years he enjoyed abundant opportunities and ample leisure to correct or modify the partialities of youthful friendship. Bnt in life's gloaming, as in life's noon, Stewart of Cromarty was still the prince of preachers.

As might have been anticipated, such a man was not a tuft hunter. In the zenith of his fame, no persuasion could induce him to go even for a single day, though often invited, to the mansions of nobility. Urgently and frequently he was pressed to accept the hospitality of the most accomplished of our Scottish nobles, yet that hospitality was invariably and most peremptorily declined. Whether it was Hugh Miller felt he had no talent for carrying duchesses off their feet, like his great countryman, Robert Burns, or whether it was the ambiguous treatment the bard received from the aristocracy, even when they professed to honour him, that made the self-taught man of science chary of their attentions, we do not presume to say; but certain it is, that with the most obdurate inflexibility did he decline their every solicitation.

> "Love had he found in huts where poor men lie,
> His daily teachers had been woods and rills,
> The silence that is in the starry sky,
> The sleep that is among the lonely hills;"

and with that love and these teachers he seemed unambitious to extend the circle of his acquaintanceship, even though it should happen to come to him all stars, garters, and coronets. Possibly he carried the feeling to the extreme of susceptibility. Yet it was not without reason he acted thus. He had cast a profoundly penetrative intellectual glance upon the hollowness of the homage offered up to the man of genius by the herd of his bustling patrons. With the tact of the accomplished journalist, and the sagacity of the astute observer of men and thimgs, he seized the opportunity afforded by a now nearly forgotten event, "The Burns' Festival," to show up the sham which hero-worship may become.

"Could we but lay open the inner springs of this tendency to man-worship, they would enable us, we are convinced, to comprehend many a curious chapter in the early history of the species. Departed greatness, enveloped by its peculiar atmosphere of reverential respect and awe, and exaggerated by distance, is suffered to retain within the bright circle of its halo many an attendant littleness and impurity that contemporaries would have at least not admired. The greatness is doubtless the staple of the matter—that which dazzles, impresses, attracts; and the littleness and impurities were accidents that have mixed with it; and yet how strange a tone do they not too frequently succeed in imparting to the worship! There was much of apology at the Burns' Festival for the errors of the poet; and it said at least something for the morals of the time, whatever it might for the taste of the speakers, that such should have been the case. In a remoter and more darkened age of the world, like those ages in which hero-worship rose into a religion, the errors would have been remembered, but the apology would have been wanting. Burns would have been deified into an Apollo, and his love passages with the nymphs Daphne, Leucothoe, and Coronis, and his drinking-bouts with Admetus and Hyacinthus, would have been registered simply as incidents in his history—incidents which, in the course of time, would have come to serve as precedents for his worshippers. We are afraid that, maugre regret and apology, there is too much of this as it is. His hapless errors, so fatal to himself, have been too often surveyed through the dazzling halo of his celebrity. The felt influence of his greatness has extended to his faults, as if they were part and parcel of his greatness. The atmosphere of the sun conceals the sun's spots from the unassisted eye of the observer; but the atmosphere of glory that surrounds the memory of Burns has not had a similar effect. To many, at least, it has the effect of making his blemishes appear less as original flaws, than as a species of beauty-spots, of a fashion to be imitated. How can we marvel that the old worshippers of the offspring of Saturn or Latona should have imitated their gods in their crimes, if in these our days of light, with the model of a perfect religion before our eyes, hero-worship should be found to exert, as of old, a demoralizing influence! But it would not be easy to say, where more emphatic or more honest warning could be found on this head than in the writings of Burns himself. We stake his own deeply-mournful prediction of the fate which he saw awaiting him, against all ever advanced on the opposite side:—

'The poor inhabitant below
Was quick to learn, and wise to know,
And keenly felt the social glow,
And softer flame;
But thoughtless follies laid him low,
And stained his name.'

"Despite the authority of high names, we are no admirers of hero-worship. We are not insensible to what we may term the natural claims of Burns on the admiration of his country, both as a writer and as a character of great bulk and power. It would be hypocrisy in us to say that we were. Were his writings to be annihilated to-morrow we could restore from memory some of the best of them entire, and not a few of the more striking passages in many of the others. Nor are we unimpressioned by the massiveness of his character as a man. We bear about with us an adequate idea of it, as developed in that deeply-mournful tragedy—his life. But we would not choose to go and worship at his festival. There was a hollowness about the ceremony, independently of the falseness of the principles on which its ritual was framed. Of the thousands who attended, how many, does the reader think, would have sympathized, had they seen the light some fifty years earlier, with the *man* Robert Burns? How many of them grappled in idea at his festival with other than a mere phantom of the imagination—a large but intangible shade, obscure and indefinable as that conjured up, by the uninformed Londoner, of Cromwell or of Johnson? Rather more than fifty years ago, the sinking sun shone brightly one fine afternoon, on the stately tenements of Dumfries, and threw its slant rule of light athwart the principal street of the town. The shadows of the houses on the western side were stretched half-way across the pavement, while on the side opposite, the red beam seemed as if sleeping on jutting irregular fronts and tall gables. There was a world of well-dressed company that evening in Dumfries; for the aristocracy of the adjacent country for twenty miles round had poured in to attend a county ball, and were fluttering in groups along the sunny side of the street, gay as butterflies. On the other side, in the shade, a solitary individual paced slowly along the pavement. Of the hundreds who fluttered past, no one took notice of him—no one seemed to recognise him. He was known to them all as the exciseman and poet, Robert Burns; but he had offended the stately Toryism of the district by the freedom of his political creed; and so—tainted by the plague of Liberalism—he lay under strict quarantine. He was shunned and neglected; for it was with the *man* Burns that these his cotemporaries had to deal. Let the reader contrast with this truly melancholy scene, the scene of his festival a fortnight since.

Here are the speeches of the Earl of Eglinton and of Sir John M'Neill, and here the toast of the Lord Justice General. Let us just imagine these gentlemen, with all their high aristocratic notions about them, carried back half a century into the past, and dropped down, on the sad evening to which we refer, in the main street of Dumfries. Which side, does the reader think, would they have chosen to walk upon? Would they have addressed the one solitary individual in the shade, or not rather joined themselves to the gay groups in the sunshine who neglected and contemned him? They find it an easy matter to deal with the phantom idea of Burns now; how would they have dealt with the man then? How are they dealing with his poorer relatives—or how with men of kindred genius, their cotemporaries? Alas! a moment's glance at such matters is sufficient to show how very unreal a thing a commemorative feast may be. Reality, even in idea, becomes a sort of Ithuriel spear to test it by. The Burns Festival was but an idle show at which players enacted their parts."

But in sternly reprobating man-worship, however exalted, Hugh Miller was not, therefore, the less just to his great countryman. None saw more clearly or could estimate more accurately the worth of his work.

"*Robert Burns was the man who first taught the Scottish people to stand erect.* Let us not be blind to the great national faults, and only lynx-eyed to the faults of the great national poet. A mean and creeping subserviency to the great,—a getting up 'to be hanged in order to please the laird,'—was the master fault of the Scotch people; and a century of persecution had failed to wean them of it. That part of the general Epistle of James which speaks of 'respect of persons,' and the undue partiality shown to men with 'gold rings and goodly apparel,' might have been more appropriately addressed to the Scotch, even after the rich had 'oppressed' and 'drawn' them 'before judgment-seats,' and 'blasphemed the Holy Name,' than to almost any other people of Europe. But the independent peasant, who, in the most trying circumstances, never bent himself before the worthless wealthy or the little great, and who in his ever-living strains asserted the dignity of manhood, taught them another lesson; and they have learned it. Yes! the Scottish people have lost the habitual stoop, and now stand erect; and all honour, say we, to the *reformer* who, more than any other, effected the change. His life, as certainly as his works, were effectual in producing it; and, had it accomplished nothing else, it would not, with all its errors and shortcomings, have been spent in vain."

Yet, though doing the amplest justice to the poet, as if to illustrate the imperfection of the justest thinking and the noblest intentions in reprobating "the sham," Hugh Miller insensibly assumed the attitude of "the cynic." With much said about the hollowness of the worship offered to the memory of Coila's bard, all must acquiesce; but it should not be forgotten, even while remembering the false, how many true worshippers of the poet met to honour his name.

The speech of the Burns' festival was neither the speech of the Lord Justice-General, of Sir John M'Neill, nor of the Earl of Eglinton; it was the speech of Professor Wilson, and the tribute of the heart Christopher North offered on that day to the memory of the bard, merited a more handsome recognition than the expressive silence Hugh Miller left to muse its praise. Nor can we divest ourselves of the impression that the genial-hearted Eglinton was only uttering the genuine sentiments of his soul, when announcing to the gathered thousands that he, the descendant of those who dwelt in the "Castle of Montgomery," only felt himself too highly honoured in being permitted to propose the memory of him who then wandered there unknown by the banks of the Fail.

Neither can we give up even Sir John M'Neill: true he has been through life what is called a Tory; but in the remembrance of the fact that this Tory was among the earliest and kindest friends of a more friendless son of genius than even Burns, the graduate of Plymouth workhouse, John Kitto, we read an earnest of the treatment the poet would have received from the ex-Crimean commissioner. Nay, was there not in the genuine pluck and faithfulness of that report of his on the mismanagement by which a herd of titled aristocrats decimated the sons of the people, perhaps the noblest recognition of the poet's creed, "a man's a man for a' that," modern times have furnished?

Later in life, we believe Hugh Miller considerably modified his opinions of some of the men to whom, in his paper on the Burns' Festival, he had done such scant justice. In the year of his death, we had the pleasure of seeing him on the same platform with not a few of these same tories, heartily co-operating in a common effort to save the monument of the bard from the vandalism of the town council of Edinburgh. The oratory on that occasion was done chiefly by Professors Aytoun and Blackie; but their speeches, so far as they bore upon the object of the meeting, were confessedly echoes of an article replete with the truest taste, the noblest eloquence, and the most ardent patriotism, which appeared in the *Witness* on the previous day.

CHAPTER XVI.

EDUCATION.

HITHERTO the course of the ecclesiastical leaders of the Free Church, and the course of the editor of the *Witness*, had run nearly parallel. Slight variations in policy and views, had, indeed, occasionally manifested themselves, but no serious disagreement was yet apparent. A crisis had, however, now arrived, when considerable discrepancy of opinion and policy was about to disclose itself. The severe labours, literary, ecclesiastical, and scientific, undergone by Hugh Miller during the first four years of the existence of the *Witness*, compelled him to forego all literary effort during the greater part of 1845 and 1846. Thus necessarily precluded from forming any very fixed views of what the church was doing, on returning in renovated health, early in January, 1847, to his editorial duties, he found her on the eve of that great educational controversy in which he was called to combat the church's entire ecclesiastical artillery, a combat which did not cease until, from his own solitary but well-appointed battery, he silenced its every gun.

No sooner had Hugh Miller returned to Edinburgh, than Dr. Chalmers, with his wonted kindness, paid him a visit of congratulation on his convalescence, and in a long and serious conversation, urged the importance of maintaining the *Witness* in honest independency, uninfluenced by cliques and parties, secular or ecclesiastical. At this interview the prospects of the Free Church educational scheme were briefly discussed. Dr. Chalmers was struck with the views of Hugh Miller, and expressed his desire to see the educational question brought at once to the columns of the *Witness*, and probed to the bottom. The opportunity for this discussion soon presented itself. The scheme of privy-council grants for educational purposes was announced by government. Dr. Candlish had got the church committed to a refusal of all participation of those grants, as inconsistent with the principles of the Free Church.

So recently disentangled from the meshes of statecraft, like the bird escaped from the snare of the fowler, it was not wonderful, they should have been chary of entering anew into friendly relations with Erastian politicians. Had this dissatisfaction based itself on legitimate grounds, and expressed itself in logical forms, even if not able to hold its own against the powerful antagonist it encountered in the *Witness*, it would, at least, have been more worthy of respect. As it was, the "*vicious Cameronianism*," as Hugh Miller styled the sentiment with which he had to contend, made but a sorry figure in conflict with the strong common sense of the editor of the *Witness*. In supporting his views of the propriety of accepting the privy-council grants, Hugh Miller employed successively every arrow in his intellectual quiver, turning at will from the gravest statement to the gayest satire. Now by a calm historical narrative, now by a piece of powerful ratiocination, anon by the liveliest wit and the broadest humour does he overthrow the positions of his antagonists. Grave and reverend seigniors, with whom wit was wickedness, were startled from their propriety, by finding themselves occasionally treated in the columns of the *Witness*, much after the manner they might have expected to have been treated in the columns of *Punch*.

As exhibiting the playful style in which he thus sometimes clothed important ideas, and the adroitness with which he could avail himself of the accidents of the hour for the illustration of permanent principles, this bit of exquisite banter will suffice. To a brother editor of opposite opinions on the education question, and somewhat alarmed at the range and freedom of illustration Hugh Miller brought to its discussions, he thus addresses himself:—

"What sort of teaching, then, we ask our cotemporary, does he expect for ten, fifteen, or even twenty pounds per annum! He remembers, we daresay, the story of Betty the cook-maid and her mistress. Betty, an old and faithful servant, on one day informing her mistress that she purposed getting married, had got a present of five pounds from her; and straightway taking her leave, she returned a morning or two after, to show the good lady her husband. The husband was little, and old, and blear-eyed, and lame of a foot, and did not take the mistress's fancy at all. 'Betty,' she said, 'is *that* the man you have got?' 'Oh! Mem,' exclaimed Betty, imploringly, 'Oh! Mem, what could we expect for five pounds?' Our respected cotemporary, who strangely enough accuses *us* of indulging in 'a variety of *facetiæ*' (we!—the sober-eyed!—the grave-featured!—the demure!—we!)—our cotemporary, we say, delights in only *grave* stories; and we are quite sure he will luxuriate on this one, for the sake, not only of its intrinsic properness and sobriety, but also for that of the high-toned moral which it bears. We ask him imploringly, in the very vein of Betty—'Oh! Mem, what can we expect for fifteen pounds!' Cheap articles are not always great bargains,—a fact of which the Free Church has already had some little experience, and regarding which, sheerly for the sake of warning in this matter, we beg leave to submit to our respected cotemporary a brief snatch of historic narrative, founded on personal observation.

"We travelled, about a twelvemonth since, through a remote part of the country, and, in the course of a single morning, passed by two Free Churches erected after the Edinburgh model. As the first came full in view, at the distance of several miles, it presented to our wondering eyes an appearance which we could not at all understand. It was the subject, evidently, of some strange mysterious operation. There were about fifty adventurous Free Churchmen clustered upon the roof, like so many triumphant Lilliputians on the prostrate Gulliver, or a crew of Dutch Greenlandmen engaged in flaying a whale,—while about a hundred more, heaving upon good ropes, or tugging at levers, swarmed thick in the area below. We could hear, as we approached, the stout 'yo heave o',' translated into Gaelic, echoing clear through the calm morning air; and by and by ascertained that the work on hand was neither more nor less than the *skinning* of a kirk. And hard work it was. A ponderous integument of felt and tar played flap, flap, flap, upon the sarking, as the tugging moiety of the party below strained in desperation at the cordage, or ever and anon relaxed their endeavours to sheer but hopeful exhaustion. At length up rose the enormous cover, in one riddled whole, from gable to gable. It stuck up on end for half a minute in mid air, as if balanced on the casement, like the ancient brocade described by Crabbe,—

'Silk beyond price, so rich, 'twould stand alone;'

and then rolling over in one immense mass on the sward, the stripped erection stood up in all its nakedness, like a flayed rhinoceros. 'What is all this about?' we asked a decent-looking bonneted man, much begrimed with pitch. 'Oh, that nasty tar!' he replied. 'Ye see, sir, we took the cheap Edinbro' roofing, an' we're noo taking it aff again to get sclate. It's no little trouble we had wi't fra first to last!' We walked on, and in about two hours after passed the second Free Church. It had got considerably in advance of its neighbour; half a dozen workmen were just closing in the last course of a capital cover of Breadalbane slate, that glanced bright in the sun, while the rejected tar-work lay in a forlorn heap beside an adjacent rivulet, like the cast-off skin of a renovated snake, or the slough of a transformed mermaid. The decent bonneted man was, we found, quite in the right—the cheap Edinburgh roofing *had* cost the Free Church a world of trouble. It did tolerably well in calm, cool, dry weather; but when the rains descended on the roof, they were sure always to descend also *through* the roof—not in the character of pure rain, but in the character of Bishop Berkeley's famous tar-water, till every Free Church, in a shower, became a sort of medicated Dropping Cave of Slaines. And then, when the sun shone in its power, down came, not water, but the tar itself. It descended in long hot trails on the worthy men at the plate, like seething pitch cast from a beleaguered tower on the heads of the besiegers,—bedaubed the Sunday toggery of the young men, till long-tailed coats looked, in their vigorous youth, as if fallen into infirm health, and stuck over with strengthening plaster,—did infinite damage to jemmy calicoes and unexceptionable Leghorns,—and stuck fast the whole membership of a congregation to their pews and to one another, as Cobbler Audley in the story, by sitting down on his prayer-book to protect himself against witchcraft, and forgetting to note, in his terror, that a ball of his rosin had insinuated itself between his inexpressibles and the cover, stuck himself fast to 'our most excellent liturgy;' or a better comparison still—as our respected contemporary * * * sticks fast to his subject. It is no doubt an excellent thing that congregations should be united; but there exists no reason whatever for sticking them together with tar. It was, however, when to a hot sun there was a high wind superadded, that the molten roofing rendered itself most remarkable. It arrested in their vagrant course wandering bits of paper, voyaging straws, and flying feathers, till they stuck up thick and manifold over the erection 'like quills upon the fretful porcupine,' and at the close of a summer gale, decent churches came to resemble huge Friezeland hens. The Edinburgh Building Committee had *tarred* the Free Kirk, all out of sheer economy, and the chapter of accidents *feathered* it."

The Free Church in its eagerness to "possess the land," and its ambition still to be reckoned the Church of Scotland, had projected a magnificent educational scheme, gathering round it a phalanx of teachers, incomparably more numerous than she had the power to support. Her principles as a church were not the less pure, nor the conduct of "the outed" ministers the less noble, that they were not able to secure the adhesion of the entire ministry of the Church of Scotland, as by law established, to their claim of rights. But in the first blush of their zeal, they could not bear to look the stern facts of their position fully in the face.

All but two years' seclusion from the turmoil of church controversy, had served to dissipate the illusion Hugh Miller had perhaps originally shared in common with the church's ecclesiastical leaders. And he came now, after that lengthened period of rustication, with a fresh eye to the consideration of the position of his party.

That position he has thus described:—

"We found in all the various schemes of the Free Church, with but one exception, its extensively-spread membership and its more active leaders were thoroughly at one; but that in that exceptional scheme they were not all at one. They were at one in their views respecting the ecclesiastical character of ministers, elders, and Church courts, and of the absolute necessity which exists that these, and these only, should possess the spiritual key. Further, they were wholly at one in recognizing the command of our adorable Saviour, to preach the gospel to all nations, as of perpetual obligation on the Church. But regarding what we shall term, without taking an undue liberty with the language, the pedagogical teaching of religion, they differed *in toto*. Practically, and to all intents and purposes, the schoolmaster, in the eye of the membership of our Church and of the other Scottish Churches, was simply a layman, the proper business of whose profession was the communication of secular learning; and, as in choosing their tailors and shoemakers, the people selected for themselves the craftsmen who made the best and handsomest shoes and clothes, so in selecting a schoolmaster for their children, they were sure always to select the teacher who was found to turn out the best scholars. All other things equal, they would have preferred a serious, devout schoolmaster to one who was not serious nor devout, just as, *cæteris paribus*, they would have preferred a serious shoemaker or tailor to a nonreligious maker of shoes and clothes. But religious character was not permitted to stand as a compensatory item for professional skill; nay, men who might almost be content to put up with a botched coat or a botched pair of shoes for the sake of the good man who spoiled them, were particularly careful not to botch, on any account whatever, the education of their children. In a country in which there was more importance attached, than in perhaps any other in the world, to the religious teaching of the minister, there was so little importance attached to the religious teaching of the schoolmaster, that when weighed against even a slight modicum of secular qualification, it was found to have no sensible weight; and with this great practical fact some of our leading men seemed to be so little acquainted, that they were going on with the machinery of their educational scheme on a scale at least coextensive with the Free Church, as if, like that church—all-potent in her spiritual character—it had a moving power in the affections of the people competent to speed it on. And it was the great discrepancy with regard to this scheme, which existed between the feelings of the people and the anticipations of some of our leading men, clerical and lay, that excited our alarm. Unless that discrepancy be removed, we said,—unless the anticipations of the men engaged in the laying down of this scheme be sobered to the level of the feelings of the lay membership of our church, or, *vice versâ*, the feelings of the lay membership of our church be raised to the level of the anticipations of our leaders,—bankruptcy will be the infallible result."

This passage contains the key to the position Hugh Miller maintained with so much pertinacity, and so much success throughout this controversy. Evangelical in his religious, he was moderate, rather perhaps we should say, national in his educational views. He loved the nationality of our schools, and turned in disgust from the attempt to make what had hitherto been common ground on which the youth of Scotland met, without distinction of party, the clerical preserve of any sect, even though that sect should happen to be his own. With such views and feelings, he naturally enough scorned the absurd proposals made to identify the teachers with the sacred office. There can be no doubt that, while following this course, and holding these views, he was much nearer the views of the Scottish Reformers on the education question than the party he opposed. Without dissociating religion from the teaching of the school, the master idea in the minds of all those men was the importance of providing for the youth of the country, what, to adopt a modern, and not altogether unobjectionable term, we may describe as a secular education. Upon this point, therefore, Hugh Miller was invulnerable. But with the peculiar opinions entertained by the Free Church—opinions for which there was a greater justification in the circumstances of society and the ideas of contemporary political and religious parties, than the editor of the *Witness* was disposed to acknowledge—the acceptance of the privy-council grants trembled on the verge of treachery to principle.

None had been more strenuous than the leaders of the Free Church in denunciation of the vicious tendency of modern statecraft to the indiscriminate endowment of all religious creeds. It was only to be anticipated, therefore, that in accepting these grants as a religious denomination, and appearing at the door of the treasury, in common with sects deemed subverters of the faith, it should be felt by not a few, they had forsaken their cherished principles. This anomalous position in which the church found itself, arose from the circumstance that its leaders only accepted half the advice given them by the editor of the *Witness*, and by Dr. Chalmers. The strong common sense of Hugh

Miller detected at once the absurdity of taking the public money as a denomination for religious purposes, under the minutes of privy council, and protesting against giving the same aid to other denominations not, indeed, so orthodox as themselves, but quite as really as themselves contributors to the public purse. His withering *exposé* of the untenable character of the original opposition to the privy-council grants, seconded by certain political influences, to which the church has often bowed, had, indeed, silenced the hostility of Dr. Candlish and the majority in the church; but though dislodged from their original position, they had not yet reached any really legitimate resting-place.

They had, indeed, taken the money of the state, but they had done nothing to secure a national, in opposition to a merely denominational education. True, religious differences interposed a powerful barrier to the accomplishment of this object; but though the barrier was powerful in the opinions alike of Dr. Chalmers and of Hugh Miller, it was by no means insurmountable. Like the editor of the *Witness*, Dr. Chalmers aimed to set up a scheme of education, which, so far as the state was concerned, should be substantially a secular education. The matured expression of his views upon the subject was embodied in a letter addressed to the then Right Hon. Fox Maule, now Lord Panmure. As the document is necessary to an accurate comprehension of Hugh

Miller's position in this controversy, we reproduce it entire:—

"It were the best state of things that we had a parliament sufficiently theological to discriminate between the right and the wrong in religion, and to encourage or endow accordingly. But failing this, it seems to us the next best thing, that in any public measure for helping on the education of the people, government were to abstain from introducing the element of religion at all into their part of the scheme, and this not because they held the matter to be insignificant—the contrary might be strongly expressed in the preamble of their act; but on the ground that, in the present divided state of the Christian world, they would take no cognizance of, just because they would attempt no control over, the religion of applicants for aid—leaving this matter entire to the parties who had to do with the erection and management of the schools which they had been called upon to assist. A grant by the state upon this footing might be regarded as being appropriately and exclusively the expression of their value for a good secular education.

"The confinement for the time being of any government measure for schools to this object we hold to be an imputation, not so much on the present state of our legislature, as on the present state of the Christian world, now broken up into sects and parties innumerable and seemingly incapable of any effort for so healing these wretched divisions as to present rulers of our country with aught like such a clear and unequivocal majority in favour of what is good and true, as might at once determine them to fix upon and to espouse it.

"It is this which has encompassed the government with difficulties, from which we can see no other method of extrication than the one which we have ventured to suggest. And as there seems no reason why, because of these unresolved differences, a public measure for the health of all—for the recreation of all—for the economic advancement of all—should be held in abeyance, there seems as little reason why, because of these differences, a public measure for raising the general intelligence of all should be held in abeyance. Let the men, therefore, of all churches and all denominations alike hail such a measure, whether as carried into effect by a good education in letters or in any of the sciences; and, meanwhile, in these very seminaries, let that education in religion which the legislature abstains from providing for, be provided for as freely and amply as they will by those who have undertaken the charge of them.

"We should hope, as the result of such a scheme, for a most wholesome rivalship on the part of many in the great aim of rearing on the basis of their respective systems a moral and Christian population, well taught in the principles and doctrines of the gospel, along with being well taught in the lessons of ordinary scholarship. Although no attempt should be made to regulate or enforce the lessons of religion in the inner hall of legislation, this will not prevent, but rather stimulate to a greater earnestness in the contest between truth and falsehood—between light and darkness—in the outer field of society; nor will the result of such a contest in favour of what is right and good be at all the more unlikely, that the families of the land have been raised by the helping hand of the state to a higher platform than before, whether as respects their health, or their physical comfort, or their economic condition, or, last of all, their place in the scale of intelligence and learning.

"Religion would, under such a system, be the immediate product, not of legislation, but of the Christian and philanthropic zeal which obtained throughout society at large. But it is well when what legislation does for the fulfilment of its object tends not to the impediment, but rather, we apprehend, to the furtherance of those greater and higher objects which are in the contemplation of those whose desires are chiefly set on the immortal wellbeing of man.

"On the basis of these general views I have two remarks to offer regarding the government scheme of education.

"1. I should not require a certificate of satisfaction with the religious progress of the scholars from the managers of the schools, in order to their receiving the government aid. Such a certificate from Unitarians or Catholics implies the direct sanction or countenance by government to their respective creeds, and the responsibility, not of *allowing*, but more than this, of *requiring*, that these shall be taught to the children who attend. A bare allowance is but a general toleration; but a requirement involves in it all the mischief, and I would add, the guilt, of an indiscriminate endowment for truth and error.

"2. I would suffer parents or natural guardians to select what parts of the education they wanted for their children. I would not force arithmetic upon them, if all they wanted was writing and reading; and as little would I force the catechism, or any part of the religious instruction that was given in the school, if all they wanted was a secular education. That the managers in the Church of England schools shall have the power to impose their catechism upon the children of Dissenters, and still more, to compel their attendance on church, I regard as among the worst parts of the scheme.

"The above observations, it will be seen, meet any questions which might be put in regard to the applicability of the scheme to Scotland, or in regard to the use of the Douay version in Roman Catholic schools.

"I cannot conclude without expressing my despair of any great or general good being effected in the way of Christianizing our population, but through the medium of a government themselves Christian, and endowing the true religion, which I hold to be their imperative duty, not because it is the religion of the many, but because it is true.

"The scheme on which I have now ventured to offer these few observations I should like to be adopted, not because it is absolutely the best, but only the best in existing circumstances.

"The endowment of the Catholic religion by the state I should deprecate, as being ruinous to the country in all its interests. Still, I do not look for the general Christianity of the people but through the medium of the Christianity of their rulers. This is a lesson taught *historically* in Scripture by what we read there of the influence which the personal character of the Jewish monarchs had on the moral and religious state of their subjects—it is taught *experimentally* by the impotence, now fully established, of the Voluntary principle—and last, and most decisive of all, it is taught *prophetically* in the book of Revelation, when told that then will the kingdoms of the earth (βασιλεῖαι or governing powers) become the kingdoms of our Lord Jesus Christ; or the governments of the earth become Christian governments.—THOMAS CHALMERS."

Within a week of the writing of this paper Dr. Chalmers was no more, and where its meaning seemed ambiguous, there was no one to whom conflicting parties might appeal for the true interpretation. Considerable controversy respecting its precise import arose in the Free Church. Those whose views it favoured naturally enough saw in it more perhaps than the writer meant they should see; and those on whose views it frowned, were reluctant to acknowledge so formidable an authority had pronounced against them. That Hugh Miller was substantially right in his interpretation of its meaning, we cannot doubt. As far as was possible for a man of strong religious sympathies, Dr. Chalmers had committed himself in favour of a state system of secular education. Any ambiguity upon that point is removed by the remembrance of the circumstances in which the paper was written. The document was prepared at the request of the Right Honourable Fox Maule, that it might form material to guide government in dealing with the general subject.

Chalmers and Miller were alike reluctant to recognize Scotland as torn into factions. Both of these great men had rather loved to look upon the nation as still a powerful unity, and in the fact that all the great sections of dissent held substantially a common faith, Miller discerned the basis of a common system of education. In discussing the question, the editor of the *Witness* entered largely into details; Chalmers only indicated general principles. But though united in principle and aim, we rather suspect they would have parted company upon these details. The editor of the *Witness* appears to have borrowed his conception of the popular basis on which he sought to place national education, from the common school-system of New England. And so utterly divested of all those centralizing features, hitherto the chief objection to modern state education, is his scheme—so completely has he made it a thing, not only for the people, but of the people, we are apt to wonder he stopped short of even the voluntary principle. Like Dr. Chalmers, however, Hugh Miller was singularly sceptical of that principle upon certain questions, though, like him also, reposing the amplest faith in its virtues with respect to others. The extremest voluntary could not have resisted the imposition of a poor-rate with more zealous tenacity than both these distinguished men. With that graphic power of illustrating a principle by the reminiscences of his experience, the editor of the *Witness* thus demonstrated to his own satisfaction the injustice of a statutory support of the pauper class.

"We resided and laboured in this part of the country (Edinburgh) for a summer and autumn about eighteen years ago, at a time when wages were high and employment abundant. There was much dissipation among the working classes of the period; and one of our brother workmen, Jock Laidlie, was an extreme specimen of the more dissipated class. Pay-day came round once a fortnight, and then we were sure to lose sight of Jock for about three days. When he came back to resume his labour, he had always a miserable, par-boiled sort of look, as if he had been simmering for half an hour in a caldron over a slow fire. He was invariably, too, in that wretched state of spirits which in those days workmen used to term 'the horrors;' and as men can't get par-boiled and into the 'horrors' for nothing, it was found in every instance, that Jock's whole wages had been dissipated in the process. And such, fortnight after fortnight, was the course pursued by Jock. Now, employment, though easily enough procured in summer and autumn in Jock's profession, was always uncertain in winter, even when the winter proved fine and open; and when frosts were keen and prolonged, and the snow lay long on the ground, there was no employment for even the more fortunate. It was essentially necessary therefore, in the busier seasons, to make provision for the seasons in which business failed. For our own part, we were desirous, we remember, to have the winter all to ourselves, and when Hallowday came round and employment failed, we found ourselves in the possession of twelve pounds, which we had laid by just at its price, if we may so speak. Twelve pounds relieved us from the necessity of labouring for twice twelve weeks. Twelve pounds were sufficient to purchase for us leisure and independence—two very excellent things—from the end of October to the beginning of May; and we were desirous to employ the time thus fairly earned in cultivating a little inheritance which in lesser or larger measure descends to all, and of which no law of appropriation can rob even working men, but which, unless resolutely broken in, and sedulously improved, must lie fallow and unproductive—of no benefit to the possessor, and useless to the community. Jock Laidlie had not laid by a single farthing. We, on a very small scale, were a capitalist determined on making an investment. Jock was a pauper; and here, in a state of great simplicity, in comes the question at issue—Had Jock Laidlie any right to our twelve pounds? To not one copper farthing of it, say we. It was all our own—all honestly earned by the sweat of our brow. We had never claimed to share with Jock in a single gill. We had never enjoyed one whiff of his tobacco. We had never meddled with his earnings; he had no right to intermeddle with ours. But Jock Laidlie had an aged mother, who, without any fault on her part, was miserably poor, just because Jock had failed in his duty towards her

Had Jock Laidlie's mother any right to our twelve pounds? No!—no right. It might doubtless be a duty to help the poor suffering woman, but her claim on us was merely a claim of compassion. She had no right, nor had any third party a right to thrust his hand into our pocket, and out of our hard-earned twelve pounds, to assist Jock Laidlie's mother."

We are not about to enter upon any argument in behalf of voluntaryism, educational or ecclesiastical: all we say of this illustration is, that it points to principles more fatal to state education than they can ever become to any argument in behalf of state provision for the poor. If the unfortunate have no right to life, what claim—what state claim, we mean, have they for instruction? As the greater includes the less, if the right to life is denied, we necessarily deny the right to education.

But we refrain from doing more than simply indicating the path on which such a discussion would inevitably lead. To enter *in extenso* upon the question of voluntary *versus* state education, would be to enter "neither a vineyard nor an oliveyard, but an intricate jungle of briers and thorns, from which those who lose themselves therein, may bring back many scratches, but no food." The issues raised by the controversy have not yet been decided, though the unsatisfactory position in which the whole question of popular education has been left during the last ten years, cannot much longer be tolerated. The chief good Hugh Miller's discussion of the subject accomplished, was an indirect good. It formed the thin edge of the wedge by which successive assemblies of the Free Church have been shattering the vicious system of management that, from the Disruption downwards, has been the bane of that important ecclesiastical organization. It may, indeed, be regretted the good was not achieved without attendant evils. The personalities with which the discussion was garnished, might have been spared, while yet the argument retained its undiminished power. But it is not given to man to accomplish unmixed good. As even the finest gold is not wholly free from alloy, so in the loftiest human wisdom there lurks a grain of folly, and in man's noblest efforts, a something amiss—

> "There's something in this world amiss,
> Shall be unriddled by and by."

The keen eye of Francis Jeffrey noted in the vigorous self-assertion of Burns, rather too fierce and defiant a tone. In the estimation of the great Reviewer, our national bard sometimes mistook the pride of the sturdy peasant for the natural elevation of a generous mind. The shadow of this same vice has occasionally marred the exquisite delicacy of taste and feeling, by which almost all Hugh Miller has done is distinguished. Esteeming him substantially right in his educational controversies, there are yet episodes in these controversies where we cannot veil from ourselves the conviction, swagger is mistaken for strength. A morbid jealousy of his independence seduced him into this error—this weakness.

We are quite aware that, from a very early period, attempts were made to control the *Witness*, and that probably any two men less resolute than its proprietors, would have succumbed to the cumulative influences that sought to seduce from its integrity the solitary independent organ of the Free Church. Dictation and intrigue were, however, equally impotent, equally futile: turning neither to the right hand nor the left, the *Witness* pursued the even tenor of its way, not only undismayed, but inflicting the most terrible chastisement upon all who presumed to cross its path. Doubtless, many of the men with whom its editor dealt so cavalierly, merited his lusty lash, but there were old friends whom the recollections of the days of other years might have spared the merciless castigations he occasionally indulged; and "glimmering through the dream of things that were," was at least one ancient friendship which needed not to have been so rudely sundered. Mistaken as was the earlier course of Dr. Candlish on the education question, he had surely done nothing that might legitimately warrant the scathing sarcasm of these sentences so replete with the extremest susceptibility. "It has been insinuated to us," says Hugh Miller, "that the *Witness* newspaper is pursuing on the educational question a course perilous to itself. We are not careful, we at once say, to answer for ourselves in this matter. The editor of the *Witness* is a humble man, but he stands on other ground than mere salaried functionaries, of whom with all deference it may be affirmed, that 'a breath can make them, as a breath has made.' It is to God, not to patronage, clerical or lay, that he owes that voice with which he addresses himself to a large circle of certainly not the least intelligent of his countrymen, nor does he fear that circle will be ultimately much contracted, should he be compelled to read in behalf of his country, and of a meritorious though neglected class ot men, an occasional sermon to a committee, or even to call a church leader to account."

Had he been content to sink into one of those mere mercenaries of the newspaper-press who frame special pleadings in the cause of party, the opportunity, not unbacked by pecuniary argument, was presented to him at least two years ere he came forward, in conscious weakness, to contend for a good cause against the hostile press of a kingdom. Had he looked to merely secular advantage, he would have quitted his exposed and thankless post of duty long ago. These remarks are unwillingly extorted, nor shall we advert further to the purely personal matter on which they touch, than in the words of our noble motto, "I am in the place where

I am demanded of conscience to speak the truth, and, therefore, the truth I speak, impugn it whoso list." Unfortunately for his own peace, rigid adherence to *his* motto who never feared the face of man, brought the editor of the *Witness* into antagonism with church leaders on other topics than popular education. On the college question, on the question of rating and kindred subjects he was generally found leading the opposition. In most instances, we think, his hostility was well-founded; but unhappily the misunderstandings that arose, the heats and jealousies kindled, had a corroding influence upon his spirit, and ultimately almost completely alienated him from taking part in the discussion of church policy. But though mingling little more in the strife of tongues, the freedom with which he had canvassed the schemes of ecclesiastical leaders, at a time when something very like a dictatorship had destroyed presbyterian parity in the general assemblies of the Free Church, bore fruit. It has been the misfortune of Dr. Candlish that his majorities in the Assembly have too often been made up of the least enlightened of her presbyteries. No one who has been present at any division in that venerable court, can have failed to note that the dexterous church leader mainly owes his success to the adroitness with which he is able to manage the "Highland Host." The prejudices of the north, and the bigotry of the west, have been the buttresses of his power. To humour northern prejudices, and to flatter western bigotry, substantial injustice has not seldom been done to the best interests of the Free Church. Hugh Miller has the honour to have been the first to break up this vicious alliance. His labours were the prelude of that liberal opposition, which, under the leadership of Dr. Hanna, is now gradually leavening the Free Church with more genial sympathies, broader views, and a higher culture, than under the old *régime* she was ever likely to attain.

CHAPTER XVII.

MODERN LIGHT LITERATURE.

TURNING aside from the thorny path of ecclesiastical polemics, Hugh Miller instinctively fell back with renewed ardour upon his favourite topics, literature and geology. As might have been anticipated, he who had so completely mastered the great novelists and essayists of the eighteenth century, had scanned with an eye scarcely less keen, if, perhaps, a little less loving, the great novelists of our own age. It was no more than to be expected that early associations would render a man like Hugh Miller partial to the favourites of his youth. Possibly, were Foster alive to subject the great writers of this age to the same terribly-impartial interrogation as that to which, in his Essays, he subjected the great writers of a past age, they too might be found wanting in much the Christian thinker desiderates. But though still far from perfect, the literary man is not now what he was in the days of Johnson and Addison, Steele and Sterne, Swift and Pope, Wycherly and Congreve. Our age will no longer tolerate the trifling of other and earlier days. In the eighteenth century even the purest *litterateurs* did not escape the taint of the times. The noxious atmosphere of the court of the Second Charles yet radiated all around. So universally had the contagion diffused itself, that Addison—the gentlest spirit of his age—Addison, who wrote of the immortality of the soul and on Christian evidences, and of whom Macaulay has said he deserved as much love and esteem as can justly be claimed by any of our infirm and erring race—even he permitted the vice of his times to become his master, and exposed himself to the coarse wit of Voltaire, who said, The best thing which he had seen come out of Joseph Addison, was the wine he had put in him. In that age literary men seem to have felt none of the responsibility which many of them are now beginning to feel.

It was this utter want of all sense of responsibility which produced that singular combination of frivolousness and fierceness by which the literature of the eighteenth century is characterized. Mingling with the pleasing and innocent prattle of Addison and Steele, might be heard the stinging and waspish satires of Pope, and the savage howl of the dean of St. Patrick's, Jonathan Swift. We have now a more healthy race of writers than that age could boast.

The age of which we write might be called the Augustan age of English literature, so far as the encouragement of literary men was concerned: they basked in the sunshine of royal favour. Addison was a secretary of state, Steele was a commissioner of the stamp-office, Prior was ambassador to France, Tickell held a similar office to Addison. Congreve, Gay, and Dennis all held offices to which very considerable emoluments were attached. But this profusion of patronage purified neither our literature nor our *litterateurs.* The muse of Wycherley and Congreve, and even Dryden, was tainted with the grossest impurity; and not until one whom there was no possibility of mistaking for a Puritan—not until Jeremy Collier lashed into decency the "godless, reckless Jezebel of his age,"—was there any improvement. For a time, indeed, Congreve maintained with Collier an unequal struggle in defence of what was utterly indefensible. At length, however, the literary libertine was compelled to succumb beneath the vigorous blows dealt by the witty high-church parson. Looking back upon that sin-stained and polluted page of our national annals, and contrasting those times with these, we think we may say, without egotism and without presumption, that the relations of literary men to society, are now of a more healthy kind than they have ever been before. No doubt there is still a large mass of our literature requiring an infusion of the moral element to tone and fit it for blessing the nation. But notwithstanding every drawback, this much has been gained: no eminent name in literature would venture to serve up to the nation the grossness and impurity in which some of the most distinguished writers of the eighteenth century revelled. Vice has not yet altogether hid its head; but no man of genius is found prepared to prostitute his powers in garnishing its grossness.

The growing sense of responsibility now animating the literary class, is already exerting a most salutary influence. The press teems with works devoted to the solution of great social problems—a proof that literary men are no longer contented merely to amuse, but are now seeking to mend mankind. This altered phase of our literature is, we are proud to think, the product of our own age. A century ago it had no existence. The *litterateurs* of that time would readily with one consent have buried for the moment their mutual animosities, and united to pooh-pooh it from amongst them as unworthy of consideration. To have a care for the *canaille* was no business of theirs. To write for the improvement of the vulgar herd would have been preposterous. Literature was a heartless, soulless thing in those days; and such as it was then, such it was a century earlier still. John Foster has, with all his peculiar and gloomy power, drawn a picture of the appalling contrast between the mass of England's population in the Elizabethan age as compared with the great men of that world-renowned epoch of our national history. "There was," he says, "then perhaps a learned and vigorous monarch, and there were Cecils, and Walsinghams, and Shaksperes, and Spensers, and Sidneys, and Raleighs, with many other powerful thinkers and actors to render it the proudest age of our national glory. And we thoughtlessly admit on our imagination this splendid exhibition, as in some manner involving or implying the collective state of the people in that age! The ethereal summits of a tract of the moral world, are conspicuous and fair in the lustre of the heavens, and we take no thought of the immensely greater proportion of it which is sunk in gloom and covered with fogs. The general mass of the population, whose physical vigour indeed, and courage, and fidelity to the interests of the country, were of such admirable avail to the purposes, and under the direction of the mighty spirits that wielded their rough agency—this great assemblage was sunk in such mental barbarism as to be placed about the same distance from their illustrious intellectual chiefs, as the hordes of Scythia from the finest spirits of Athens." Thanks to an extended culture, there is now no such marked disparity between teacher and taught, between sage and swain. If the swain has not quite shot up into the philosopher, he is at least capable of understanding him. We look upon this progress with unbroken, unalloyed delight. We are no believers in the sounding nonsense talked by the Twickenham bard about the dangerousness of a little knowledge. Nor do we homologate a statement often in the mouths of the idolaters of the past, that what culture gains in breadth it will inevitably lose in depth—that in the rage for light literature and periodical reading, profound thinkers and profound thinking will disappear. We have often suspected, that those who are loudest in this outcry belong to a class who measure profundity by bulk. Let a man only write some folio volume, and instantly he acquires a reputation for profundity, though inane prolixity and senility be apparent on every page; while if even a more than Plato were to communicate his thoughts through the medium of a magazine or a novel, these solemn fools would designate it a dissipation of your mental energies to trouble yourself with his divine philosophy.

We have a firm faith that God will never leave the world without its legitimate quota of profound thinkers; and if there be any truth in that fine fancy of the poet, found on all lips, which points us to the many mute, inglorious Miltons who walk our earth, what so likely as an extended culture to give to them a tongue and a voice, that thus they may make earth vocal with their melody, and gladden the world with their song? Talk not of the cumulative influences now at work to seduce the thinkers of the age from a profound into a superficial treatment of the problems they are called upon to solve. Every age has its temptations—earlier times were no more without them than our own. To our thinking, the alternating superstitious dread and senseless adulation to which the pioneers of thought were subjected, must have exerted a more wintry influence upon their spirits than any adverse influences their successors are called to combat. From the vague and imperfect knowledge of science, and the dim and shadowy conceptions of the material universe which filled their minds, the thinking of those much-lauded times was necessarily as often puerile as profound. No man of letters need now, as many men of letters in those ages did, build up a seemingly goodly structure reflecting the highest lustre upon their ingenuity and acuteness, but which, from its utter want of any basis of facts, proved nothing better than a card-castle, which the first breath of the zephyr might blow into dust. With all due deference, then, to those who venerate with an idolatrous reverence the bulky tomes of our literary sires, we believe that in the present we shall find as profound thinkers as in any past time. Nor should such a statement be deemed at all extravagant: if, as Carlyle truthfully and humorously remarks, the world has been under way ever since Noah left the ark, we ought to have made some progress—at least, there should be no retrogression, no degeneracy. And we have only to scan our present position, to find there really has been none. We see no necessity for allowing the gloom which clouds the souls of some, as they contrast the past with the present, to cast its pall over our spirits. The bow of God and the everlasting arch of heaven's azure as really o'erspans our horizon as it did all our fathers'. A question very naturally suggests itself here, To what do we owe this advancement of society—this progress of the race! We stay not to indicate all the varied elements which have combined to produce so gratifying a result. Our business now is with the purely literary element. That *it* has imparted a very powerful and very salutary impetus to society, will, we presume, be disputed by none, except perchance the autocrat whose attempts to throttle it have been thwarted, or some college of cardinals who have beheld their darling dogmas toppling to their fall beneath its influence.

We know no more interesting study than tracing the progress of this power from its state of nonage to its present maturity and position. In its earlier and infantile condition, we find it alternately flattered and frowned upon by the great ones of the earth, as they imagined it either served or subverted their purposes —seconded or thwarted their ambition. Now, it has grown into an authority which, on occasion, makes the mighty of the earth tremble. Formerly statesmen could afford to dispense with the aid of literature, and could affect to despise its paper-shot; now there is no measure they can hope to carry until it has been thoroughly ventilated by the press. Formerly ecclesiastical corporations and ecclesiastical courts could riot, unchecked, in the caprices of tyranny or rapacity; now every indication of the exercise of the one, or the indulgence of the other, is instantaneously denounced by this subtle and lynx-eyed power.

Not the periodical press alone, but the novelist has found in these abuses material to interest the people while influencing authority. Conspicuous among those who have almost become a political power through the popular novel, is Charles Dickens. It may be a question with critics how far Dickens has, in his more recent writings, been sacrificing permanent fame for immediate effect, by entering this fertile and inviting field; but there can be no question about the effect. Lawyers have reclaimed against the treatment they have met with in "Bleak House;" and had only lawyers complained, they might perhaps have been left to nurse their sorrow and their wrath. Unfortunately, from caricaturing Chancery, Dickens passed to caricaturing Christianity. Like the late Lord Jeffrey, Hugh Miller enjoyed the most exquisite gratification from the genial and genuinely English writings of the prince of modern novelists. Nevertheless, he was unable to refrain from embodying in one of his latest and most elaborate articles, a stern dissent from the mode in which Dickens has abused the opportunities of the novelist in burlesquing the sanctities of a day, the sole relic of an innocence that is no more, and still the sacrament of benison and blessing sin cannot destroy:—

"Never was Burke more essentially wrong, and never was he more popularly right, than, when speaking of the high tone of civilization in the court of France, he described it as that unbought grace of life 'by which vice itself loses half its evil by losing all its grossness.' It is not vice, but the accessories of vice, that shock the feelings of worldly men. A fine gentleman of the Feejee Islands, when he happens to quarrel with one of his wives, and is resolved that her fate shall be an example to the rest, takes her into a field, and orders her to prepare and heat a native oven; which being done, he clubs her, and putting her into the oven, coolly sits down till she is sufficiently baked, when he devours her at his leisure. On hearing of such an atrocity, the good-natured world holds up its hands in horror and amazement; while a plain story of every-day murder excites very little attention. In like manner, it is not virtue, but the mere adjuncts of virtue, that command the admiration of the vulgar. And these, in order to please the popular taste, must be painted in the most glaring and exaggerated colours, like Tony's 'Bet Bouncer of these parts,' who had 'two eyes as black as sloes, and cheeks as broad and red as a pulpit-cushion.' Well did our old writers of romance know this failing of humanity; and, therefore, when vice was to be pourtrayed, it stalked forth

'A monster of such hideous mien,
As, to be hated, needs but to be seen;'

and when virtue was brought on the stage, she appeared in pure white muslin and all sorts of bedizenments, like the heroine of a provincial theatre. Our popular romancer, Mr. Dickens, has improved on this ancient plan. He has the same sort of audience to deal with; he also must consult the taste of the groundlings; but, to diversify the entertainment he has contrived to clothe his vicious characters with some of the most attractive attributes of virtue, and to exhibit virtue in some of the most repulsive habiliments of vice. His Newman Noggs and Dick Swivellers,—characters which, if met in actual life, would be studiously avoided by all who had a character to lose,—he invests with the most amiable qualities, borrowed, like their garments, from better men. On the other hand, his Pecksniffs and Dombeys, who, we doubt not, were very virtuous and excellent men in their own way, it is his delight to depict as the most detestable of human beings. To give still greater zest to this strange compound, another ingredient has been thrown in. Born in an age when religion appears as 'life in earnest,'—when its influence cannot be gainsaid, and its fruits cannot be hid,—Mr. Dickens is yet a professed worshipper of nature. And, as the result of this anachronism, many of the warmest admirers of his genius (and we profess ourselves among the number) cannot fail to regret that, while he has invested his anything-but-devotional characters with all that is pure, and lovely, and of good report, he has uniformly exhibited his would-be religious ones with every quality that can excite odium and contempt. Nor is this all. We fear we must add, that to religion he has transferred all the grossnesses of vice; and that, borrowing without acknowledgment from the wardrobe of religion, he has clad nature in all the graces of virtue. His heroes and heroines are held up as spotless and charming without religion; alas! all the more spotless and charming because without it. Now, we are no ascetics, and few things excite our bile more than the fopperies of some pretended religionists. Nothing gives us more pleasure than to see the mask torn off from the unmanly face that would employ the cant of pietism to gloze over selfishness or sensuality; or to look at a good caricature of the unwomanly zeal which would parade a Christianity without charity, or a charity that begins anywhere but at home. But if we know anything of Christianity, it is the very perfection of charity, and of everything that is pure, and lovely, and blessed. Why, then, present it only in its caricature? We like to see the bad shilling nailed to the counter; but where is the genuine metal? 'Surely, Mr. Dickens,' one feels compelled to exclaim, 'you must have been singularly unhappy in the specimens of Christianity you have met with. If one may judge from the figure which it cuts in your pages, you must never have seen it apart from the sulky scowl of the bigot, the odious squint of hypocrisy, or the greasy dawdling simper of half-crazed fanaticism. On no occasion can it have been your lot to see Christian principle and piety in alliance with manly dignity or female loveliness. For certainly, in all the brilliant creations of your genius, religion seldom if ever appears, except in the form of a grim sprite, casting its cold shadow on every scene of innocence and gaiety into which it intrudes.'

"What 'Little Dorrit' may turn out to be it is not for us, who are seated before the curtain, to say; but already has the reader been prepared for a stroke at the inner sanctities of religious life, in the form of an attack on some of the most questionable of its outer demonstrations. A gentleman of the name of Clennam is introduced, overcharged with melancholy, which is traced to a stern religious training, and which, strangely enough continues to hang about him, even after spending twenty summers in China. This middle-aged gentleman gives a sad account of his parents. 'Staid people, as the phrase is, professors of a stern religion, their very religion was a gloomy sacrifice of tastes and sympathies that were never their own, offered up as a part of a bargain for the security of their possessions. Austere faces, inexorable discipline, penance in this world and terror in the next, —nothing graceful or gentle anywhere, and the void in my cowed heart everywhere; this was my childhood, if I may so misuse the word as to apply it to such a beginning of life.' This hideous sketch, however, only forms the back-ground to the picture that follows, in which we see the reflection of the past, with its dark shades and slimy reptiles crawling over the imagination of the religion-haunted man:—

"'Mr. Arthur Clennam sat in the window of the coffee-house on Ludgate Hill, counting one of the neighbouring bells, making sentences and burdens of songs out of it in spite of himself, and wondering how many sick people it might be the death of in the course of a year. As the hour approached, its changes of measure made it more and more exasperating. At the quarter it went off into a condition of deadly lively importunity, urging the populace in a voluble manner to Come to Church, Come to Church, Come to Church! At the ten minutes it became aware that the congregation would be scanty, and slowly hammered out in low spirits, They won't come, they won't come, they won't come! At the five minutes it abandoned hope, and shook every house in the neighbourhood, for three hundred seconds, with one dismal swing per second, as a groan of despair.

"'Thank Heaven,' said Clennam, when the hour struck, and the bell stopped.

"'But its sound had revived a long train of miserable Sundays, and the procession would not stop with the bell, but continued to march on. 'Heaven forgive me,' said he, 'and those who trained me. How I have hated this day!"

"And then come 'the dreary Sunday of his childhood,'—'the sleepy Sunday of his boyhood,'—'the interminable Sunday of his nonage,'—and 'the resentful Sunday of a little later, when he sat glowering and glooming through the tardy length of the day, with a sullen sense of injury in his heart, and no more knowledge of the beneficent history of the New Testament than if he had been bred among idolaters. There was a legion of Sundays, all days of unserviceable bitterness and mortification, slowly passing before him.' All this might have passed as a satire upon certain Puritanic habits which may have existed in England at some remote period; and the exception made in favour of 'the beneficent history of the New Testament,' may be held a sufficient, though certainly a very cheap method for buying off a dark suspicion, which might otherwise militate rather expensively against the reputation of the writer. But Mr. Dickens has left us no room to doubt that his object is, under cover of reprobating a forced observance of Sunday, which is as ridiculous as it must be rare, to aim at the citadel of the Sabbath itself, and to vindicate a loose un-English observance, or rather non-observance, of that day, in the style in which it has been advocated by the Holyoakes and other disciples of the naturalist school. The following description identifies him with the party:—

"'Everything was bolted and barred that could by possibility furnish relief to an overworked people. No pictures, no unfamiliar animals, no rare plants or flowers, no natural or artificial wonders of the ancient world,—all *taboo* with that enlightened strictness that the ugly South Sea gods in the British museum might have supposed themselves at home again. Nothing to see but streets, streets, streets. Nothing to breathe but streets, streets, streets. Nothing to change the brooding mind, or raise it up. Nothing for the spent toiler to do, but to compare the monotony of his seventh day with the monotony of his six days, think what a weary life he led, and make the best of it, or the worst, according to the probabilities.'

"Nothing is easier, with such a fancy as that of Dickens, than to cull out of an overgrown metropolis materials for the gloomy sketch he has drawn; though, even to the eye of a poet, the spectacle of London's mighty heart quieted for one day from the incessant throbbings of the week, and the hard-toiled artisan permitted to enjoy a day of unbroken rest of body and mind in the bosom of his family and the devotions of the sanctuary, might have suggested a more pleasing, and certainly more rational picture. The scene of repose of which Dickens has given such a doleful view, if transferred to the country, would suggest only images of delight; and why should the overwrought sons of labour in towns be denied the opportunity of visiting such scenes, except on the only day which religion has provided for them? We confess we cannot understand the mawkish sentimentalism which would deny them a single hour during the week, which is the property of man, and then, with an affectation of great liberality, hand them over a present of the day which is the property of God. But, indeed, the world would rob man even of that day, if it could; and, instead of shut shops and silent streets, we should soon have the unremitting sweat and swelter, roar and revelry of a Parisian Sunday. We recollect of being struck, on a certain holiday, when the gay crowds, released from their employments, were jostling and jesting along the streets, by seeing a hearse pass mournfully along, with all the dismal pomp and paraphernalia which seems such a mockery of woe. And as it moved onward, shaking its plumed head with ominous meaning at the happy faces turned up to it, how true it is, we thought, that death keeps no holiday. And were it not for Christianity, Mammon would keep no holiday. His grating wheels would roll on with ruthless intermission; and to every cry from its agonized slaves, the answer would be that of the Egyptian monarch, 'Ye are idle, ye are idle: therefore ye say, Let us go and do sacrifice. Go now, therefore, and work.'

"Every one has his own taste; but to ours, we confess, melancholy as is Mr. Dickens's account of stern sabbatarianism, there is something still more gloomy in the thought of genius cringing at the feet of vulgar vice, and pandering to the low tastes and worse passions of a London mob. It reminds one of the days of Moloch, and irresistibly suggests the image of smiling childhood, garlanded with flowers, and sacrificed, amidst music and frankincense, to some bloodthirsty deity. And perhaps the most dangerous and seductive form which irreligion assumes in the present day, is that which affects the language of natural religion, rears crystal palaces in which to offer the fruits of the ground as sacrifices, appropriates the Sabbath as the best and the only day for this species of Cain-worship, and engages as its priests and hierophants our men of science and the most popular writers of the day. It may be vain to reason with such men, so long as their minds remain so obtuse to the paramount claims of religion, and so long as they maintain the low-minded faith, that man's enjoyments and aspirations are limited to the present life. It may be vain to remind them, that ere the common people can appreciate natural beauty, they must be trained by previous moral and mental culture; else Nature, viewed in her loveliest forms and her loftiest moods, will fail to quench a single lust, or inspire a single generous emotion. It may be equally vain to impress upon them the weighty words of Pope, that 'He who considers this earthly spot as the only theatre of his existence and its grave, instead of the first stage in a progressive being, can never view nature with a cheerful, or man with a benevolent eye.' But there is another view of the matter to which, as more immediately touching themselves, they may be presumed more accessible. The most earthly-minded secularist is not willing to forego, in behalf of his writings, the immortality which he disclaims for himself. And yet, nothing is more certain than that literary productions that have been prostituted to the service of vice and irreligion, are incapable of long life. They want the principle of vitality; their wages is death. Dryden, with all his genius, and Butler, with all his wit, have not been able to preserve, the one his licentious plays, or the other his once famous satire, from a neglect bordering on oblivion. The filth and garbage of our literature, which pleased for a time the lovers of such stuff, have sunk to the bottom, leaving only what was pure and fresh to flow down the stream of time into immortality. Bad as mankind may be, they have no idea of erecting monuments to the memory of people whose sole distinction was their agility in pulling down the fences and trampling on the sanctities of moral obligation. Even though they may be amused with such antics, they have no respect for the performer, whom they may inwardly despise, as the profligate shuns by day the scene of his nightly debauch.

Entertaining, as we do, a real liking to the man, as well as admiration of the writer, fain would we whisper in the ear of Mr. Dickens, that his is a genius too genial, as well as lofty, to become the common drudge of metropolitan rascality, or the common drain for carrying off and diffusing throughout the country the fetid streams which can only raise a crop of rank and unwholesome vegetation; that we dread the effect of such writing as he has chosen to indulge in on young and ardent minds; and that his own reputation depends on devoting his talents, which are so well fitted for the task, to the moral elevation of his fellow-men. Let us respectfully remind him that the Romans at first had a joint temple dedicated to virtue and honour, and afterwards, when they allotted separate fanes to them, they were so placed that no one could enter the temple of honour without passing through that of virtue. And let us kindly part with him in the words of the poet of immortality,—

> 'Virtue alone out-builds the Pyramids;
> Her monuments shall last when Egypt is no more.' "

This elaborately severe reprehension of certain marked tendencies of the writings, while rendering the amplest homage to the genius of Dickens, may possibly be looked upon by southern admirers of the great novelist as only an amusing illustration of Scottish narrowness.

Our Gallic neighbours have a theory, that English thought partakes of the limitation and isolation of England's soil. Something very similar to prepossessions which on the further shores of the straits of Dover are found so freely cherished respecting Albion, would seem to have taken possession of Englishmen regarding Scotland. Such of our countrymen as wander south and get metamorphosed into cockneys, may be permitted to pronounce upon the merits of southern authors; but criticism by a Scotchman who has not crossed the border, is for the most part looked upon, not in the light of its own merits, but through the blinding mists of national prejudices. That Hugh Miller's opinion of Dickens is an opinion pretty prevalent among the more reflective portion of Scotchmen does not, we presume, admit of doubt, however much southern friends may dispute the competency of Scottish taste to decide on English wit.

We should not, perhaps, be disposed altogether to acquiesce in the charge of pandering to a debased popular sentiment, which, if not directly made, is rather broadly hinted as a sin of the novelist. Dickens is, we believe, in this respect altogether above suspicion. The author who has not stooped to humour "the throne," is not likely to be guilty of any mean compliances to humour the mob. The truth is, Dickens owes his immense popularity to the fact, that at once in his faults and excellencies, his strength and weakness, he is a perfect representative of the English mind, minus the theological element; and so feeble is that element in a large section of Englishmen, its absence from the writings of their favourite author is hardly felt. But while this is the condition of England, Scotland has been, so to speak, saturated with theology; and to a man like Hugh Miller, on whom almost a double portion of the national tendency and predilection had fallen, nothing was more natural than to imagine what never, unless by design and the most studied intention, could be overlooked or misrepresented by himself, must have been intentionally misrepresented by the novelist.

Calvinian theology, so universally the theology of Scotland, has found but comparatively little favour south of the Tweed. We are quite aware, some of England's greatest theologians have been Calvinists; but at this hour the writings of these theologians are more read and more reverenced by Scotchmen than by Englishmen. Veneration for usages and ideas understood to be peculiarly associated with Calvinistic tenets, has never been very great in England. Knox brought with him from Geneva an idea of the man Calvin, which, blending with the dogmas of his theology, left an image of greatness and power that for ever associates itself in the Scottish mind with the memory of the stern Genevan reformer. Among Englishmen, even Englishmen hold ing substantially a Calvinistic creed, no such hallowed conception of the great Frenchman is found to exist. Cowper's theology is well known, yet Cowper could say of Calvin:—

"Religion, in him intolerant, austere,
Parent of manners like himself severe,
Drew a rude copy of the Christian face,
Without the smile, the sweetness, or the grace."

Dickens's caricatures of religious characters, are little more than an amplification of Cowper's lines; indeed, the epithets which the bard of Olney has brought together in this single verse, would almost exhaust the portraits of religious life Dickens has drawn. Given a character intolerant, austere, with a needless severity of manner, and lacking the smile, the sweetness, and the grace of Christianity, and we realize to the life the glowing asceticism of Dickens's religious characters.

Noticing not only in Dickens, but in other scarcely less popular modern English novelists, pious people always painted of the same obnoxious school, we suspect it must surely be a degenerate Calvinism compared with the Scottish type—a sort of parasitic plant that has entwined itself with a certain order of the English mind. In Kingsley's "Alton Locke" we recognize the same disgusting features in the religious characters, that so sicken us in the novels of Dickens. They are Calvinistic clergymen who devour Widow Locke's house, and for a pretence make long prayers during the process. It may, therefore, be possible that Scotchmen do English authors an injustice in sometimes mistaking for caricature what has been copied from the life. It may be that, like plants which flourish luxuriantly in their own proper latitude, but which get dwarfed so soon as transferred to a less genial soil, some forms of faith may acquire a maturity, a strength, and a nobleness among certain peoples, which degenerate into a puerile fanaticism among peoples less fitted to profit by their peculiar power.

CHAPTER XVIII.

SCIENCE.

As years rolled away, Hugh Miller felt his early passion for science growing upon him. The storms of ecclesiastical controversy had subsided, and though he bore himself nobly and as a man of honour throughout the great church struggle, yet the editor of the *Witness* made no secret of the regret he felt for some of the more personal controversies in which he had been engaged. It was occasionally his lot, during the latter years of his life, to meet some of those towards whom, in the earlier part of his connection with the *Witness*, he had violated the dictates of good taste. When he found men on whom in other days he had poured the vials of his sevenfold wrath, forgetful of the past and all that had been personal between them, had nothing for him save honour and attention, the recollection of these rencounters was intolerable.

Nor was the recoil of such feelings weakened by the mode in which some he had served only too well, were disposed to treat his labours. His fame was indeed no longer in the keeping of any sect or party. But to a man with the deep attachments of which Hugh Miller was capable, the approbation of his party would naturally often be set above the fame which came from a more extended arena. When therefore he discovered that approbation could only be purchased by stooping to the immoralities of party, and laying the *Witness* at the feet of a conclave of ecclesiastical censors, was it wonderful his manly but sensitive heart sickened, and became suspicious of the combination of mendacity and meanness with which his work was rewarded. We hope we shall not be misunderstood here. It was no vulgar reward Hugh Miller sought. Indeed, such recognitions of service as are usually only too highly esteemed in this world, had not been wanting. The money originally invested in the *Witness*, was offered him through Dr. Chalmers, as something of a honorarium for his eminent services, but as resolutely declined as it was handsomely tendered.

When, at a subsequent period, Professor Miller representing a select circle of opulent Free Churchmen, waited upon him to intimate a resolution to bestow a testimonial in the form of a mansion, the proposal met the same fate. "I know," said the editor of the *Witness* in reply to his friend, "I know that, as the defender of Free-church principles, my intentions have been pure and loyal, but I am not quite sure I have always been successful in doing the right thing, nor have I done anything that is worthy of such consideration from my friends. I believe my way is to make yet." But though perfectly aware he possessed a large body of the sincerest admirers, he was also aware his independent conduct had created numerous jealousies among that considerable section of the clergy of the Free Church, who possess no higher idea of the function of a newspaper editor, than that he should be the echo of their every crotchet and every whim. Naturally enough these gentlemen felt irritated "this courser of the sun could not be yoked in the harness of the dray-horse." It was only to be anticipated the consciousness such feelings were entertained respecting him would have strengthened his distaste for ecclesiastical controversy; and during several of the last years of his life, he took but little interest in those squabbles which furnish so much excitement to polemical divines. He saw, moreover, what too many ecclesiastics did not see—that since the Disruption other foes to truth, and other antagonists to Christianity had arisen, than any against whom the Free Church had lifted her protest. Not some mere outwork or unimportant position of the evidences of revealed religion was now called in question, but its most fundamental verities. A pseudo-philosophy sought to supersede creation by development. "Vestiges of the Natural

History of Creation," and the discoveries of good Mr. Crosse, it was thought, were about to resolve life into a compound of albumen and electricity, and track the genealogy of man through a maze of degrading links down to not the monkey only, but the mollusc. Based upon the speculations of Lamark and Oken, and gathering into itself whatever seemed the semblance of support from all the realms of science, written in a popular and fascinating style, the "Vestiges" had nearly as great a run as the last novel. In its unprecedented popularity, Mr. Miller felt a call to put forth what he deemed the theory of true science on the subjects it mainly treated. Without loss of time, the "Footprints of the Creator" was got ready. From the facts of science, and on the soundest principles of the inductive philosophy, did Hugh Miller demolish the specious sophisms of the "Vestiges." This work largely enhanced his reputation. The "Footprints" were noticed with approbation by the most eminent savans of Europe. A reply was attempted in the sequel to the "Vestiges," but no effectual rejoinder was made to the argument of Mr. Miller, while the breastwork of facts with which he had fortified his theory remained unshaken. Meanwhile Lord Rosse's telescope exploded the nebular hypothesis. The basis of his theory overthrown, the author of the "Vestiges" was taught, in a sense more saddening than Campbell sung them, the truth of those well-known lines—

> "When science from creation's face
> Enchantment's veil withdraws,
> What lovely visions yield their place
> To cold material laws."

Friends who knew the growing devotion of Mr. Miller to purely scientific studies, and who rejoiced in the splendid results of those studies, from this time bethought themselves if it were not possible to procure for him some position where he might give himself unreservedly to the work to which he seemed eager to consecrate his best energies. His own high literary and scientific fame, the devotion with which he had served the cause of the Disruption, together with the admirable business arrangements of his copartner in the proprietary of the *Witness*, Mr. Fairley, had made of that journal an excellent newspaper property. What was wanted was simply that Mr. Miller might be secured some situation where he would not be subjected to the incessant toil constant contribution to a public journal necessarily entails. At this juncture he was offered, through the Marquis of Breadalbane, a Government situation, very similar to the situation Wordsworth so long held. The duties would have been merely nominal, but he would have been responsible for considerable sums of money passing through the hands of his subordinates. The appointment would have yielded a salary of some £800 per annum, and what of work he would have required to do, was of a nature which his early training in the bank would have enabled him to discharge with the utmost ease. He had been all but persuaded to accept the situation. His friends, Drs. Guthrie and Hanna, accompanied him to the chambers of the political agent who would have ratified the formalities of the appointment. Before entering the office he hesitated, asked his friends a few minutes for further consideration, and pacing up and down Heriot Row, he suddenly stopped, and addressing Dr. Hanna, said, "Doctor, I have made up my mind to refuse. I find my memory not now so good as it was formerly. I forget things I was wont to remember with ease. I am not clear in such circumstances about taking upon me any money responsibility." Remonstrance was vain; his resolution was fixed. No persuasion of friends could induce him to alter his resolve. He felt he could not conscientiously take the situation. Was this confusion of memory which already haunted him, a premonition of that more awful confusion in which not memory alone, but reason and life, were ultimately extinguished?

Such was, we believe, the first and the last attempt made to secure for Mr. Miller a position where he might have given himself wholly to the special duties in which he felt so paramount an interest. At an early period of his connexion with the *Witness*, he had been offered a situation on the *Times*. The salary was such as showed the high estimate of his powers entertained in Printing House Square; but circumstances precluded its acceptance. Afterwards, in the city of his adoption, and in connection with the university, chairs were vacant none could have filled more worthily, but no chair was ever offered him. Had the author of "The Old Red Sandstone" been appointed Professor of Natural History in the University of Edinburgh, in a few years his class would have become as popular as were the moral philosophy classes of Dugald Stewart, Thomas Brown, and Professor Wilson, or as was the class of logic and metaphysics under Sir William Hamilton. And yet, now that all is done, perhaps there is a greater symmetry about the life of this self-made man as it is, than had fortune lifted him out of the peculiar sphere in which he had gathered so much renown, into any government or municipal appointment.

In the last years of his life, awakened to a conception of the importance of diffusing a taste for science among his countrymen, throwing aside his constitutional reserve, Mr. Miller betook himself to the lecture-room, and on not a few platforms, both in his native land and across the border, did he discourse on his favourite study. The date, we believe, of his first appearance in this new capacity is 1852. His audience, on the occasion of his maiden effort, was an audience of working men: his chairman was the Duke of Argyle.

The earliest opportunity we enjoyed of hearing him discourse on the mysteries of geology was in the City Hall of Glasgow, when fulfilling an engagement with the Young Men's Christian Association. The next time we had the pleasure of listening to his oral instructions was in Queen Street Hall, Edinburgh, when fulfilling an engagement with the philosophical Institution of the metropolis. On that occasion, just recovering from a somewhat protracted illness, his friend, Professor Miller, did the duties of reader with admirable effect, himself describing the specimens and fossils brought from his museum, to illustrate the lectures. Two of the finest papers in his last work were read upon the occasion. At these lectures it was we first saw her whose name and story are now imperishably associated with his own. There on a front bench of Queen Street Hall, amidst that numerous and brilliant auditory, not unjustly elate, we may presume, with the magnificent reception of the lecturer, sat,

> "The prudent partner of his blood.
> Wearing the rose of womanhood."

Unfortunately Mr. Miller took the field too late in life ever to acquire the fluency necessary to render his platform appearances altogether comfortable to himself.

Even as a lecturer, however, though utterly unacquainted with the tricks of art, he was highly popular. Wherever he went, crowds flocked to listen. In Glasgow and in London, taking into account the recondite character of the topics he discussed, he was the most acceptable man that appeared before the Christian institutes of these cities; while, at the Edinburgh Philosophical Institution, of all the eminent men whom that admirably-conducted association brought to Edinburgh, no one commanded such audiences as assembled in Queen Street Hall to listen to his prelections. Such services were always cheerfully and readily given, so far as time and strength would allow—often, indeed, beyond his strength, solely for the luxury of doing good. With his friend, Professor Miller, he began his career as a lecturer; both of these gentlemen, with an equal generosity, gave whatever services they have been able to render the cause of popular education entirely gratuitously. Hugh Miller, though he might have pocketed thousands by such labours, preferred to do what work he could accomplish in that way without fee or reward. In this disinterested trait of character we are reminded of Burns, who, not as a hired soldier, but as a patriot, would strive for the glory of his country; so, casting from him the poor six-pence a-day, he served zealously as a volunteer.

The "Testimony of the Rocks" may be deemed the

memorial of his platform labours, and with characteristic affection it is dedicated to Professor Miller. Dr. Miller was regarded by the editor of the *Witness* as one of the best men he had ever met—a genuinely leal-hearted friend, and was, we believe, the only man from whom he ever could accept a favour, without the acceptance weighing upon his spirits in a most unaccountable and uncomfortable manner. So completely knit in feeling and sympathy were the two men, any obligation the professor might confer upon the geologist, was received at once in the spirit it was tendered. Indeed so little did the feeling in question,—overpowering on all other occasions and with all other individuals, attach itself to the good offices of Dr. Miller, that in the dedication of "The Testimony" he had almost forgotten to notice the professional kindness to which he owed so much. On reading the dedication in manuscript to Mrs. Miller, the quick eye of Lydia detected the omission; and gently reminding her husband at once of his own neglect and Dr. Miller's character, by a couplet in which the bard of Twickenham described an eminent, and benevolent as eminent, physician of his day, on the recital of the lines, Hugh Miller instantaneously rose from his desk, and taking a volume of Pope from one of the shelves of his library, he added to the dedication the tasteful recognition of Dr. Miller's services embodied in this sentence—

"Your kind attentions and advice during the crisis of my illness, were certainly everyway suited to remind me of those so graphically acknowledged by the wit of the last century, when he bethought him of

> "Kind Arbuthnot's aid,
> Who knew his art, but not his trade."

Of this latest effort of Hugh Miller's genius, this is not the place to speak, except in so far as it is connected with the personal history of the closing scene of his existence. It is enough to say, it nobly crowns the labours of a noble life, and will take rank with the works of the fathers of English geology, even for the profundity of its science; while in affluence of illustration, in wealth and beauty of poetic diction, it is unapproached by either Buckland or Murchison, Sedgewick or Lyell.

It may indeed be admitted, that Mr. Miller's sacred hermeneutics are not equal to his scientific attainments. It was not in the region of Biblical criticism his great strength lay. Hosts of much inferior men distanced him in that domain. We do not expect, therefore, the purely critical, and what may be called the exegetical portion of "The Testimony of the Rocks" will be received with the same unqualified admiration, or will command the same unhesitating acceptance, as the speculations of Mr. Miller in the field of pure science have never failed to call forth. Other readings of the story of the first chapter of Genesis will be resorted to, and possibly "The Vision," set in all the glory of his most superb descriptive efforts, may be found without foundation, save in his imperial imagination. Yet even were it so—even if the hypothesis embodied in that vision was thrown aside as untenable, "The Testimony of the Rocks" would never fall into that class of works, the productions of second-rate minds, working at second-hand upon materials which higher genius and deeper culture had brought near to them. Its science, its eloquence, its poetry, are all too original to admit of it ever being overtaken by such a fate.

To such of our readers as have not met the work we commend the following selections, made, not indeed upon any consecutive plan, but only with a view to give an idea of the power and style of "The Testimony"—

CREATION PROGRESSIVE.

"Whether we look to the inspired record in Genesis, or the disclosures of geology, we are taught that the work of creation was a progressive one. First, there may have been a time when the earth was simply mineral; then it appears clothed with plants; animals in due time come forth to browse upon them: and, as the completion, man stands up to gaze with intelligent eye upon the whole. There is a unity of plan running along all this series. The plant, when it comes, is higher than the mineral—a new power, the vital, has been superinduced; but still the organic is dependent for nourishment on the inorganic, and all the forces which operate in the mineral are active in the plant. Look at the more complicated crystals—look at the frostworks on our flagstones and windows, so like the tree in their ramifications—and you at once see that powers are operating there which are to appear in a more advanced form in the plant. When the animal appears, it has something not in the plant—in particular, it has a power of sensation and voluntary motion; but still it retains all the power that is in the mineral, and is dependent for food on the vegetable; and so clearly are the plant and the brute allied, that it is difficult to draw a line which will decidedly separate the higher forms of the one from the lower forms of the other. And when man walks forth to contemplate all these objects, it is evident that there is a higher principle in him, which is not in the mineral, or in the plant, or in the brute; but it is just as clear that he has affinities with the lower creation, arising from the lower creation tending upwards towards him. Made of the dust of the ground, his bodily frame is subject to all the inorganic laws of the world, and at last returns to the dust, out of which it was formed. As an organism, he is subject to all organic laws; he needs breath and food from without, and has an allotted period of existence. As an animal, his bones and his muscles, his very nerves and brain, are after the same model as those of the brutes; like them, he needs organized matter whereon to feed; and, like them, he is susceptible of pleasure and pain. It may be maintained that the lower animals are, in a sense, anticipations of humanity, and have appetites, instincts, attachments—as for offspring and home—perceptions, and a sort of intelligence, which, though not identical with, are homologous to, certain of the lower endowments of man.

"All this does not prove, as some would argue, that man is merely an upper brute—possibly sprung from the monkey, or removed from it only as one species is from another. In his bodily frame he may be simply a new species—the highest of animated organisms—with the fore limbs turned into hands, and his frame raised into an upright attitude,—and even in this, so far anticipated by the ape. But in his soul, endowed with the power of discovering necessary and immutable truth, and of discerning the difference between good and evil: capable of cherishing voluntary affections—which alone (and not mere instinctive attachments) are deserving of the name of love,—and of rising to the knowledge of God, and of communion with him; by reason of this soul—responsible and immortal—he belongs not merely to a new species or genus of nature, but to a new order in creation. In respect of this, his nobler part, he is made not after the likeness of the brute, but after the image of God. He stands on this earth, but with upright face he looks upward to heaven.

THE FIRST BEE.

"The first bee makes its appearance in the amber of the Eocene, locked up hermetically in its gem-like tomb,—an embalmed corpse in a crystal coffin,—along with fragments of flower-bearing herbs and trees. The first of the Bombycidæ, too—insects that may be seen suspended over flowers by the scarce visible vibration of their wings, and sucking the honied juices by means of their long, slender trunks, —also appear in the amber, associated with moths, butterflies, and a few caterpillars. Bees and butterflies are present in increased proportions in the latter tertiary deposits, but not until that terminal creation to which we ourselves belong, was ushered on the scene, did they receive their fullest development. There is exquisite poetry in Wordsworth's reference to 'the soft murmur of the vagrant bee'—

'A slender sound, yet hoary Time
Doth to the soul exalt it with the chime
Of all his years; a company
Of ages coming, ages gone,
Nations from before them sweeping.'

And yet, mayhap, the naked scientific facts of the history of this busy insect are scarcely less poetic than the pleasing imagination of the poet regarding it. They tell that man's world, with all its griefs and troubles, is more emphatically a world of flowers than any of the creations which have preceded it; and that, as one great family—the grasses—were called into existence, in order, apparently, that he might enter in favouring circumstances upon his two earliest avocations, and be in good hope a keeper of herds, and a tiller of the ground; and as another family of plants—the Rosaceæ—was created in order that the gardens which it would be also one of his vocations to keep and to dress, should have their trees 'good for food and pleasant to the taste;' so flowers in general were profusely produced just ere he appeared, to minister to that sense of beanty which distinguishes him from all the lower creatures, and to which he owes not a few of his most exquisite enjoyments. The poet accepted the bee as a sign of high significance: the geologist also accepted her as a sign. Her entombed remains testify to the gradual fitting up of our earth as a place of habitation for a creature destined to seek delight for the mind and the eye, as certainly as for the grosser senses, and in especial marks the introduction of the stately forest trees, and the arrival of the delicious flowers.

THE LIASSIC AGES.

"There are tridactyle footprints in the red sandstones of Connecticut that measure eighteen inches in length from the heel to the middle claw, nearly thirteen inches in breadth from the outer to the inner toe, and which indicate, from their distance apart in the straight line, a stride of about six feet in the creature that impressed them in these ancient sands,—measurements that might well startle zoologists who had derived their experience of the ornithic class from existing birds exclusively. . . . I have already referred to flying dragons,—real existences of the Oolitic period,—that were quite as extraordinary of type, if not altogether so huge of bulk, as those with which the seven champions of Christendom used to do battle; and here are we introduced to birds of the Liassic ages that were scarcely less gigantic than the roc of Sinbad the sailor. They are fraught with strange meanings, these footprints of the Connecticut. They tell of a time far removed into the by-past eternity, when great birds frequented by myriads the shores of a nameless lake, to wade into its shallows in quest of mail-covered fishes of the ancient type, or long extinct molluscs; while reptiles equally gigantic, and of still stranger proportions, haunted the neighbouring swamps and savannahs; and when the same sun that shone on the tall moving forms beside the waters, and threw their long shadows across the red-sands, lighted up the glades of deep forests, all of whose fantastic productions,—tree, bush, and herb,—have even in their very species long since passed away. And of this scene of things only the footprints remain, 'footprints on the sands of time,' that tell us, among other matters, whence the graceful American poet derived his quiet, but singularly effective and unmistakeably indigenous figure.

MAN'S DESTINY.

"The appearance of man upon the scene of being constitutes a new era in creation; the operations of a new *instinct* come into play,—that *instinct* which anticipates a life after the grave, and reposes in implicit faith upon a God alike just and good, who is the pledged 'rewarder of all who diligently seek Him.' And in looking along the long line of being,—ever rising in the scale from higher to yet higher manifestations, or abroad on the lower animals, whom instinct never deceives,—can we hold that man, immeasurably higher in his place, and infinitely higher in his hopes and aspirations than all that ever went before him, should be, notwithstanding, the one grand error in creation—the one painful worker, in the midst of present trouble, for a state into which he is never to enter—the befooled expectant of a happy future which he is never to see? Assuredly no. He who keeps faith with all his humbler creatures—who gives to even the bee and the dormouse the winter for which they prepare—will to certainty not break faith with man—with man, alike the deputed lord of the present creation, and the chosen heir of all the future. We have been looking abroad on the old geologic burying grounds, and deciphering the strange inscriptions on their tombs; but there are other burying grounds and other tombs,—solitary churchyards among the hills, where the dust of the martyrs lies, and tombs that rise over the ashes of the wise and good; nor are there wanting, on even the monuments of the perished races, frequent hieroglyphics and symbols of high meaning, which darkly intimate to us, that while *their* burial yards contain but the debris of the past, we are to regard the others as charged with the sown seed of the future.

MEMORY—TRADITION.

"There are events so striking in themselves, or from their accompaniments, that they powerfully impress the memories of children but little removed from infancy, and are retained by them in a sort of troubled recollection ever after, however extended their term of life Samuel Johnson was only two and a half years old, when, in accordance with the belief of the time, he was touched by Queen Anne for the 'Evil;' but more than seventy years after, he could call up a dream-like recollection of the lady dressed in the black hood, and glittering with diamonds, into whose awful presence he had been ushered on that occasion, and who had done for the cure of his complaint all that legitimate royalty could do. And an ancient lady of the north country, who had been carried when a child, in her nurse's arms, to witness the last witch execution that took place in Scotland, could distinctly tell, after the lapse of nearly a century, that the fire was surrounded by an awe-struck crowd, and that the smoke of the burning, when blown about her by a cross breeze, had a foul and suffocating odour. In this respect the memory of infant tribes and nations seems to resemble that of individuals. There are characters and events which impress it so strongly, that they seem never to be forgotten, but live as traditions, sometimes mayhap very vague, and much modified by the inventions of an after time, but which, in floating downwards to late ages, always bear upon them a certain strong impress of their pristine reality. They are shadows that have become ill-defined from the vast distance of the objects which cast them—like the shadows of great birds flung, in a summer's day, from the blue depths of the sky to the landscape far below—but whose very presence, however diffuse they may have become, testifies to the existence of the remote realities from which they are thrown, and without which they could have had no being at all. The old mythologies are filled with shadowy traditions of this kind—shadows of the world's 'gray fathers,'—which, like those shadows seen reflected on clouds by travellers who ascend lofty mountains, are exaggerated into the most gigantic proportions, and bear radiant glories about their heads"

CHAPTER XIX.

DEATH.

The labour to which Hugh Miller had been subjected in the preparation and final revision of the "Testimony of the Rocks," was the melancholy means of unhinging his intellectual powers, and leaving him the prey of those spectral illusions, those paroxysms of horror and despair, amidst whose deep and awful shadows he so gloomily perished. In such a state of mind as was his during the last months of his life, intellectual effort of any kind ought to have been strictly forbidden and rigidly foregone. Yet even long prior to these months, the mischief was done. Conjugal love had thrown a veil of the most inviolate secrecy over the earlier attacks of the insidious malady, so that not even his physicians knew how deep-seated was the calamity they at length became aware, only when too late, had smitten him, as it has smitten many of the most gifted of earth's sons.

The form which the malady latterly assumed, was precisely of the nature we might have expected from the peculiar mental and physical characteristics of Mr. Miller. To his medical advisers, to his partner, and to his family, he talks of strange dreams and awful visions which, in hours when deep sleep falleth upon men, came up before him as from the Spirit-land. Indeed, through life the dark cloud had been gathering over his mental powers; a predisposition to insanity lurked in that magnificent intellect. The student of his "Schools and Schoolmasters" will have noted that, even when a stripling, he was the subject of peculiar attacks, in one of which he bit the nails from his fingers. Nor can it have escaped the notice of any who have perused with care his "Scenes and Legends of the North of Scotland" how deep a hold the supernatural had taken upon his mind. With Hugh Miller, these northern superstitions were not—as they would have been to Sir Walter Scott—merely the raw material of the artist. We shall not insult the memory of the great Departed, by insinuating a vulgar belief in a tithe of the floating traditions he has perpetuated by the magic of his style; but without asserting so much, it is not too great a license to assert, that they were more to him than mere legends. These northern traditions, in which the beliefs of pagan and christian times were often curiously and grotesquely blended, mantled his spirit with the weird gloom of the supernatural, which his peculiar geological studies contributed still further to deepen. In the pursuit of the investigations to which he had devoted himself, he left the society of men to commune with the stones of the field; and in the gorge of the wave-lashed rock, or deep in the bowels of mother earth, did he gather up those records of the past through which he deciphered the story of an earlier world. On such a mind as Hugh Miller's, the reflection brought home by these studies, with a force and vividness those who only read of it can have no conception—that this earth of ours was but one vast mausoleum and burial-pyramid—could not fail to have exerted a surpassing power. Hugh Miller did not share the scepticism of those who believe the annihilation which has swallowed up in turn all the races of the past, will one day, like a mountainous wave, overtake man also; leaving nought to tell he had ever been, save those traces of his existence the fossils of the rock may perpetuate. Those doubts the discords of nature inspire, and which Tennyson has so vividly portrayed, did not perplex him. He knew there had been given to man a life that bears immortal fruit, and that beyond the verge of the present existence was the brightness of eternal day. He knew, "the song of woe is after all an earthly song," yet its melancholy moan had touched his spirit. In the last days of his earthly pilgrimage, "the light that shone when Hope was born" burned low; and in the hour when reason reeled, all those shadows of the past, all those shapes of the supernatural, which haunted him even in the vigour of his powers, hurried to take possession of the throne from which the monarch had fallen.

> "O life! as futile, then, as frail—
> Oh for thy voice to soothe and bless!
> What hope of answer or redress
> Behind the veil, behind the veil?"

The story of the closing scene of Hugh Miller's existence, so far as man could tell it, has been told in the columns of the *Witness* by Dr. Hanna, with a minuteness, a fidelity, a pathos, and an eloquence which leave almost nothing to be added:—

"In the belief," says the accomplished biographer of Chalmers, "that nothing touching the character and memory of such a man can be regarded with other than the deepest interest, the friends of Mr. Hugh Miller have thought it due at once to his great name and to the cause of truth, to lay fully before the public a statement of the most mournful circumstances under which he has departed from this life. For some months past his overtasked intellect had given evidence of disorder. He became the prey of false or exaggerated alarms. He fancied—if, indeed, it was a fancy—that occasionally, and for brief intervals, his faculties quite failed him—that his mind broke down. He was engaged at this time with a treatise on the 'Testimony of the Rocks,' upon which he was putting out all his strength—working at his topmost pitch of intensity. Hours after midnight the light was seen to glimmer through the window of that room, which, within the same eventful week, was to witness the close of the volume and the close of the writer's life. This overworking of the brain began to tell upon his mental health. He had always been somewhat moodily apprehensive of being attacked by footpads, and had carried loaded fire-arms about his person. Latterly, having occasion sometimes to return to Portobello from Edinburgh at unseasonable hours, he had furnished himself with a revolver. But now, to all his old fears as to attacks upon his person, there was added an exciting and overmastering impression that his house, and especially that his museum, the fruit of so much care, which was contained in a separate outer building, were exposed to the assault of burglars. He read all the recent stories of house robberies. He believed that one night lately an actual attempt to break in upon his museum had been made. Visions of ticket-of-leave men prowling about his premises haunted him by day and by night. The revolver, which lay nightly near him, was not enough; a broad-bladed dagger was kept beside it; whilst behind him, at his bed-head, a claymore stood ready at hand. A week or so ago, a new and more aggravated feature of cerebral disorder showed itself, in sudden and singular sensations in his head. They came only after lengthened intervals. They did not last long, but were intensely violent. The terrible idea that his brain was deeply and hopelessly diseased—that his mind was on the verge of ruin—took hold of him, and stood out before his eye in all that appalling magnitude in which such an imagination as his alone could picture it. It was mostly at night that these wild paroxysms of the brain visited him; but, until last Monday, he had spoken of them to no one. A friend, who had a long conversation with him on the Thursday of last week, never enjoyed an interview more, or remembers him in a more genial mood. On the Saturday forenoon another friend from Edinburgh found him in the same happy frame. On the forenoon of Sunday last he worshipped in the Free Church at Portobello; and in the evening read a little work (*the Pole Star of Faith*) which had been put into his hands—penning a brief notice of it, his last contribution to the *Witness*. About ten o'clock on Monday morning, he took what with him was an altogether unusual step. He called on Dr. Balfour in Portobello, to consult him as to his state of health. 'On my asking,' says Dr. Balfour, in a communication with which we have been favoured, 'what was the matter with him?' he replied, 'My brain is giving way. I cannot put two thoughts together to-day; I have had a dreadful night of it; I cannot face another such; I was impressed with the idea that my museum was attacked by robbers, and that I had got up, put on my clothes, and gone out with a loaded pistol to shoot them. Immediately after that I became unconscious. How long that continued I cannot say; but when I awoke in the morning I was trembling all over, and quite confused in my brain. On rising, I felt as if a stiletto was suddenly, and as quietly as an electric shock, passed through my brain from front to back, and left a burning sensation on the top of the brain, just below the bone. So thoroughly convinced was I that I must have been out through the night, that I examined my trousers to see if they were wet or covered with mud, but could find none.' He further said—'I may state that I was somewhat similarly affected through the night twice last week, and I examined my trousers in the morning to see if I had been out. Still, the terrible sensations were not nearly so bad as they were last night; and I may further inform you that, towards the end of last week, while passing through the Exchange in Edinburgh, I was seized with such a giddiness, that I staggered, and would, I think, have fallen, had I not got into an entry, where I leaned against the wall, and became quite unconscious for some seconds.' Dr. Balfour stated his opinion of the case; told him that he was overworking his brain, and agreed to call on him on the following day, to make a fuller examination. Meanwhile the quick eye of affection had noticed that there was something wrong, and on Monday forenoon Mrs. Miller came up to Edinburgh to express her anxiety to Professor Miller, and request that he would see her husband. 'I arranged,' says Professor Miller, 'to meet Dr. Balfour at Shrubmount (Mr. Hugh Miller's house), on the afternoon of next day. We met accordingly at half-past three on Tuesday. He was a little annoyed at Mrs. Miller's having given me the trouble, as he called it, but received me quite in his ordinary, kind, friendly manner. We examined his chest, and found that unusually well; but soon we discovered that it was head symptoms that made him uneasy. He acknowledged having been night after night up till very late in the morning, working hard and continuously at his new book, "which," with much satisfaction, he said, "I have finished this day." He was sensible that his head had suffered in consequence, as evidenced in two ways: first, occasionally, he felt as if a very fine poniard had been suddenly passed through and through his brain. The pain was intense, and momentarily followed by confusion and giddiness, and the sense of being "very drunk"—unable to stand or walk. He thought that a period of unconsciousness must have followed this—a kind of swoon, but he had never fallen. Second, What annoyed him most, however, was a kind of nightmare, which for some nights past had rendered sleep most miserable. It was no dream, he said; he saw no distinct vision, and could remember nothing of what had passed accurately. It was a sense of vague and yet intense horror, with a conviction of being abroad in the night wind, and dragged through places as if by some invisible power. "Last night," he said, "I felt as if I had been ridden by a witch for fifty miles, and rose far more wearied in mind and body than when I lay down." So strong was his conviction of having been out, that he had difficulty in persuading himself to the contrary, by carefully examining his clothes in the morning to see if they were not wet or dirty; and he looked inquiringly and anxiously to his wife, asking if she was sure he had not been out last night, and walking in this disturbed trance or dream. His pulse was quiet, but tongue foul. The head was not hot, but he could not say it was free from pain. We came to the conclusion that he was suffering from an overworked mind, disordering his digestive organs, enervating his whole frame, and threatening serious head affection. We told him this, and enjoined absolute discontinuance of work—bed at eleven, light supper (he had all his life made that a principal meal), thinning the hair of the head, a warm sponging-bath at bed-time, &c. To all our commands he readily promised obedience, not forgetting the discontinuance of neck-rubbing, to which he had unfortunately been prevailed to submit some days before. For fully an hour we talked together on these and other subjects, and I left him with no apprehension of impending evil, and little doubting but that a short time of rest and regimen would restore him to his wonted vigour.' It was a cheerful hour that was thus passed, and his wife and family partook of the hopeful feeling with which his kind friend, Professor Miller, had parted with him. It was now near dinner hour, and the servant entered the room to spread the table. She found Mr. Miller in the room alone. Another of the paroxysms was on him. His face was such a picture of horror, that she shrank in terror from the sight. He flung himself on a sofa, and buried his head, as if in agony, upon the cushion. Again, however, the vision flitted by, and left him in perfect health. The evening was spent quietly with his family. During tea he employed himself in reading aloud Cowper's "Castaway," the "Sonnet on Mary Unwin," and one of the most playful pieces, for the special pleasure of his children. Having corrected some proofs of the forthcoming volume, he went up stairs to his stndy. At the appointed hour he had taken the bath, but, unfortunately, his natural and peculiar repugnance to physic had induced him to leave untaken the medicine that had been prescribed. He had retired into his sleeping-room—a small apartment opening out of his study, and which, for some time past, in consideration of the delicate state of his wife's health, and the irregularities of his own hours of study, he occupied at night alone—and lain some time upon the bed. The horrible trance, more horrible than ever, must have returned. All that can now be known of what followed is to be gathered from the facts, and next morning his body, half-dressed, was found lying lifeless on the floor—the feet upon the study rug, and chest pierced with the ball of the revolver pistol, which was found lying in the bath that stood close by. The deadly bullet had perforated the left lung, grazed the heart, cut through the pulmonary artery at its root, and lodged in the rib in the right side. Death must have been instantaneous. The servant, by whom the body was first discovered, acting with singular discretion, gave no alarm, but went instantly in search of the doctor and minister; and on the latter the melancholy duty was devolved of breaking the fearful intelligence to that now broken-hearted widow, over whose bitter sorrow it becomes us to draw the veil. The body was lifted and laid upon the bed. We saw it there a few hours afterwards. The head lay back, sideways on the pillow. There was the massive brow, the firm-set manly features we had so often looked upon admiringly, just as we had lately seen them—no touch nor trace upon them of disease—nothing but that overspread pallor of death to distinguish them from what they had been. But the expression of that countenance in death will live in our memory for ever. Death by gun-shot wounds is said to leave no trace of suffering behind; and never was there a face of the dead freer from all shadow of pain, or grief, or conflict, than that of our dear departed friend. And as we bent over it, and remembered the troubled look it sometimes had in life, and thought what must have been the sublimely terrific expression that it wore at the moment when the fatal deed was done, we could not help thinking that it lay there to tell us, in that expression of unruffled majestic repose that sat upon every feature, what we so assuredly believe, that the spirit had passed through a terrible tornado, in which reason had been broken down; but that it had made the great passage in safety, and stood looking back to us, in humble, grateful triumph, from the other side.

On looking round the room in which the body had been discovered, a folio sheet of paper was seen lying on the table. On the centre of the page the following lines were written—the last which that pen was ever to trace:—

Dearest Lydia.—My brain burns. I *must* have *walked;* and a fearful dream rises upon me. I cannot bear the horrible thought. God and Father of the Lord Jesus Christ have mercy upon me. Dearest Lydia, dear children, farewell. My brain burns as the recollection grows. My dear, dear wife, farewell.

Hugh Miller.

What a legacy of love to a broken-hearted family! and to us and all who loved him, how pleasing to observe that in that bewildering hour, when the horror of that great darkness came down upon that noble spirit, and some hideous shapeless phantom overpowered it, and took from it even the capacity to discern the right from the wrong, humility, and faith, and affection, still kept their hold—amid the ruins of the intellect, that tender heart remaining still unbroken! These last lines remain as the surest evidence of the mysterious power that laid his spirit prostrate, and of the noble elements of which that spirit was composed—humble, and reverent, and loving to the last.

On Friday, at the request of friends, and under the authority of the procurator-fiscal, a *post-mortem* examination of the body took place. We subjoin the result:—

Edinburgh, Dec. 26, 1856.

We hereby certify on soul and conscience, that we have this day examined the body of Mr. Hugh Miller, at Shrubmount, Portobello.

The cause of death we found to be a pistol-shot through the left side of the chest; and this, we are satisfied, was inflicted by his own hand. From the diseased appearances found in the brain, taken in connection with the history of the case, we have no doubt that the act was suicidal, under the impulse of insanity.

James Miller.
A. H. Balfour.
W. T. Gairdner.
A. M. Edwards.

How abrupt, how mysterious this adieu to earth. Nothing in the circumstances or position of the editor of the *Witness* foretokened the great darkness amid which he descended into the valley of the shadow of death. His life was no catalogue of abortive schemes, blighted hope, baffled ambition. His name was inscribed upon the noblest page of our modern history as the ablest literary defender of those ecclesiastical principles, and that ecclesiastical polity Scotland's sons received a spiritual heritage from the heroes of the Reformation; with a European reputation as the most eloquent living expositor of the profoundest truths of geological science. All this achieved while his eye is yet undimmed, and his natural force yet unabated, it might in the course of nature have been anticipated, that this man so greatly beloved would have been spared to the republic of letters, spared to the cause of science, and to the cause of religion for at least another decade; that so, in the gloaming of his years, he might have gathered up the fruits of his maturest knowledge and ripest wisdom into that great work he had meant should round the circle of his scientific labours—"The Geology of Scotland." But it had been otherwise determined, and that bright particular star which had hitherto shone with so lustrous a light, suddenly sunk amidst the murkiest gloom; and not the broken arch nor the fallen column, tells the story of the ruin of earth's mightiest empires in language more impressive than do the tragic circumstances in which the editor of the *Witness* was taken hence, teach the vanity of even the loftiest human ambition. One feels that there is something of awe and mystery about the departure of so gentle a spirit from amongst the generations of the living, in this sudden and violent manner. Chalmers went his way in an equally unexpected moment; but he was found sleeping his last sleep upon the couch of rest. His latter end was peace, and he went up from that Assembly he was so eager to meet, to "the general assembly and church of the first-born, whose names are written in heaven." In the case of Hugh Miller death did its work by more violent means, and that heart which erewhile throbbed with the noblest and most generous emotion, is torn by bullets, shattered by a revolver.

Through the kindness of a personal friend of Mr. Miller, the Rev. Mr. Mackenzie of Dunfermline, we are enabled to close this memorial with one of the last of Mr. Miller's letters, so characteristic of the man, so genuine in its affection, and so genial in the touch of humour which irradiates it. Mr. Mackenzie will let the reader understand its point and allusions:—

Mr. Miller had engaged to be present at a lecture to be delivered in my church by Alexander Macansh, a self-taught genius, in whom Mr. Miller took much interest. His letter was in reply to one from me, fixing the day. He had arranged an excursion to Fordel, three or four miles from Dunfermline, to see what the country folks called a fossil man, found some time before in a quarry there. The fossil is, of course, nothing more than ferruginous stains in the rock, presenting the rude outline of a human figure.—Yours, &c.

J. MACKENZIE.

To the Rev. James Mackenzie, Dunfermline.

Shrubmount, Portobello, 16th Dec., 1856.

MY DEAR JAMES,—I have been set aside by one of my severe colds for a fortnight, and on Saturday, when I got your note, did not exactly know what to say in reply to it. But I have been getting steadily better for the last three days, and trust I may be able to be with you on the 29th. You may at least depend on my making an exertion; and if, notwithstanding, the fates forbid, must just get somebody else to sit in my place. Try, meanwhile, and find out the whereabouts of the Fordel man. With kind regards to Mrs. M.

Yours affectionately,

HUGH MILLER.

On the 29th December a funeral procession is taking its way from Shrubmount, Portobello, to the Grange cemetery. The funeral is such as has not been seen in Edinburgh since the death of Chalmers, and it is the dust of the editor of the *Witness* that is about to be laid by the dust of the great Scottish theologian. In that general assembly of the inhabitants of the metropolis that followed his bier, men of all ranks, all classes, and of all creeds, vied with each other in doing homage to the mighty dead. It was no common loss the land mourned; and, amidst a nation's lamentation, was he borne to his long rest.

> "He is gone who seem'd so great—
> Gone! but nothing can bereave him
> Of the force he made his own,
> Being here; and we believe him
> Something far advanced in state,
> And that he wears a truer crown
> Than any wreath that man can weave him.
> But speak no more of his renown;
> Lay your earthly fancies down,
> And in the vast cathedral leave him:
> God accept, and Christ receive him!"

APPENDIX.

THE articles contributed to the *Witness* by its editor, during the last month of his existence, exhibit all the great powers of the great journalist in the fullest play. His papers on "The Forces of Russia," "The Felons of the Country," and "Modern Poetry," are characterized by the same wide grasp of thought, the same powerful sweep of imagination, the same felicitous grouping, and the same richness of literary allusion that had ever distinguished his finest productions. We give—all our limits will permit—the last thing he penned for the *Witness*, written only three days before in such sadly-tragic manner he bade farewell to earth. We also subjoin his favourite prayer:—

HUGH MILLER'S LAST ARTICLE.

"THE POLE STAR OF FAITH. Bath: Binns & Goodwin. London: Hamilton, Adams, & Co.

This is a sound little volume—simple in its plan, but excellent in its matter. It at once introduces the reader to an interesting circle of neighbours in a country locality, representative, in the several members of which it is composed, of some of the leading religious aspects of the time. There is a clever young man, tinged, though still untainted, by the prevailing neologic infidelity; a young lady, his sister, who has just begun to dream of stained glass, carved images, crosses, candlesticks, and mystic Gothic steeples that point upwards, and whose embryo Popery, taken up rather as a matter of taste than feeling, forms the true complementary colour, if we may so speak, to the incipient infidelity of her brother. Their aunt is represented as an old-fashioned Scottish Episcopalian lady, amiable and simple-hearted, but whose religion consisted mainly in attending, on Sabbaths and the principal holidays, the services of her church, and whose religious adviser is well hit off as an equally old-fashioned clergyman of the same persuasion, who, so far as his light extends, is an honest man, but very considerably *moderate* in his leanings, and not a little teased and annoyed by the newly-awakened rage for the mediæval which he saw prevailing around him. Such are the *dramatis personæ* on the one side. Those on the other are a lady and son, earnest evangelical Christians; and an able and thoroughly excellent clergyman of the same vital school. There is scarce any incident in the work; but much ingenious and interesting dialogue, and many a sound and judicious reflection; and all is represented as coming right in the end. The semi-infidel becomes wholly a believer, influenced not more by the argument than by the disinterested excellence of his friend, and by his devotion to the Christian cause, for which he is described as giving up fair prospects of advancement in life, and welcoming the hardships and perils which encircle the life of the missionary. And the Puseyite lady loses in thoroughly awakened feeling, all her fancies, and discovers that religion is not a coloured window or a symbol, but a great life-influencing reality, that has its home in the heart. As a work of art the story is defective; but from the concluding sentences, we infer that it is *not* a work of art, but a sketch from nature, and that the mingled tissue of argument and reflection which forms the prevailing tissue of so many of the chapters, has been woven with an eye to the benefit of actual characters, who stood in need of the teaching thus imparted. We need scarce say that the doctrines specially dwelt upon are emphatically Protestant, and that the 'Pole Star of Faith' by which the work teaches to steer, and from which it borrows its title, is the guiding star of Divine Revelation."

Hugh Miller's Favourite Prayer, Made by John Knox at the First Assemblie of the Congregation, when the Confession of our Faithe and whole Orders of the Church was there red and approved.

"O Lord God Almightie, and Father moste mercifull, there is none lyke thee in heaven nor in earthe, which workest all thinges for the glorie of thy name and for the comfort of thyne elect. Thow dydst once make man ruler over all thy creatures, and placed hym in the garden of all pleasures; but how soone, alas, dyd he in his felicitie forget thy goodness! Thy people Israel, also, in their wealth dyd evermore runne astray, abusinge thy manifold mercies; lyke as all flesh contynually rageth when it hath gotten libertie and external prosperitie. But such is thy wisdome adjoyned to thy mercies, deare Father, that thou sekest all means possible to brynge thy chyldren to the sure sense and lyvely feelinge of thy fatherly favour. And therefore, when prosperitie wyll not serve, then sendest thow adversitie, graciously correctinge all thy chyldren whome thow receyvest into thy howshold. Wherefore we, wretched and miserable synners, render unto thee most humble and hartie thankes, that yt hath pleased thee to call us home to thy folde by thy fatherly correction at this present, whereas in our prosperitie and libertie we dyd neglect thy graces offered unto us. For the which negligence and many other grevous synnes whereof we now accuse ourselves before thee, thow myghtest most justly have gyven us up to reprobate mynds and induration of our hartes, as thow hast done others. But such is thy goodness, O Lord, that thow seemest to forget all our offences, and haste called us of thy good pleasure from all idolatries into this citie most Christainlye refourmed, to professe thy name, and to suffer some crosse amongest thy people for thy truth and gospell's sake; and so to be thy wytnesses with thy prophets and apostles, yea, with thy dearely beloved Sonne Jesus Christ, our head, to whome thow dost begynne here to fashion us lyke, that in his glorie we may also be lyke hym when he shall appear. O Lord God, what are we upon whome thow shuldest shewe this great mercie? O most lovynge Lord, forgyve us our unthankfulness and alle our synnes, for Jesus

Christ's sake. O heavenly Father, increase thy Holy Spirit in us, tc teach our hartes to cry Abba, dear Father! to assure us of our eternal election in Christ; to revele thy wyll more and more towards us; tc confirme us so in thy trewthe, that we may lyve and dye therein; an l that by the power of the same Spirit we may boldely gyve an accompt of our faith to all men with humbleness and mekeness, that whereas they backbyte and slaunder us as evyll doers, they may be ashamed and once stopp their mowthes, seinge our good conversation in Christ Iesu, for whose sake we beseche thee, O Lord God, to guide, governe, and prosper this our enterprise in assemblinge our bretherne to prayse thy holy name. And not only to be here present with us thy chyldren, according to thy promesse, but also mercifullie to assist thy lyke persecuted people, our bretherne, gathered in all other places, that they and we, consentinge together in one spirite and truethe, may (all worldly respectes set a part) seke thy onely honour and glorie in all our and their assemblies. So be it."

THE END.

CATALOGUE

OF THE

PUBLICATIONS

OF

RUDD & CARLETON,

130 GRAND STREET,

(BROOKS BUILDING, COR. OF BROADWAY,)

NEW YORK.

NEW BOOKS

And New Editions Just Published by

RUDD & CARLETON,

130 GRAND STREET,

NEW YORK (BROOKS BUILDING, COR. OF BROADWAY.)

N.B.—RUDD & CARLETON, UPON RECEIPT OF THE PRICE, WILL SEND ANY OF THE FOLLOWING BOOKS, BY MAIL, *postage free*, TO ANY PART OF THE UNITED STATES. THIS CONVENIENT AND VERY SAFE MODE MAY BE ADOPTED WHEN THE NEIGHBORING BOOKSELLERS ARE NOT SUPPLIED WITH THE DESIRED WORK.

NOTHING TO WEAR.

A Satirical Poem. By WILLIAM ALLEN BUTLER. Profusely and elegantly embellished with fine Illustrations on tinted paper, by Hoppin. Muslin, price 50 cents.

MILES STANDISH ILLUSTRATED.

With exquisite *Photographs* from original Drawings by JOHN W. EHNINGER, illustrating Longfellow's new Poem. Bound in elegant quarto, morocco covers, price $6 00

BOOK OF THE CHESS CONGRESS.

A complete History of Chess in America and Europe, with Morphy's best games. By D. W. FISKE, editor of *Chess Monthly* (assisted by Morphy and Paulsen). Price $1 50.

WOMAN'S THOUGHTS ABOUT WOMEN.

The latest and best work by the author of "John Halifax, Gentleman," "Agatha's Husband," "The Ogilvies," &c. From the London edition. Muslin, price $1 00

VERNON GROVE;

By Mrs. Caroline H. Glover. "A Novel which will give its author high rank among the novelists of the day."—*Atlantic Monthly.* 12mo., Muslin, price $1 00

BALLAD OF BABIE BELL,

And other Poems. By Thomas Bailey Aldrich. The first selected collection of verses by this author. 12mo Exquisitely printed, and bound in muslin, price 75 cents.

TRUE LOVE NEVER DID RUN SMOOTH.

An Eastern Tale, in Verse. By Thomas Bailey Aldrich, author of "Babie Bell, and other Poems." Printed on colored plate paper. Muslin, price 50 cents

BEATRICE CENCI.

A Historical Novel. By F. D. Guerrazzi. Translated from the original Italian by Luigi Monti. Muslin, two volumes in one, with steel portrait price $1 25.

ISABELLA ORSINI.

A new historical novel. By F. D. Guerrazzi, author of "Beatrice Cenci." Translated by Monti, of Harvard College. With steel portrait. Muslin, price $1 25.

DOCTOR ANTONIO.

A charming Love Tale of Italy. By G. Ruffini, author of "Lorenzo Benoni," "Dear Experience," &c From the last London edition. Muslin, price $1 00.

DEAR EXPERIENCE.

A Tale. By G. Ruffini, author of "Doctor Antonio," "Lorenzo Benoni," &c. With illustrations by Leech, *of the London Punch.* 12mo. Muslin, price $1 00

LECTURES OF LOLA MONTEZ.

Including her "Autobiography," "Wits and Women of Paris," "Comic Aspect of Love," "Gallantry," &c. A new edition, large 12mo. Muslin, price $1 25.

EDGAR POE AND HIS CRITICS.

By Mrs. Sarah Helen Whitman. A volume possessing many attractions and which has created considerable interest among the *literati.* 12mo. Muslin, price 75 cts

THE GREAT TRIBULATION;

Or Things coming on the Earth. By Rev. John Cumming, D.D., author of "Apocalyptic Sketches," &c. From the English edition. First Series. Muslin, price $1 00.

THE GREAT TRIBULATION.

Second Series of the new work by Rev. Dr. Cumming, which has awakened such an excitement throughout the religious community. 12mo. Muslin, price $1 00.

ADVENTURES OF VERDANT GREEN.

By Cuthbert Bede, B.A. The best humorous story of College Life ever published. 80*th edition*, from English plates. Nearly 200 original illustrations, price $1 00

CURIOSITIES OF NATURAL HISTORY.

By Francis T. Buckland, M.A. A sparkling collection of surprises in Natural History, and the charm of a lively narrative. From 4th London edition, price $1 25.

BROWN'S CARPENTER'S ASSISTANT.

The best practical work on Architecture; with Plans for every description of Building. Illustrated with over 200 Plates. Strongly bound in leather, price $5 00

THE VAGABOND.

A volume of Miscellaneous Papers, treating in colloquia sketches upon Literature, Society, and Art. By ADAM BADEAU. Bound in muslin, 12mo, price $1 00.

ALEXANDER VON HUMBOLDT.

A new and popular Biography of this celebrated *Savant*, including his travels and labors, with an introduction by BAYARD TAYLOR. One vol., steel portrait, price $1 25.

LOVE (L'AMOUR).

By M. JULES MICHELET. Author of "A History of France," &c. Translated from the French by J. W. Palmer, M.D. One vol., 12mo. Muslin, price $1 00.

WOMAN (LA FEMME).

A sequel and companion to "Love" (L'Amour) by the same author, MICHELET. Translated from the French by Dr. J. W. Palmer. 12mo. Muslin, price $1 00.

LIFE OF HUGH MILLER.

Author of "Schools and Schoolmasters," "Old Red Sandstone," &c. Reprinted from the English edition. One large 12mo. Muslin, new edition, price $1 25.

AFTERNOON OF UNMARRIED LIFE.

An interesting theme admirably treated. Companion to Miss Muloch's "Woman's Thoughts about Women." From London edition. 12mo. Muslin, price, $1 00.

SOUTHWOLD.

By MRS. LILLIE DEVEREUX UMSTED. "A spirited an well drawn Society novel—somewhat intensified bu bold and clever." 12mo. Muslin, price $1 00.

DOESTICKS' LETTERS.

Being a compilation of the Original Letters of Q. K. P. Doesticks, P. B. With many comic tinted illustrations by John McLenan. 12mo. Muslin, price $1 00

PLU-RI-BUS-TAH.

A song that's by-no-author. *Not* a parody on "Hiawatha." By Doesticks. With 150 humorous illustrations by McLenan. 12mo. Muslin, price $1 00

THE ELEPHANT CLUB.

An irresistibly droll volume. By Doesticks, assisted by Knight Russ Ockside, M.D. One of his best works. Profusely illustrated by McLenan. Muslin, price $1 00.

THE WITCHES OF NEW YORK.

A new humorous work by Doesticks; being minute, particular, and faithful Revelations of Black Art Mysteries in Gotham. 12mo. Muslin, price $1 00

TWO WAYS TO WEDLOCK.

A Novellette. Reprinted from the columns of Morris & Willis' *New York Home Journal.* 12mo. Handsomely bound in muslin. Price $1 00,

HAMMOND'S POLITICAL HISTORY.

A History of Political Parties in the State of New York. By Jabez B. Hammond, L.L.D. 3 vols., octavo, with steel portraits of all the Governors. Muslin. Price, $6 00.

ROMANCE OF A POOR YOUNG MAN.

From the French of Octave Feuillet. An admirable and striking work of fiction. Translated from the Seventh Paris edition. 12mo. Muslin, price $1 00

THE CULPRIT FAY.

By JOSEPH RODMAN DRAKE. A charming edition of this world-celebrated Faery Poem. Printed on colored plate paper. Muslin, 12mo. Frontispiece. Price, 50 cts.

THE NEW AND THE OLD;

Or, California and India in Romantic Aspects. By J. W. PALMER, M.D., author of "Up and Down the Irrawaddi." Abundantly illustrated. Muslin, 12mo. $1,25.

UP AND DOWN THE IRRAWADDI;

Or, the Golden Dagon. Being passages of adventure in the Burman Empire. By J. W. PALMER, M.D., author of "The New and the Old." Illustrated. Price, $1,00.

THE HABITS OF GOOD SOCIETY.

An interesting handbook for Ladies and Gentlemen; with thoughts, hints, and anecdotes, concerning social observances, taste, and good manners. Muslin, price $1 25.

RECOLLECTIONS OF THE REVOLUTION.

A private manuscript journal of home events, kept during the American Revolution by the Daughter of a Clergyman. Printed in unique style. Muslin. Price, $1,00

HARTLEY NORMAN.

A New Novel. "Close and accurate observation, enables the author to present the scenes of everyday life with great spirit and originality." Muslin, 12mo. Price, $1,25.

MOTHER GOOSE FOR GROWN FOLKS.

An unique and attractive little Holiday volume. Printed on tinted paper, with frontispiece by Billings. 12mo. Elegantly bound in fancy colored muslin, price 75 cts.

www.ingramcontent.com/pod-product-compliance
Lightning Source LLC
LaVergne TN
LVHW010155110826
845151LV00002B/525

9781425537203